The Strangers Book

HANEY FOUNDATION SERIES

A volume in the Haney Foundation Series,
established in 1961 with the generous support
of Dr. John Louis Haney

The Strangers Book

The Human of African American Literature

Lloyd Pratt

PENN

UNIVERSITY OF PENNSYLVANIA PRESS

PHILADELPHIA

Published by
University of Pennsylvania Press
Philadelphia, Pennsylvania 19104-4112
www.upenn.edu/pennpress

Printed in the United States of America
on acid-free paper
1 3 5 7 9 10 8 6 4 2

Library of Congress Cataloging-in-Publication Data
Pratt, Lloyd, 1967– author.
The strangers book : the human of African American literature / Lloyd Pratt.
    pages cm.— (Haney Foundation series)
Includes bibliographical references and index.
ISBN 978-0-8122-4768-8 (alk. paper)
    1. American literature—African American authors—History and criticism.
2. American literature—19th century—History and criticism.   3. African Americans—
Race identity—History—19th century.   4. Strangers in literature.   5. Blacks in
literature.   6. Humans beings in literature.   I. Title.   II. Series: Haney Foundation
series.
PS153.N5P73   2016
810.9'896073—dc23
                                                                    2015013295

For the Katrina people
(those who made it, those who did not)

But our humanity is our burden, our life; we need not battle for it; we need only to do what is infinitely more difficult—that is, accept it.

—James Baldwin, "Everybody's Protest Novel," in *Notes of a Native Son*

Il ne m'est pas nécessaire que je le "comprenne" pour me sentir solidaire de lui, pour bâtir avec lui, pour aimer ce qu'il fait. Il ne m'est pas nécessaire de tenter de devenir l'autre (de devenir autre) ni de le "faire" à mon image.

[To feel in solidarity with him or to build with him or to like what he does, it is not necessary for me to grasp him. It is not necessary to try to become the other (to become other) nor to "make" him in my image.]

—Édouard Glissant, "Pour l'opacité"/"For Opacity," in *Poetics of Relation*

Toute conviction sincere mérite le respect, et la conscience de l'homme est un sanctuaire sacré pour l'homme, un asile où Dieu seul a le droit de pénetrer comme juge.

[Every sincere conviction deserves respect, and a man's conscience is his hallowed sanctuary, a haven where God alone has the right to enter and judge.]

—Félicité de Lamennais, qtd. in *Les Cenelles*

People are different from each other.

—Eve Kosofsky Sedgwick, *Epistemology of the Closet*

CONTENTS

When the *Times-Picayune* returned to print four days after Hurricane Katrina made landfall, its plaintive headline broke down the fourth wall of the fourth estate. Desperation was reflected in the headline's outsized typeface, which shouted down the paper's customary flat editorial voice with an insistent "HELP US, PLEASE." The storied newspaper of New Orleans had been reduced to an act of petition. Upon closer examination the quotation marks cordoning off the headline came into focus. In a deft displacement undertaken at a moment of great crisis, the newspaper shifted responsibility for its petition to Angela Perkins, the woman pictured in the large-scale color photograph appearing below the headline. In the photograph, Angela Perkins wears a close-fitted, cropped yellow top with spaghetti straps. Her black capri pants are screen-printed with large cabbage roses. Her head, feet, and shoulders are bare; her hands are clasped. Bending slightly forward, she kneels in a street clogged with spent water bottles. Perkins is at an oblique angle to the camera's lens, and her clasped hands lift toward her chest. Her eyes are closed, but the tendons in her neck look strained to the point of breaking. Her mouth is open. Crowds of people stand and sit on the curb behind her. The caption reads "NEW ORLEANS: A distraught Angela Perkins screams 'Help us, please!' outside the Ernest N. Morial Convention Center on Thursday. A cloud of desperation settled over the hundreds of hungry, homeless people at the Convention Center, creating an atmosphere of fear and hopelessness." The inauspicious history of such cagey ventriloquism should be well known. Its legacy explains why you will have already guessed that Angela Perkins is black.

White antebellum abolitionists treasured images of petition. Attached to the plaintive "Am I not a man and a brother?," the figure of a kneeling black man was ubiquitous. Here, Angela Perkins becomes the paper's proxy; it is she, not the paper or the city, who requires witness and assistance. The paper draws on her presence while nevertheless associating her with the disorder it describes in a smaller headline. "After the disaster," the *Times-Picayune* reports, "chaos and lawlessness rule the streets." The very same streets where Angela Perkins kneels. Although the "us" of the newspaper's headline would, therefore, appear to include Angela Perkins or even to issue from her, a second us organized around her exclusion is in the making. This second us invoked by the paper's headline is the you implied in its address to its readers. "You, help us, please." This second us, or you, is the U.S. national audience that the *Times-Picayune*, many New Orleanians, and Louisiana's leaders sought to rouse to action when the nation-state made clear that it had no plans for saving the city from this ongoing and preventable event. This particular mode of address led to the destruction of New Orleans being figured in the days that followed Katrina as a source of national shame, which, of course, it was. It is nevertheless worth acknowledging how this event and its aftermath were used to rehabilitate the idea of a national audience at a historical moment committed to hyping the emergence of a globe unencumbered by national, racial, or other boundary limits. The rhetoric of aid and sympathy emerging from Katrina sought to reconstitute the nation in a way that even the Second Iraq War had failed to accomplish. In our moment of distraction, the category of the human came to be figured as isomorphic with the nation. We became Americans again and so did you. Other options were available.

Print and the Human

The Strangers Book uses the occasion of two bodies of writing to clarify the relation between entering into print and acquiring a human profile in a specific time and place. It does so by making clear the transformative work undertaken by a group of African American men who were committed to reframing the meaning of the human. They also sought to make participation in their revised category of the human more widely available than had been the case in earlier and different humanisms. The first body of writing consists of Frederick Douglass's editorials, correspondence, addresses, lectures, and autobiographies; the second is the antebellum criticism and poetry of a circle of francophone free men of color who wrote in New Orleans. Although Douglass's name attaches to the first body of writing, it will become clear how this writing was as much a group performance as was that created by the *hommes de couleur libres* responsible for *Les Cenelles: Choix de poésies indigènes* (1845). The latter is the acknowledged first anthology of African American literature, and it was published in New Orleans in the same year as Douglass's *Narrative* (1845). The writing in *Les Cenelles* both is collective and is not, a quality that exemplifies the overall thrust of my argument, which insists on the presence of given and proper names in the context of an arguably coterie publication. The parameters circumscribing the specific time and place that interest me emerge in the chapters that follow, as will a sense that this writing is a site of overlapping worldviews. More will also be said about why this particular constellation of writers and writing makes for a suitable object of analysis.

My central claim is that these two bodies of writing were part of a political-aesthetic project aimed at constructing what the theorist Ellen Rooney calls a "semiprivate room."[1] The semiprivate room under construction by these men would permit and even require its entrants to practice what I will call a "stranger humanism." In this room, which is a space both rhetorical and material, people discover their differences from one another, but they are barred from trying to appropriate or penetrate those differences. This discovering of difference facilitates the coming-into-selfhood of those who elect to enter the room. This discovering of difference also forms the groundwork of democracy. In order for this to happen, this room must be governed by rules that manage the encounters it shelters. The first and inviolable rule is never to mistake another's request for solidarity, for aid, or for witness as an invitation to remake or displace her or him. This antebellum project in this sense anticipates Édouard Glissant's views in "Pour l'opacité"/"For Opacity" (1990). "To feel in solidarity with [the other]," Glissant writes, "it is not necessary for me to grasp him." We can stand in solidarity with those who are unlike us, which is to say each and every human being, and understand that they are "for themselves" rather than "for us." The second unbreakable rule is to take the humanness of African Americans as a given. The rest of the rules are subject to ongoing renegotiation by those who elect to enter this semiprivate room, and by those they in turn choose to admit, but the rules must evolve through accretion and addition rather than by a forgetful overturning of what has been. Only strict attention to the decorum appropriate to this semiprivate room can ensure the unfolding of a democratic humanism, which is conceived of in these men's writing as a stranger humanism.

It will be clear that my vocabulary for describing stranger humanism echoes other intellectual traditions. I will return to these traditions, but I want first to identify two features of these antebellum African American men's stranger humanism that differentiate it from other humanisms. On the one hand, the literary-formal practices adopted in the writing of these men indicate the centrality of multiparty disclosure and multiparty witness to their vision of stranger humanism. On the other hand, the organizing practices of these men acknowledge that in order for stranger humanism to function as it should, the right material conditions must be in place in order to support such disclosure and witness. On the first issue, the African American men whose work I describe here indicate by way of their writing and their organizing practices that intersubjective recognition must be conceived of as involving not two or even three subjects but many of them at once. On the second, they consider that those subjects must have access not only to apt rhetorical constructions, but also to appropriate physical formats (book formats, literal rooms, periodical formats) in which to pursue that multiparty recognition. These men understand the space of democracy to emerge from the joining of rhetorical practice to the physical world. "The space of democracy" must never be mistaken, therefore, for a metaphorical phrase; neither should it be reduced to a single given chamber, a single rhetorical figure, or a single gathering of people. Hence these men's emphasis on writing together, publishing together, meeting together, reading together, and witnessing each other's human becoming together. This accounts as well for what I will suggest is their interest in cultivating an apostolic openness to others that inflects their stranger humanism with a deep generosity. At the same time, this apostolic openness should not be misperceived as an open invitation with no binding requirements. There is a price to pay for participation in stranger humanism, the price of decorum appropriate to the occasion, and those who refuse to pay it are not welcome.

In order to lay the groundwork for these arguments, I want to use the rest of this introduction to formulate an initial response, which will be elaborated over the course of this book, to the following query from Alexander G. Weheliye regarding the category of the human: "What different modalities of the human come to light," Weheliye has asked, "if we do not take the liberal humanist figure of 'man' as the master-subject but focus on how humanity has been imagined and lived by those subjects excluded from this domain?"[2] The chapters that follow will, in turn, supplement Weheliye's question with this one: What does the human look like when we attend not only to how it is "imagined and lived by those subjects excluded from" the major lines of liberal humanist thought, but also to the formal and institutional structures that facilitate and constrain that imagining? This book remains sensitive throughout to what the entry into print entailed for these considered few, rather than all, African Americans by attending to the forms and institutional contexts that characterized their writing. The Strangers Book thus considers how the formal and institutional circumstances that framed their entry into print, as well as their own revision of those circumstances, conditioned the extent to which these writers realized their redefinition of the human as a consequential practice.

Fantasies of Print, Past and Present

What did mid-nineteenth-century African American writing do? Given a world seemingly intent on hounding black people out of print and into bondage, why did African Americans bother to write at all? As Jeannine DeLombard explains, one answer to these questions long predominated.[3] Historians and literary critics early on identified antebellum African American writing, in general, and the fugitive slave narratives, in particular, as cornerstones of a tradition in which African Americans used print to secure recognition of their humanity. This notion surfaced first in the fugitive slave narratives themselves. In particular, Frederick Douglass's *Narrative* argues for the humanizing payoff of reading and of writing. As he did on other issues, Douglass would later revise this view. His early sense that black people's engagement with print could secure recognition of their humanity has nevertheless structured histories of African American literature into the recent past. Access to printed matter was as a result understood to remediate black people's exclusion from the category of the human. One important aspect of this belief was the supposition that once white people learned black people were capable of engaging with the printed word, this lesson would in turn precipitate white acknowledgment of black humanness. Critics and historians conceded that fugitive slave narratives and the African American literary tradition, more generally, did other work too. Where slaveholders sought to bar black people from accessing their history and genealogy, for example, fugitive slave narratives and African American historical novels were understood to reconnect broken kinship ties. In the context of a Western intellectual tradition in which a print presence continued to signify the humanity of any people or person, the most notable feature of black writing nevertheless remained the fact that it existed at all.

For some time now, it has been recognized that this generalizing approach to early appearances of African Americans in print came at a high cost. As DeLombard shows, it obscured how early entrances of black people into print by way of gallows literature and published criminal confessions secured a persistent sense of their inadequacy as candidates for inclusion within the ranks of the desirably human, while at the same time allowing black people to count as legal persons for the purposes of criminal prosecution.[4] This particular scene of entry into print effaced the divide separating thing from person, but it did so by making criminal culpability a main testament to the personhood of black people. The sense that not all print culture is the same print culture is reflected as well in Leon Jackson's survey of early African American print culture studies, in which Jackson suggests that the very notion of a generalized print culture obscures the many different ways to attach oneself to print, or to be attached to it, as a black person; he also enumerates the deep reserves of scholarship on this topic.[5] These views complement a long tradition of African American critical theory stipulating that adequate attention be paid to "black expressive culture," to evoke Houston Baker's still-resonant phrase, which points up the error of taking print to be the only significant register of black meaning-making.[6] Perhaps most important, Frances Smith Foster's recent anthology of early African American writing on love and marriage is a potent reminder, to anyone who had forgotten, that these writers had other things on their minds than simply proving to white people that they were human.[7]

This shared interest in developing a more finely grained analysis of how black writing functioned as a tool for achieving recognition of black human-ness, or failed to do so, has developed in tandem with a mounting sense of the need to revisit this last category, the human, and its evolving meaning in the African diaspora. As more than one person has pointed out, there is and always has been more than one approach to conceiving of the human. Sylvia Wynter goes so far as to interpret much antihumanist leftist critique as a miscued argument targeting a designedly restrictive view of the human emerging from the exact discursive tradition that the antihumanist cri-tique sets out to counter.[8] Arguments focused on rejecting the category of the human because it has sometimes been deployed for pernicious ends too readily concede this category, Wynter argues, to its worst offenders rather than acknowledging its better, often darker angels. According to Wynter, it is worth attending with as much care to how people who have been excluded from dominant fictions of the human define it as we have devoted to parsing the thinking of those who commit crimes in its name. Wynter in this way reprises a long tradition of African diasporic thought and practice calling for serious attention to the nuances of black political theorizing. She anticipates Nancy Fraser's more recent proposition that the study of political philoso-phy must accord folk theories of justice the same sustained analysis devoted to even the most casual writings of a figure such as Kant. Her comments also align with Paul Gilroy's proposal that "vernacular cultures and the stub-born social movements that were built upon their strengths and tactics have contributed important moral and political resources to modern struggles in pursuit of freedom, democracy, and justice."[9] Ultimately, Wynter and these others insist on the need to engage routinely, and in depth, the many African diasporic vernacular theories of the human, as well as the material circum-stances that informed them, both of which are part and parcel of humanity's inheritance from the past.

Being with Strangers

Reading Frederick Douglass's writing from this period together with fran-cophone African American writing from New Orleans highlights one facet of this inheritance: an interest in specifying the practices required for an experience of politics, or of being-with-strangers, that might successfully displace the more familiar, racist humanisms. Douglass's fraught encounters with white U.S. abolitionists inform his interest in this issue. The writing and thought of the *Les Cenelles* poets trace the Creole of color community's efforts to temporize with their recently changed fortunes in the city of New Orleans, where the tensions among the city's white Creoles, recent white European immigrants, and the expanding white American presence were at an all-time high. Most important, though, this writing engages U.S. and international conversations concerning the category of the human and its place in modern life. This writing concerns itself with local, national, and international, as well as ancient and modern, frameworks for thinking through the relations among democracy, literateness, and the human.

In a cumulative fashion, this writing comes to maintain that the human condition demands a polis committed to the deliberate refinement of practices of stranger humanism.[10] It does not on balance merely recycle flawed notions of humanity's easy access to a shared repertoire of common experiences and emotions. It instead solicits and preserves a sense of the binding strangeness of each to all, and it takes this solicitous preservation of strangeness to be the only available avenue of approach to a viable notion of the human. Although this writing therefore depicts strangerhood in its most general sense as a condition of (modern) life, its key transformative moments supplement agnostic acknowledgment of modern humans' strangeness to one another with exploratory efforts at growing the distances between human agents in order to cultivate a preferred style of strangerhood. In central episodes, in other words, this writing passes over into presenting a form of distance as the ground on which a human demos, or a feasibly humanist community, finds its firmest footing. This distance, which is the ground of the semiprivate room, can be understood as the place of convergent opacities that Glissant has described. "Opacities can," he writes, "coexist and converge, weaving fabrics. To understand these truly one must focus on the texture of the weave and not on the nature of its components."[11] In its most intriguing moments, the antebellum African American men's writing considered here does not misapprehend or misrepresent this woven distance, or the opacity to one another of those who stand on it, either as unchanging or simply as given. Neither is this distance understood as a barrier to political life. It comes to count instead as one element of a historically conditioned life held in common whose character sanctions, supports, and necessitates democracy.

Ill-chosen forms, flawed institutional contexts, or some combination of these two often short-circuited this writing's antiracist stranger humanism.

However, this writing nevertheless worked to realize a way of being-with-strangers that avoided familiar idioms of individualism, on the one hand, and reflexive attachment to static cultural difference, on the other. This writing thus did something illegible when viewed from the most common scholarly angles of approach to early writings on and by African Americans. This writing does not exclusively reproduce the liberalism/republicanism binary dominating early America. Neither does it anticipate precisely the concerns of the Jim Crow United States. Nor does it tolerate the melancholy attachment that Ian Baucom associates with modern practices of stranger witnessing.[12] In this sense, these writers are neither merely imitating U.S. and European (white) political theory, philosophy, and aesthetic practices nor reflexively reacting to them. They are in constructive dialogue with those practices and with one another. They envision a racially integrated democracy whose contours the judicial and legislative crimes of Reconstruction and Jim Crow would work hard to render unimaginable in the future and unremembered from the past.

This writing in this sense tarries with the cultivation of something that can be described as akin to Hannah Arendt's "condition of plurality." In *The Human Condition*, Arendt proposes that the historicity of human life means that each human will be different from any other human who has ever lived, lives, or will live; over time each human will as well differ from themselves. For Arendt, this condition of plurality constitutes the horizon of possibility for politics. Rather than suppress it, she argues, plurality should be acknowledged and even nurtured. As Arendt also insists, however, and as this mid-century writing anticipates, there can be no definitive claim about human nature, only an identification of that which historically conditions, in a transitive sense, being human. What "the human" is remains impossible to determine. All that is known is that humans will be as different from each other as they are from themselves over time.[13] Fundamentally, then, Arendt's is an argument about the historicity of human being, and this constitutes its main solidarity with the writing considered here.

In certain striking moments, this writing not only permits something like plurality to come into view; its orchestration of a defined range of formal gestures within thoughtfully managed institutional contexts establishes plurality as a ground of commonality. In these fleeting moments, this writing joins the recompensing risks and rules of the semiprivate room to the necessary protections afforded by places of sanctuary.[14] In these moments, this writing's formal protocols and thematic concerns encounter favorable material conditions that encourage the fullness of plurality to lift its head above the horizon. As helpful as other critics and theorists can be to limning its outline, however, no extant political-theoretical or literary-aesthetic vocabulary offers an adequate name for what is of interest here. This is because the successful collation of form and institutional conditions is a short-lived thing; it can be achieved only in passing moments. The rules and results of stranger humanism are always occasional. This is also because the forms of being-with-strangers that this writing pursues do not permit the creation of some greater whole—whether a public or a romantically conceived nation— that is superordinate over its members. The strangers book of my title will therefore have to serve to figure the venue that emerges in passing moments and without a discernible product, but with many discernible consequences. (In saying this, I do not mean to overvalue the unknowable or the more simply not yet known; hence, a figure, the strangers book, rather than a proper name, describes my main object of study. Characterization by way of figures best describes what was there while at the same time connoting a sense of life in motion. Figurative language never really claims to name the exact thing. It attempts to point to something like it. Discussions of sublimity or the unknowable do the opposite: They focus on what is not there in order to designate that which exceeds or stands outside of historical experience. The former is the goal; the latter is a hazard of critical and historical inquiry.)

Douglass and the *Les Cenelles* poets were, moreover, much more concerned than is Arendt to detail how social relations, broadly conceived, are the most significant site of origin for plurality's initial emergence. Arendt gives us the tools to conceptualize the human as a contingent rather than a transcendent formation, in other words; this writing does so as well, but it is also keen to specify the social scenarios that predicate and maintain any given human being. To put this point a different way, this writing insistently documents the permanent and necessary relation of every I to a constituting we. As I argue in Chapter 1, this is the relation of stranger-with-ness. This writing does so without imagining that this constituting we has any special claim to that I save that this particular we was present in the first place. All the same, that constituting we never surrenders its claim to the aforesaid I. Absent this specification, which is tracked in this writing's tendency to adopt practices of social citationality that repeatedly footnote its scenes of composition (rather than to wrap the author in a mantle of self-possession), the account of the human described here might recall either the type of liberal individualism that Saidiya Hartman characterizes as "burdened individuality"[15] or the spiritual communitarianism associated with many Afrocentrist and Christian frameworks. The moments of writing under consideration instead present a specific mode of derived strangerhood as a credible pathway to an experience of the human that departs from those other well-traveled roads.

This writing presents the particular experience of the human signified by the figure of the strangers book as credible only to the extent that this experience remains apposite to, and mainly discouraging of, sympathetic identification. In pivotal moments, the fully human emerges in this writing from open-ended and multiparty disclosure, both of which are presented as essential elements of the intersubjective recognition required of good politics. As the reference to multiparty disclosure would suggest, one of the key ways that the pitfalls of intersubjective recognition are avoided is to overcome the one-on-one-ness conventionally implied by the term intersubjective. While this writing in this way presents its own reaching toward a particular inflection of stranger relationality as an escape route from sympathy's dubious terrain, it also seeks to identify the protocols, rules, and inbuilt limitations of an antiracist stranger humanism at midcentury.

To borrow a useful, if necessarily inadequate, vocabulary, this writing is organized around a sense that "one becomes an individual subject only in virtue of recognizing, and being recognized by, another subject" understood as "equal and also as separate," and it also anticipates recent work in the political philosophy of recognition that stipulates "parity of participation" as a condition of the encounter known as recognition.[16] It furthermore points to and pursues reforms understood as elements essential to this parity.[17] These reforms are simultaneously formal, cultural-institutional, industrial, and governmental. They involve dismantling the master's tools; they aim to redistribute the distribution of the sensible.[18] This writing additionally seeks to displace the subject-to-object/subject-to-subject dynamic with a relation more irreducibly plural, but one whose irreducibility is historical rather than given. In this writing, for the we to have been there is required. The we having been there is also the only thing that validates its claim to the I.

This writing's interest in equal and in separate does not (simply) indicate its insistence on certain experiences of slavery or blackness remaining beyond the ken of white readers. Clearly it does. To overemphasize this point would nevertheless be to participate in the Jim Crow thinking recalled by the proximity of the words "equal" and "separate." Neither is this writing retailing a commitment to individualism borrowed from the white populism of the period. Nor is it reinvesting in the body, affect, or collective experience as a locus of political knowledge.[19] This writing reaches for something appreciably different from a self-alienating disembodiment in print, which, scholars have argued, contemporaneous and earlier models of citizenship presented as the proper basis of political community and the benefit of the print public sphere. At the same time, it seeks to avoid the appropriative gestures of identification politics often associated with sympathy. This writing at key moments therefore deflects analogical practices of reading, rejecting the notion that anyone's experience may be substituted with or for the experience of another person. It also demands intersubjective recognition of an unfamiliar kind, bringing into view a polis predicated on a form of multidirectional encounter rather than the radical individualism of either sympathetic identification or disinterested personhood. Antiracist stranger humanism emerges in these brief episodes as an alternative to republican universalism. It also offers a place of respite from liberal individualism where the burdened individual can release his burden.

This writing's antiracist stranger humanism permits the coming into being of a self that is a function of tethered relations with necessary equals who are acknowledged as such. The price of this equality is taken to be a shared acceptance that what it means to be human is to be in a state that renders humans always strangers to those whom they encounter. Humans are strange to one another because their persistent coming into being, which is to say their historicity, forbids identification, to the extent that identification requires a relation to a static imago rather than an unfolding personhood.[20] Stranger humanism properly engaged is therefore an encounter without end in which the parties to the encounter never reach a concluding moment of full mutual intelligibility; they instead have the opportunity to participate in recognition predicated on emerging difference. These acts of recognition accelerate the emergence of a tenable demos. The encounter itself acknowledges the writ for democracy by granting that no party will ever attain the transcendent knowledge required to obviate collective deliberation and debate. The encounter is itself fully democratic only if and when material conditions permit its universal availability; the simple reaching toward such an encounter nevertheless makes clear when those conditions are and are not present.

From the slave narrative's fugitive stranger to Paul Laurence Dunbar's mask to W. E. B. Du Bois's veil, African American men's writing includes many examples of seeming stranger personae. Those personae have often been read as subtractions of the self from view or as reclamations of the right to privacy.[21] John Stauffer argues, for example, that Douglass's "public self differed from his private self."[22] He also suggests that Douglass "was (and is) extremely difficult to penetrate and know as a private individual."[23] Strangerhood furthermore frequently registers in African American writing as the undesired consequence of forced alienation. In Lose Your Mother, Saidiya Hartman recalls the pain of being referred to, and addressed, as "stranger," *obruni*, during an extended visit to Ghana. Those moments of stranger address index for Hartman the great crime of natal alienation and an attendant desire for impossible scenes of homecoming in the motherland. Echoing the title of James Baldwin's memorable essay, Hartman writes, "I was the stranger in the village, a wandering seed bereft of the possibility of taking root."[24] Baldwin's essay "Stranger in the Village" (1955) in turn recalls the masthead of a short-lived but significant African American newspaper from the 1850s, *The Aliened American*, whose title signals the condition of being made stranger to a village that is (or at least should be) one's own nation-state. However, in Douglass's post-1845 work and in the writing and sociality of New Orleans's *hommes de couleur libres*, something other than an authentic self that lies behind or prior to the stranger's face emerges as a primary concern. Neither is strangerhood understood to be a condition always and forever bereft of belonging. Strangerhood comes to be figured as having the potential to become a proper mode of human existence. In this writing, what is not shared is not always mistaken for what is not human.

In disappointing ways, this writing's production of a felicitous strangerhood does sometimes trade in the public/private distinction that grounds many politics of the public sphere, and that has historically required a cultivation of depth and coercive gender norms.[25] From antiquity through the nineteenth century, that distinction also took slavery as its developmental antecedent. In this sense, this writing's reaching toward an antiracist stranger humanism exceeded its grasp in its own time. It left in its wake both a legacy of disappointment and intimations of opportunities to come. In Frederick Douglass's Civil War–era "Address for the Promotion of Colored Enlistments," which he delivered in Philadelphia on July 6, 1863, and then published in *Douglass' Monthly* in August 1863, Douglass writes, "Do I hear you say still that you are a son, and want your mother provided for in your absence?—a husband and want your wife cared for?—a brother, and want your sister secured against want? I honor you for your solicitude. Your mothers, your wives, and your sisters ought to be cared for, and an association of gentlemen, composed of responsible white and colored men, is now being organized in this city for this very purpose." Contextualize Douglass's statement as much as you like, it is difficult to ignore its cultivated display of *oikos* doing service to androcentrism, even if it also aims at love and honor. The dedication of the *Les Cenelles* poets' *choix de poésies*, which reads "*au beau sexe louisianais*," can be understood in related terms.

This writing contains as well an alternative to the view that represents the movement from private to public life as the only pathway to political personhood. It reveals without adequately remediating the limitations of models of selfhood and democracy organized around notions of domestic interiority, patriarchal privacy, and *oikos*.[26] Although it does not always admit as much, it highlights how such models invite a static notion of selfhood as internally given or as grounded in relations of domination premised on gender difference and slavery. At its best, this writing's experimentation with the possibilities of strangerhood previews, and occasionally introduces into being, a self that is contingent upon other persons, evolving, and in these terms equal to all others. Such an understanding vitiates the logics of patriarchy and racism, but it cannot itself bring either of these structural inequities to an end. The best practices of these texts in this sense outpace the daily politics of many of their authors, their readers, and the wider world. To this extent, these texts confirm a basic lesson of political life: Visionary anticipation and formal innovation are necessary but insufficient ingredients of social transformation, especially when it comes to the shorter-term struggles that ultimately establish long-term conditions of political possibility.

If the study of these works does not overcome all of the many intractable problems of masculinist writing, when we attend to its stranger humanism, a different light is cast on the depleting potential of certain familiar critical idioms of loss and deficit, while at the same time we can acknowledge the perpetuity of the struggle for democracy, justice, and selfhood. As African American feminist literature and theory has long argued, it is essential not only to acknowledge that the experiences of strangerhood associated with abstract personhood, lingering strategies of warning out, the emergence of the police power, and the historical displacements of the slave trade came at an unforgivable cost, but also to insist that nineteenth-century African America was neither an affective void nor an intellectual impasse nor a social wasteland.[27] This pertains even, and perhaps especially, to the seemingly most atomistic, and therefore the most masculinist, of African American personae: the (male) stranger. Even this outwardly singular figure must be understood in different terms. Although these black male writers, the personae they deploy, and the characters they depict sometimes appear to be strangers seeking solitude, the voice that these writers develop is always (and admittedly) less solitary than it might at first seem. Even the solitude that this writing does in fact sometimes value breaks with conventional notions of solitude's shape and its recompense. This writing reconfigures standing notions of strangerhood and solitude, and in doing so it yields rewards significantly different from those previously on offer.[28] By the middle of the nineteenth century, this writing had identified a specific form of stranger-with-ness as a desirable destination. The African American pursuit of stranger humanism arguably declined with the onset of the U.S. Civil War, Reconstruction, and Jim Crow, but it never entirely disappeared from the landscape of African America. One key lesson to be drawn from Hazel Carby's *Race Men* is that much of what is thought of as modern black masculinity is a post-Reconstruction project.[29] This is not to suggest that all antebellum African American men were radical gender egalitarians, although some arguably were, but it does raise the possibility that the exact contours of black masculinity in this period might be worth further study. In other words, rather than reproduce what Carby identifies as Du Bois's tendency to frame the history of black political achievement as the history of individual black men's achievement, and instead of responding to Du Bois's history as if it were the only way of telling the history of black achievement, it might be more productive to view this writing as a window onto a notion of black masculinity that was closed down by the crimes of Reconstruction. In addition to allowing for the rethinking of African American men's writing, addressing the question of African American stranger-with-ness raises significant questions about antebellum African American women's writing. How, for example, does the reliance of so much African American women's writing from this period on the authority of a singular, unbroken relation to God measure up against the standard of a stranger humanism? Given the reading of the *Les Cenelles* poets that I offer in the relevant chapter in this book, can that reliance be understood in different terms than as a private—to the point of being privative— relation to God?

Of course, like any writing, the writing of these men is often at variance with itself; some of those variances are trivial ones, but others are more consequential. A selective focus on the more successfully transformative moments in the writings of Douglass and the *Les Cenelles* poets nevertheless has the merit of directly calling to account the academic standards of intelligibility that once governed the critical study of antebellum African American writing. One of the main contributions of Afrocentrist and black aesthetics to the study of African America has been to argue that the scholarly standards of intelligibility that were originally (and are sometimes still) applied to black culture borrow from white Western critical traditions fit for confirming whether a particular people or person should count as human, but that those same critical traditions were much less adept at interrogating the nature of the humanness being measured, especially when black people were the subject of interest. White Western critical traditions often specified, in other words, a version of the human inadequate to a democratic humanism comprehensive of black life. For this reason, there has commonly been some-thing of a mismatch of critical paradigm to actual African American writ-ing. To put the point a different way, white Western critical traditions long addressed this writing with the following question: Do these works testify to the humanity of black people? This writing turns out to be interested in a more radical question: Human, yes, but how?[30]

Targets of Address

The writings of Douglass and the *hommes de couleur libres* of *Les Cenelles* pursue something more than the end of slavery and of racism. These objects of its political desire come markedly into focus when this writing attends to the management of address. There is, for instance, Douglass's careful manip-ulation of address when writing to his former master, both directly and in published open letters, described in this book in Chapter 3. There is also the peculiar way, considered in Chapter 2, that Armand Lanusse, the editor of *Les Cenelles*, positions his *Les Cenelles* writing companions and himself in relation to readers. Then there is the point in Douglass's career when his voice joins with others to stage scenes of collective address in published con-vention "sentiments," a topic to which I turn in Chapter 1. Finally, there is the tendency of the *Les Cenelles* poets to address one another across the poems collected in that volume, another subject of Chapter 3. In these instances, and many others like them, something significant is happening. Here, as else-where, address has everything to do with how notions and experiences of the human emerge from practices of being-with-strangers contingent upon the developing formal, industrial, and institutional idioms of print culture.

Barbara Johnson argues that how one configures an address to another has profound consequences for all parties involved. "'I' and 'you' are per-sons," she writes, "because they can either address or be addressed, while 'he' can only be talked *about*. A person who neither addresses nor is addressed is functioning as a *thing* in the same way that being an *object* of discussion rather than a *subject* of discussion transforms everything into a thing."[31] From Johnson's perspective, which draws from Émile Benveniste, the only way to count as human is to enter into a specifically configured relation of address. You and I can be many things without having to articulate or take up a form of address, but you and I can never be human without access to the manners and the means of effective address. Recalling Martin Buber's *I and Thou* (1923), Johnson furthermore argues that certain modes of address are powerful enough to "transform an 'I-it' relationship into an 'I-thou' relationship, thus making a relation between persons out of [what] was in fact a relation between a person and non-persons."[32]

The political context of mid-nineteenth-century African American writing makes it tempting to infer that the person/nonperson relation was at issue in this writing's management of address. From this perspective, antebellum African American writing would be broadly understood as an attempt to establish a person-to-person relationship where a person-to-thing standoff once obtained. The matter of address immediately brings to mind, after all, the de facto and de jure regulation of black-to-white address in the antebellum United States, including the enforced use of honorifics when addressing white children, the sometimes deadly consequences of innocent scenes of cross-gender verbal address on city sidewalks, and the theft of black people's right to petition the state for a redress of grievances as epitomized in Congress's refusal to give antislavery petitions an in-house reading.

Importantly, however, the most interesting moments of address in this writing are more concerned to reorganize the meaning of the human. Something more is going on here than black people petitioning white people for recognition of black people as perspicacious enough to count as human. Dissatisfied with the version of the human on offer, this writing manifests its discomfort with, and pulls away from, what is at core a racist humanism. This writing furthermore revises the standing account of the human, or in other words racist humanism, in its considered figures of address, as well as in its exploitation of the opportunities for the management of address that follow from new methods of reprinting, variations in print format, and strategic embedding within cultural institutions. This management of address has to do with an ongoing pluralization of both the origin(s) and the target(s) of address, one that allows for the measure of plurality that recognizes human singularity without absenting the individual from either history or social relations.

* * *

My first chapter, "The Making of Self-Evidence," centers on the histories of Andrew Jackson's two addresses "To the Free Colored Inhabitants of Louisiana" (1814), William Lloyd Garrison's *Thoughts on African Colonization* (1837), and the Colored National Convention of 1853's "Address . . . to the People of the United States" (1853). In order to give a sense of how African American and antiracist writers have established the conditions of possibility for their transformation of the meaning of the human, I illustrate how they engaged with the antebellum "culture of reprinting" and invested in a process that I term "self-evidencing."[33] Here I trace the movement of Jackson's addresses through several abolitionist and antiracist, intellectual and political circles, including those established by free men of color from New Orleans and those occupied by the African American abolitionists and antiracists of the Colored National Convention of 1853. I also document an African American refusal through elision of the burdened individuality characteristic of the American nineteenth century that extends into the twentieth and twenty-first centuries. In so doing, I demonstrate how these men established and refined the character of these groups, and of the stranger relationality inherent to them, as well as how they worked with the enduring question of who stands within and outside of the circle. I moreover show that in doing the latter they probed the pressing issue of how the circle might be expanded without becoming indiscriminate and as a consequence politically ineffectual.

The next two chapters build on this initial account of how the making of self-evidence permitted African American men to engage in a fundamental refashioning of the human in theory and in practice. These chapters also track how the attribution of collective authorship present in the Colored Convention's "Address" signals an important element of these men's work on the human. The overall structure of *The Strangers Book* maps, then, one of its primary aims: to explore in detail the account of the human on offer in African American men's writing, from this period and in the decades that follow, but only after taking the question of petition off the table. Once these two tasks have been accomplished, I turn in the final two chapters to the methodological consequences of these men's account of stranger-with-ness.

In Chapter 2, I take up Frederick Douglass's sustained interest in the figure of the stranger in his writing from the fifteen years that led up to the U.S. Civil War. I read Douglass's engagement with the figure of the stranger and his investment in the editorial and organizing practices of black men in this period as indications of his sense that inhabiting and refiguring the stranger persona would be a key element in the achievement of African American male political and social enfranchisement. Douglass's inhabitation of the stranger persona is a canny acknowledgment of the mixed fortunes of the biblical stranger, who was a common figure in much antislavery discourse; it also responds to the limitations of a civic presence predicated on hospitality rather than on human right. Douglass's thoughtful tinkering with several different modes of address in his writing additionally exploits, I suggest, the surging literary view of the stranger as a symptom of modernity. His writing thus conjoins two versions of the stranger—a biblical one and the stranger as modern man—to make a case for a polis founded in scenes of stranger-with-ness. The new form of strangerhood that Douglass anticipates would release the stranger from his former roles in the anachronistic civic republicanism characterizing white abolitionism; it also sidesteps the stranger's recruitment into the project of liberal individualism. It furthermore rejects the patronizing offer of mere hospitality.

Chapter 3, "Les Apôtres de la Littérature and *Les Cenelles*," turns to an understudied volume of francophone poetry published in New Orleans. *Les Cenelles* has suffered a certain amount of neglect due to the social standing and formal habits of its authors. The francophone free men of color who contributed to the book did not participate in the founding scenes of the vernacular tradition in African American literature that in the 1980s came to justify the study of early African American writing. By the measures of vernacular criticism, this poetry is no more than a pale imitation of French romanticism. This chapter argues, however, that these writers do more than half-heartedly reflect the stylistic choices of Alphonse de Lamartine or Pierre-Jean de Béranger. The way that they use the figure of apostrophe and its relation to literary apostleship, in particular, as well as their commitment to extravagant social citationality represent reformations of both the republican and the liberal political traditions of speech. These reformations also resonate with Douglass's own interest in the stranger. Their tendency to address one another across the space of the volume; their inclusion of the songs to which their poems should be sung, in the manner of the French *chansonniers*; and their tracing of a seemingly lyric voice in highly populated settings all conduce, I argue, to this poetry's cultivation of stranger-with-ness by way of apostolic address.

These first three chapters cover, then, specific case studies of how African American men produced a sense of their own self-evident humanness; developed a stranger persona neither sacred nor secular but political in nature; and manufactured a way of being-with-strangers emergent from the production of an apostolic lyric address. In the final two chapters and in the Epilogue, I use these observations to rethink the methodological preoccupations of early African American literary studies. In particular, I seek to address a tension between, on the one hand, the long-standing and resurgent interest in respecting and preserving *le droit à l'opacité*, to recall Glissant's term, and, on the other, a commitment to figuring the archives of the African diaspora as the scene of an obfuscating crime. Although both positions are defensible, I suggest that they have also been difficult to reconcile with each other.

If the opacity of the African diasporic archive registers a traumatic crime, can opacity also be understood as an ethical and political stance in the battle against rac(ial)ism in a diasporic context? As an alternative to these two positions, I offer a practice of stranger history.

Chapter 4, "The Abundant Black Past," takes up the question of the broken archive by way of Jacques Rancière's account of the "equality of intelligences," Edward P. Jones's novel *The Known World* (2003), Douglass's "The Heroic Slave" (1852), and György Lukács's understanding of historical totality in *History and Class Consciousness* (1923). Through an extended reading of recent critical and historical work on nineteenth-century African American historiography, as well as the reflected image of this scholarship in critical theories of the African American postmodern, I suggest that a line of continuity connects these two late twentieth- and twenty-first-century frameworks. Both of them read absences and elisions as symptoms of white racist crimes against the African American archive, on the one hand, and as the sign of the sublime horror of the slave trade and life under slavery, on the other. These two views do agree on at least one thing: The primary contribution of African American writers, whether black historians writing in the nineteenth century or postmodernist black authors, has been to point up the impossibility, and the undesirability, of histories of totality. I suggest, however, that this view mistakes the identification of a problem (i.e., damage done to the archive) with one particular approach to solving it (i.e., a metacritical stance that rejects master narratives). I read Jones's novel, as well as a longer tradition of African American writing, as taking up the specific challenge of writing a total history of the black past, which in this tradition is equivalent to a history of totality. In this literary and historiographic tradition, scenes of strangers-in-relation drawn from the black past are all that is needed to tell the history of totality. In order to arrive at this total history, what Rancière calls the "equality of intelligences" must be assumed.

In Chapter 5, "How to Read a Strangers Book," I take these questions about opacity more deeply into the extraliterary archive. This chapter centers on two documents to theorize the aims and procedures of stranger history. The first document is a register of free people of color kept by the city of New Orleans from 1840 to 1864, at the insistence of the Louisiana Legislature, but whose pages exclude most of New Orleans's long-standing families of color, who were exempted from the Legislature's call to register with the authorities. The second is the Strangers Book kept by the Nantucket Atheneum, where Douglass gave a pivotal speech in 1841, in which entrants to the Atheneum who were not shareholders were registered. While these documents provide limited detail of the lives of the men and women whose names they record, they do offer a stable record of the procedures used to reckon dominant conceptions of strangerhood during this period, as well as the widespread nature of strategies of stranger management. By bringing the register of New Orleans's free people of color into dialogue with the Atheneum Strangers Book, I demonstrate a pervasive white attempt to regulate access to desirable forms of strangerhood. I also suggest a way of reading these strangers books against their grain so as to produce a form of stranger history productive of the total black history described in the previous chapter. In the Epilogue, "Stranger Literature," I conclude with the suggestion that attending to these antebellum African American men's vernacular theory of the human demands a further redefinition of the categories of judgment that determine what is and what is not literature.

CHAPTER ONE

The Making of Self-Evidence

À Mes Vers
Vous êtes, ô mes vers, orphelins sur la terre,
Car dès ce jour mon nom grossit l'obituaire
Des bardes fatigués qui brisèrent leur luth.
Ainsi donc, mes enfants, défendez-vous vous-mêmes;
Ne criez pas—A moi!—quand les astres sont blêmes,
Marchez sans appui vers le but!

[*Dear verses*
You are, dear verses, my orphan'd lonely heirs,
As this day on I have enrolled in the prayers
For the bards laid to rest, weary of applause.
And thus, my wards, you must now fight your own fight;
Cry not for help by the moon's fading light,
March, unflinchingly, for the cause!]

—M. Tullius St.-Céran, poet and printer,
Les Louisianaises: Poésies nouvelles (1840)[1]

One of the central activities of modern life is debating the topic of the human. Many who engage in this debate risk nothing in its practice. Whatever they say about the human, they have title clear to its dispensations. The same cannot be said for people of African descent contending with the racist West. It has taken a very long time for the humanness of African Americans, in particular, to be widely taken as self-evident. For some, then, the debate over what constitutes the human has had the appearance of an advanced parlor game. For others, it has meant asserting the simple right to be, while also examining the more complex aspects of being human. For better or for worse, the latter activity of thinking through advanced questions concerning the human, and being seen to do so, was historically the only thing that could secure the simple right to be. It is important, then, that nineteenth-century African American writers who focused on difficult questions regarding the human condition are often misrecognized as undertaking nothing more than a form of petition. Such misrecognition amounts to a cultivated practice of erasure. As Kwame Anthony Appiah has written: "[T]horoughgoing ignorance about the ways of others is largely a privilege of the powerful."[2] It is also one of the practices by way of which the powerful retain their power.

In the larger framework of this book, this chapter attempts to redress this erasure in two ways. First, it documents an idiomatic antiracist practice of reprinting that played a central role in establishing the self-evidence of African American humanness. Second, it makes manifest a political desire common to two groups of nineteenth-century African American men: one in the anglophone American North, the other in francophone New Orleans. My book's central aim is to give a reasonably responsive account of what their writing and their publishing suggest that these men wanted from the human, which differs from what is often imagined to have been the case. Although the chapters that follow focus on the cultivation of plurality in this writing's forms and institutional frameworks, as well as the consequence of that cultivation for African American literary study and historical inquiry, here I consider more narrowly how antebellum antiracist reprinting practices helped to secure the self-evident humanness of African American men. I also propose that those practices involved rejecting an account of the human that was common in this period and which entailed, as I show in later chapters, a congeries of suspect-stranger-making practices. These practices have often overshadowed the presence of a more radical stranger humanism in the making in this writing, which I also take up in the chapters that follow.

My discussion centers on General Andrew Jackson's 1814 addresses "To the Free Colored Inhabitants of Louisiana"; William Lloyd Garrison's 1837 *Thoughts on African Colonization*; and the 1853 "Address, of the Colored National Convention, to the People of the United States." Both Garrison and the Colored National Convention reprinted Jackson's 1814 addresses. However, the 1853 "Address" reprinting deletes from view, I will argue, the notion of burdened individuality that Saidiya Hartman identifies as the most durable impediment to African American advancement in Reconstruction and Jim Crow America.[3] The notion of burdened individuality is anticipated in

Jackson's first 1814 address, it emerges even earlier in the slave code of Spanish Louisiana, and it structures Garrison's *Thoughts*. The convention's 1853
"Address," though, cancels its representation. The "Address" thus makes a
consequential claim about the human condition by virtue of an elliptical
subtraction, offering a critique of a notion of transactional selfhood that
had origins in eighteenth-century natural-rights theory and in older Roman
legal traditions concerning enslavement that were reflected in the Spanish
and French colonial governance of Louisiana. This critique understands
itself to have ramifications for all people. In this sense, this stranger humanism is a humanism for all humans. In order to see these African American
men's claims and critique for what they are, however, it is necessary to identify first what those claims and critique are not. What they are not is a form
of petition. Neither do they have a single point of origin or a single target
of address.

Défendez-vous vous-mêmes

The story of this critique begins with the American colored national convention movement, a series of political conventions that briefly lay dormant
after the Cleveland Convention of 1848. The passage of the most aggressive of
America's fugitive slave laws, in 1850, would prompt a call for a new national
meeting in what was then Frederick Douglass's hometown of Rochester, New
York. As was the case with other colored conventions, the pamphlet issuing
from the Rochester Convention, which finally took place in 1853, included
the meeting's edited minutes, a description of its major events, and a statement of its general "sentiments." The pamphlet, known as the *Proceedings*,
also reprints General Andrew Jackson's 1814 addresses "To the Free Colored
Inhabitants of Louisiana." Douglass himself chaired the convention's committee on sentiments, which was responsible for the convention's "Address
. . . to the People of the United States" and for the reprinting of Jackson's texts.
Douglass also brought the *Proceedings* to press in the Rochester office of his
paper. The first printing of the committee's "Address" nevertheless appears
with authorship attributed to all members of the convention's committee
on sentiments. The *Proceedings* also records the full convention's deliberation over, and appointment of, that committee's members. The *Proceedings*
tells us that the committee on sentiments included, in addition to Douglass, the poet James Whitfield; the journalist and barber H. O. Wagoner; the
teacher and ordained minister the Reverend A. H. Freeman; and the lawyer

George B. Vashon. Such detailed attributions of collective authorship will prove important.[4]

By the time the Colored National Convention of 1853's committee on sentiments turned its attention to Jackson's addresses, the addresses had already been canonized as sacred texts of antiracist organizing. The fame of the first one had spread quickly forty years earlier, when Jackson ordered it published as a broadside in Louisiana. It also appeared in newspapers throughout the United States. Jackson drafted the first address in the autumn of 1814, as the British threatened to take New Orleans. Jackson was then commanding general of the U.S. forces responsible for defending New Orleans, and he was scrambling to muster troops to secure the area. With the aid of his guerrilla-like Tennessee Volunteers and with free men of color from Louisiana, Jackson would defend the city from British attack at the Battle of New Orleans. One of the modern world's infamous untimely conflicts, the Battle of New Orleans occurred on January 8, 1815, after the treaty officially concluding the war had been signed, sealed, and was being delivered.

In the months before the battle, Jackson was recruiting troops when and where he could. Jackson's first address is an artifact of those recruitment efforts; it aims to encourage Louisiana's free men of color to enlist in the federal militia. The second address congratulates those men who did enlist on their valorous service. Following their initial publication and first reprintings in 1814, these addresses accrued considerable significance. U.S. abolitionists and antiracists would present them as direct acknowledgments of black men's human and civil rights, much in the same way that abolitionists had canonized certain passages of the Bible for deployment in antislavery occasional texts, as will be seen in Chapter 2.

Not all reprintings of Jackson's addresses assumed what is elsewhere taken to be their obvious moral and political import. This first class of reprintings might be called the "newsy" ones. Jackson's initial address appears reprinted, for example, without comment and tucked among the war news in the December 3, 1814, issue of *Niles' Weekly Register* not long after Jackson ordered it to be issued. The *Register* was an icon of nineteenth-century information culture and a national resource for news from the Capitol. It focused on details of U.S. national political significance, including reports from Congress, accounts of foreign affairs, and coverage of white political conventions taking place around the nation. It was in this sense that *Niles'* was a register, or weekly chronicle, of events, and it was so in a much more limited sense than either of those terms (register or chronicle) would now suggest in a paper's masthead. It was intended as a register and as nothing more. That same day a more local paper, the *Engine of Liberty* of Uniontown, Maryland, would also present Jackson's first address, lacking either comment or editorial gloss and among its national news. The *Engine of Liberty*'s paucity of supplementary analysis and lack of commentary reflected the emerging conventions of factual news reporting, as well as the widespread practices of clipping and reprinting common in this period.[5]

A different want of interpretation characterizes many other reprintings of Jackson's addresses. From the moment of their first appearance, this second, "self-evidentiary" class of reprintings would begin to establish the central role that Jackson's addresses were to play in the work of antiracism. In this second class of reprintings, the absences surrounding and interrupting Jackson's addresses, including the paucity of interpretation and citation, as well as the introduction of many unmarked elisions, attached an aura of self-evidence to black men's humanness. Mechanical reproduction was made responsible, in other words, for generating the aura known as self-evidence. To see how this aura was produced, it is helpful to consider the organization of a text such as Julius Ruben Ames's *"Liberty." The Image and Superscription on Every Coin Issued by the United States of America* (1837). *Liberty* is a 231-page compendium of documents ancient and modern, U.S. and international, all of them compiled to serve the main goals of its publisher, the American Anti-Slavery Society. *Liberty* reprints the U.S. Constitution, Joel Barlow's poetry, Bible verse, extracts from biographies of Toussaint L'Ouverture, and many other documents. It reprints these materials largely without gloss or interpretation. It also reprints Jackson's addresses. The only bibliographic note attached to the addresses is a header above the second one indicating that it was originally issued in French.

Before turning to the larger significance of these facts about *Liberty*, it is worth noting that Jackson's addresses would resurface again and again, into the nineteenth, twentieth, and twenty-first centuries. They turn up in William Lloyd Garrison's *Thoughts on African Colonization* (1837); William Yates's *Rights of Colored Men to Suffrage, Citizenship and Trial by Jury* (1838); the *Minutes of the* [1851] *State Convention* [of the] *Colored Citizens of Ohio*; *The Schenectady* (N.Y.) *Cabinet* of March 24, 1857; *The* (San Francisco) *Elevator* of December 11, 1868; and *The* (Chicago) *Broad Ax*'s September 5, 1914, account of U.S. Congressman Martin B. Madden's address to the U.S. House of Representatives. Many similar examples exist. By 1838, Yates was already describing these addresses as Jackson's "celebrated proclamations"; Garrison had characterized the second one in 1837 as Jackson's "famous Proclamation."

The 1914 instance reports Congressman Madden's speech to the U.S. House of Representatives arguing against the proposed segregation of people of color who worked for the federal government. That speech also refers to Jackson's addresses. The most recent examples appear on heritage websites that reproduce the *Niles' Weekly Register* reprinting; such sites are established for descendants of New Orleans's antebellum soldiers of color.

It is true that each reprinting, including the one in *Liberty*, uses the addresses to somewhat different ends. It is also the case that on the whole antiracists came to present Jackson's addresses as almost scriptural in their self-evident meaning. We see this implication of self-evidence figured in the positioning of Jackson's first address in Ames's *Liberty*, where it is presented as a self-explanatory testament to be read alongside other sacred and secular scripture, as compared to its placement in *Niles' Weekly Register*, where it was made into news. In *Liberty*, Jackson's addresses are made to validate the a priori nature of human liberty, and they are made to do so in a way that recalls the function of the coin's seal pictured on the opening page of the volume. As presented, the documents included in the volume do not argue for black men's human liberty in the manner of a syllogistic proposition. They instead certify it, as might a seal invested with the force of law vis-à-vis a documentary legal record. The bibliographic and editorial apparatuses attached to reprintings of Jackson's addresses are accordingly minimal in texts, such as this one, that signify self-evidence. Sometimes those apparatuses are nonexistent. As in the *Liberty* reprinting, an implicit recourse to the authority of a *sola scriptura* model of absented reading instead identifies human liberty, like God's word, as self-evidently meaningful upon a first sighting. Such reprintings of Jackson's addresses in this sense strip these documents of their significance as items of war news and insert them into a continuing story of self-evident humanness spread across the length and breadth of history. In *Liberty*, and elsewhere, the Bible, the Constitution, and Jackson's addresses are made to tell, or made to be assumed to tell, the same story of a self-evidently universal humanity inclusive of black men. Like these other documents, Jackson's addresses are presented as requiring only limited comment, as going without saying: They testify to the humanity and consequent liberty of African American men without having to say an audible word on the subject. This silent testimony permits a crucial shift: These reprintings foreclose the redundant and morally repugnant exercise of debating whether black men should be considered human.

This turning toward self-evidence as the ground of African American political speech will be familiar to students of African American intellectual history. As the nineteenth century wore on, the dual frustrations of mounting racism and unending racial slavery led antiracist African American thinkers to resist anything resembling a definitional debate over the ontological status of black people and the rights attending that status. The January 29, 1847, issue of *The Liberator*, for example, published Frederick Douglass's response to Henry C. Wright, which Douglass had written from St. Ann's Square, Manchester, United Kingdom, on December 22, 1846. Explaining his decision to accept the efforts of his antislavery colleagues to purchase his "free papers" from his then-"legal" owner, Douglass states: "From every view I have been able to take of the subject, I am persuaded to receive the papers, if presented,—not, however, as a proof of my right to be free, for *that is self-evident*, but as a proof that my friends have been legally robbed of £150, in order to secure that which is the birth-right of every man." Douglass's statement first locates one of the main rhetorical challenges of nineteenth-century antiracist agitation: how to make self-evident a birthright denied by (white) people asserting the "privilege of unknowing."[6] Douglass then circumvents the typical discussion: Rather than allow those "free papers" to signify freedom, Douglass turns them into nothing more than the signature of a petty theft of £150. His liberty and his rights have nothing to do with it.

The key rhetorical challenge facing antiracists such as Douglass on this front remained the fact that reprinting Jackson's addresses as a form of evidence could be seen to undermine those addresses' status as self-evidentiary. (The same might be said of Douglass's asserting his "*self-evident*" "right to be free.") The self-evident should never need to be restated through reprinting; it should never have required stating or printing in the first instance.[7] The self-evident should tell its tale in silence. From another perspective, however, it is possible to understand these multiple reprintings as having sutured self-evidence to these statements rather than simply as giving the lie to the claim to self-evidence. Reprinting from this perspective takes what argument and interpretation previously or elsewhere make evident and transforms it into the now-self-evident. The mechanism of reprinting affixed self-evidence to Jackson's addresses by way of adjunctive assembly and disassembly, both across space and over time, distributing the task of making self-evidence across several instances of media production. Reprinting in this way helped to relieve black antiracist humanists, in particular, of the unseemly and debilitating task of making evident something whose self-evidence was routinely denied: their humanity and the rights attaching to it.

How did self-evidencing work? A third class of reprintings of Jackson's addresses laid the groundwork for the affixing of self-evidence by including with Jackson's addresses an exegesis of them. This class of exegetical reprint-ings established the set of queries that could be taken as pertinent to the addresses, while at the same time making a set of answers to those queries "evident." In more or less simultaneous venues located elsewhere within the same frame of circulation, as well as in chronologically later ones, other self-evidentiary reprintings of Jackson's addresses disappeared those (heu-ristically) primary instances of exegetical reprinting, or made glancing ref-erences to them. Those glancing references invoke the (again, heuristically) primary exegesis that took place earlier or elsewhere and that had articulated the sort of reading community needed to make self-evidence possible. (This notion of the heuristically primary recalls Hans Robert Jauss's idea of a read-er's induced "horizon of expectations," as well as Talal Asad's reminder that medieval Christians "learnt the meanings of elaborate allegories used in the mass through authorized commentaries.")[8] Exegetical reprinting takes pains to make a text's meaning evident to a range of readers, a range wide enough to make that meaning ipso facto self-evident in another reprinting. Reprint-ing in this context entails a moment of nearly simultaneous interpretation-plus-forgetting-of-interpretation that turns what has been made evident into the self-evident. This was a critical undertaking in the natural rights–based culture of the nineteenth-century United States.

Crucially, this creation of self-evidence through the process of reprint-ing licensed African American thinkers to take their humanity as a given. To state this point a different way, African American writers were able to take their humanity as a given by having it given "there" or "then," without having to say it "here" or "now." As the temporal and spatial coordinates of that statement suggest, the process of self-evidencing depends on auspicious conditions making reprinting possible. These auspicious conditions included functional presses, adequate circulation, capital backing, and felicitous con-ditions of copyright. All of these remained central concerns of antislavery and antiracist agitators throughout the nineteenth century. These things also concerned proslavery and racist activists, as is clear from their attacks on abolitionist presses, their interference with U.S. postal regulations, and their efforts to control the interstate flow of funds. Few social movements have been as attentive to the nodes in its communication circuit as were the ante-bellum movements to end slavery and racism. If there is a more attentive movement, it is probably antebellum proslavery racism. Without a highly developed communication circuit, self-evidencing simply could not happen; self-evidencing requires a readerly horizon of expectation that follows from a document's more or less simultaneous evidencing and self-evidencing.

Self-evidence turns out to be contingent not just on formal choices such as mode of address. It also relies on Douglass having a press available to print the *Proceedings of the Colored National Convention* of 1853; William Lloyd Garrison or someone close to him reading French well enough to translate Jackson's second address; the 1853 Colored National Convention's committee on sentiments having access either to Garrison's *Thoughts on African Colonization* or to some other reprinting of Jackson's addresses; and the abolition and colored national convention movements having distribution networks on hand to ensure that none of these documents died on the vine.

Lessons in Self-Evidence

Tracing the lives of Jackson's two addresses between the time of their initial appearance in 1814 and their reprinting by the 1853 Colored National Convention demonstrates the role that antiracism's robust reprinting apparatus played in this process of self-evidencing. It also begins to bring into focus the advanced work on the human that this apparatus enabled. One of the early and influential contributions to the cause of making evident the meaning of Jackson's addresses, and therefore a main and early agent in the process of their self-evidencing, was William Lloyd Garrison's *Thoughts on African Colonization: Or an Impartial Exhibition of the Doctrines, Principles and Purposes of the American Colonization Society. Together with the Resolutions, Addresses, and Remonstrances of the Free People of Color* (1832). Garrison's *Thoughts* is a curious polemic whose goal is to recant Garrison's own earlier endorsement of the American Colonization Society (ACS), a position that he had come to regret, not without some committed urging from his black co-agitationists.

Although it appears that Garrison intended to appease his black critics with *Thoughts*, it is difficult to see how he imagined that this would work, because *Thoughts* finds Garrison at his most egotistical and self-regarding. In it, he describes at length his reasons for his early support of the ACS and his recent change of view. Across its many lines, including those condemning the ACS, *Thoughts* tracks Garrison's recurrent problems with the management of address. Its initial pages include his dedication of *Thoughts on African Colonization* to his "countrymen, in whose intelligence, magnanimity and humanity [he] places the utmost reliance." The dedication sustains this intercourse with Garrison's "countrymen" as follows: "Although they have long suffered themselves to be swayed by a prejudice as unmanly as it is wicked, and have departed widely from the golden rule of the gospel, in their treatment of the people of color, to suppose that they will always be the despisers and persecutors of this unfortunate class is, in my opinion, to libel their character."[9] Garrison's decision to address his "countrymen" in this way initially appears to be an informed one, as is clear from the potential for slippage between the nominal and actual addressees of his statement. It is nevertheless also the case that Garrison runs into trouble when he isolates as his countrymen only those who are not people of color. In particular, the potential for a productive slippage between a nominal and an actual addressee begins to close down when Garrison presents African Americans as an "unfortunate class" deserving charitable concern. The countrymen captured by that "they" in Garrison's opening lines (i.e., racist whites) seem initially to be only the nominal addressees, with the actual addressees comprising anyone who shared Garrison's political stance and who could therefore participate in an ironic distancing from Garrison's (white racist) countrymen. This might include enslaved and free African Americans. With its identification of people of color as an "unfortunate class," Garrison's dedication shuts down this opening onto a polis constituted around nothing more than a shared commitment to antiracism, which is to say a polis constituted around nothing more than a politics. Garrison in this sense opens on the wrong note. In the lengthy argument that follows he will seek to establish that people of color warrant the honorific address of "my countrymen." This occurs despite the fact that Garrison's dedication of *Thoughts* has already displaced people of color from that category. Garrison further conflates "my countrymen" and racist whites a few pages later, when he shifts from the volume's dedication to its "Introductory Remarks." In these remarks, Garrison states his intention to "address [himself] to high-minded and honorable men, whose heads and hearts are susceptible to the force of sound logic."[10] Who are those "high-minded and honorable men?" The same racist whites addressed earlier. All of this happens in full view of Garrison's stated concerns, found in his "Address to the People of Color, delivered in various places in June, 1831," which is also reprinted in *Thoughts* and in which Garrison claims to repudiate the ACS ideologists, who "generally agree in publishing the misstatement, that you [people of color] are strangers and foreigners."[11] Notwithstanding the noble sentiments of that reprinted 1831 "Address to the People of Color," Garrison had already, in the dedication of *Thoughts*, positioned this particular (African American) "you" as outside the realm of "countrymen." "You" were precisely "strangers and foreigners" of the inassimilable kind. He positions "you" as suspect-strangers. As elsewhere, Garrison has a hard time aligning his form with his content. (Sometimes even his content seems misaligned with itself.)

That misalignment matters. Whether it is a symptom of Garrison's racism, his egomania, or his rhetorical genius is initially difficult to discern.

By the conclusion of his introductory remarks, the last possibility will seem unlikely. Closing his introduction with an explanation of why he took up rhetorical arms against the ACS, Garrison writes, "Wherever my ear caught a sound, I heard nothing but excessive panegyric. No individual had ventured to blow the trumpet of alarm, or exert his energies to counteract the influence of the scheme."[12] That statement likely came as something of a surprise to those of Garrison's white comrades who had waged more than one battle against the ascendance of the ACS. It would have surprised too the signers of a document that Garrison reprints in *Thoughts* under the heading "A Voice from Philadelphia." This "Voice" he dates to 1817, or fifteen years before the publication of his *Thoughts*, and it takes up the question of colonization. It is attributed to "Rev. Absalom Jones, Rev. Richard Allen, James Forten, Robert Douglass, Francis Perkins, Rev. John Gloucester, Robert Gordon, James Johnson, Quamoney Clarkson, John Summersett, Randall Shepherd."[13] It opens as follows:

> At a numerous meeting of the people of color, convened at Bethel Church, to take into consideration the propriety of remonstrating against the contemplated measure, that is to exile us from the land of our nativity; James Forten was called to the chair, and Russell Parrott appointed secretary. . . .
>
> Resolved, That we never will separate ourselves voluntarily from the slave population in this country; they are our brethren by the ties of consanguinity, of suffering, and of wrong; and we feel that there is more virtue in suffering privations with them, than fancied advantages for a season.[14]

For this "numerous" people of color, at least, the undesirability of the colonization scheme was clear, its danger present, and the necessity of marking both facts in print indisputable. If this is not a "trumpet of alarm," then I do not know what is.

Garrison reprints the Philadelphia resolution, or "Voice," after his initial "Thoughts," which take up two-thirds of Garrison's hefty document. The Philadelphia "Voice" appears in a second section reprinting materials from the African American community, which are allocated a scant third of the volume. This Part II, "Sentiments of the People of Color," opens with Garrison discussing the patriotic feeling, the "love of home and country," common to any sentient being.[15] Garrison acknowledges that many (racist whites) have suggested that "the people of color cannot cherish [an] abhorrence of migration, because here they have no 'continuing city,' and are not recognised as fellow-countrymen." Again, he claims to have demonstrated in Part I that this sentiment is libelous: It is white "colonizationists," he purports to have shown, who "artfully represent [people of color] as aliens and foreigners, wanderers from Africa—destitute of that *amor patriae*, which is the bond of union— seditious—without alliances—irresponsible—unambitious—cherishing no attachment to the soil—feeling no interest in our national prosperity—ready for any adventure—eager to absent themselves from the land—malignant in their feelings toward society—incapable of local preference—content to remain in ignorance and degradation—&c. &c. &c."[16] Garrison concludes his recitation of these slanderous charges, which he seems to savor the rhetorical effect of repeating, with a fiery denunciation:

> Every such representation is a libel, as I shall show in subsequent pages. The language of the people of color is,—"This is our country: here were we born—here we will live and die—we know of no other place that we can call our true and appropriate home—here are our earliest and most pleasant associations—we are freemen, we are brethren, we are countrymen and fellow-citizens—we are not for insurrection, but for peace and equality." This is not the language of sedition or alienated affection. Their *amor patriae* is robust and deathless: like the oak, tempests do but strengthen its roots and confer victory upon it. Even the soil on which the unhappy slave toils and bleeds, is to him consecrated earth.
>
> African colonization is directly and irreconcilably opposed to the wishes of our colored population as a body.[17]

If nothing else, we learn two things from that last line: Garrison is content to think of the "colored population" as "a body" or mass; he also considers that massive body to be "ours." Lucky us.

Dismissing Garrison in the way that I have begun to do grows considerably more difficult when the legacy of *Thoughts* is fairly considered. The document's aggressive denunciation of ACS aims and practices functioned, it turns out, as a source text for many later antiracists and abolitionists, both white and black, and it played a prominent role in the ongoing circulation of Jackson's addresses. It furthermore cements the familiar methodological principle that will organize much nineteenth-century antislavery and antiracist reprinting: On its title page, and as an epigraph to the full two-volume codex, Garrison includes an amalgam of Luke 19:22 and Job 15:6: "Out of thine own mouth will I condemn thee." Such is the general logic of antebellum abolitionist and antiracist agitation, whose strategies of citation and reprinting were at the core of these movements.

Consider in these contexts William Yates's 1838 *Rights of Colored Men to Suffrage, Citizenship and Trial by Jury: Being a Book of Facts, Arguments and Authorities, Historical Notices and Sketches of Debates—with Notes.* This volume identifies and directs itself toward a specific problem in the history of African America: the inattention in antiracist discourse to distinctions between free men of color and enslaved men of African descent. According to Yates, antiracists had ignored free men of color's citizenship rights, and their right to trial by jury, in favor of a perhaps justified, but still problematic, interest in the fortunes of enslaved persons in the U.S. South. Yates suggests that this interest has been consequential for free men of color:

> The condition of the slave—all that relates to him—the multiplied wrongs he is subject to—the sundering of domestic ties—his scourgings—unrequited toil—mental and moral deprivations—and even his food and sleep; all have been examined and re-examined with minutest care. But the kindred duty we owe to the freeman of color—has it been discharged with equal fidelity? Have the same pains been taken to guage [*sic*] the height and depth of his embarrassments [*sic*], aggravated by prejudice, and the legal disabilities which cripple and hinder his progress?[18]

For Yates the answer is no, and this oversight is untenable. He seeks to remedy it through the compilation of extracts from addresses, legal arguments, correspondence, histories, and other modes of discourse, all of which he presents as testimonials to the rights of free men of color. As Yates understands it, Jackson's original addresses participate in this fight and are on the right side of it (to a degree).

Yates subdivides his aims in the early pages of *Rights of Colored Men* into three: He hopes to prove the right of suffrage, the right to citizenship, and the right to trial by jury, as each of these rights is separately demonstrated in the documentary records of the United States, Europe, and antiquity. When he turns to his consideration of Jackson's first and second addresses, he states the following: "General Jackson, in his celebrated proclamations to the free colored inhabitants of Louisiana, uses these expressions: '*Your* WHITE fellow-citizens;'—and again: '*Our* brave *citizens are united,* and *all* contention has ceased *among them.*'"[19] Whether a pedant, a scholar, or a bit of both, Yates next includes a parenthetical header, "(Extracts)," which appears above Yates's main reprinting of Jackson's first address. His notice that these are extracted passages is in addition to a meticulous list, at the outset of the volume, noting "ERRATA ET ADDENDA." Although no ellipses mark the precise location of the elision that extracting requires, Yates does concede the tenuousness of mobilizing his extracts from Jackson to a cause any larger than the very limited one that Jackson appeared to have intended: "Now, to turn language employed as this was for a special object and without premeditation," Yates writes, "into a ground of inference, to establish or defeat a particular doctrine or theory, would, it is true, in the absence of other testimony, be rather slight and inconclusive."[20] Notwithstanding this initial concession that perhaps the evidentiary status of Jackson's addresses was subject to debate, the telltale "surely" in the phrase that will follow signals Yates's initial move toward a claim for self-evidence relying precisely on the "absence of other testimony," or what is really the disappearing of that testimony, and its replacement with a new set of frames that makes Jackson's addresses sensible in a different way. "[B]ut in this case," Yates continues, "as far as it goes, and especially as taken in connexion with other proof, [Jackson's address] strongly affirms the citizenship of the free colored people; for surely, if *white* men are *fellow*-citizens with free colored men, as the general's language implies, free colored men themselves must needs be citizens."[21] The watertight nature of Yates's initial hazarded syllogism gets called into question by the "surely" and the "implies," as well as by the invocation of "other proof," with this last reference to "other proof" shifting the ground of argumentation from an assertively deductive logic to the dependence on external proof characteristic of induction. Yates wants to have it both ways.

When Yates and his typesetter turn to the mechanics of reprinting the two addresses, which is to say the process of choosing and setting type, any lingering respect for the integrity of the earlier documents dissolves. Yates is scrupulous enough to include, in addition to his cautionary warning that these are extracts, a citation for his reprinting of the first address, which, as it turns out, is one of the papers with which we began: "*Niles' Weekly Register,* Dec. 3, 1814, vol. vii p. 205." A fair number of typographical and editorial liberties are taken, however, with the actual typeface and extracting. The *Niles' Weekly Register* variant includes a discreetly italicized "*To the free colored inhabitants of Louisiana*" and "*Headquarters*" in the signature line; "ANDREW JACKSON" is also fully capitalized. It is otherwise a picture of roman rectitude. In this sense, *Niles' Weekly Register* largely mirrors the copy found in Jackson's letterbook from the field, with a few key exceptions to be considered shortly. By comparison, Yates's variant of Jackson's first address manipulates type in such a way as to call explicit attention to Jackson's figures of address. Yates's reprinting is not a welter of typefaces, but it does array typebound emphasis in purposeful ways. Yates is especially attentive at this level to Jackson's patterning of second-person pronominal address and his assignment of national belonging: "you," "fellow-citizens," "Americans," and other similar words and phrases stand out in italics, full majuscules, or some combination of the two. Similar things happen in his reprinting of Jackson's second address. What the second address's reprinting noticeably lacks is a citation trail. This is unusual in the context of *Rights*. Elsewhere Yates is at pains to trace his sources to their origin. Why reprint Jackson's second address in an unattributed form that invites hostile questions regarding authenticity, especially in the context of an antebellum United States preoccupied with the issue of certifying any testimony having to do with black people's subjection? Perhaps because Yates's likely source was Garrison's *Thoughts*, a document whose overtly politicized tone would undercut the scholarly patina that Yates seeks to associate with his *Rights of Colored Men*. Better no clear source than a trail leading to Garrison: The self-evident must be seen to emerge from the nature of human nature, rather than from arguments about it.

Lay Down Your Burden (Before You Pick It Up)

The earliest record of Andrew Jackson's first address to the "free colored inhabitants of Louisiana" appears in his letterbook from the field, which includes transcriptions of Jackson's incoming and outgoing correspondence. One line in particular stands out as essential to the critical significance of this address. That line is crucial because it is absent from the reprinting of Jackson's address in the 1853 *Proceedings of the Colored National Convention*. This fourteen-word redaction reveals much about the racist humanism already on offer, as well as antiracist African American interventions into standing accounts of the human. We will return to those fourteen words in a moment.

The letterbook draft of Jackson's first address follows upon the transcription of a telling correspondence between Jackson and William Charles Cole Claiborne, the first elected governor of the State of Louisiana. The first inkling of what will become the address appears in a letter from Claiborne to Jackson dated August 12, 1814. In that letter, Claiborne explains that Louisiana's

French and Spanish colonial administrations had relied on men of color in times of martial need. The practice extended back to 1732, when the French Company of the Indies enlisted enslaved men of African descent to defend the commercial colony at New Orleans. Since its acquisition by the United States, in 1803, however, Louisiana's U.S. territorial and state governments had resisted the mustering of black troops. In the first decade of the nineteenth century, as head of the territorial administration, Claiborne had lobbied hard to reinstate the colonial practice of enlisting troops of color. Creole free men of color had come to see their history of military service as an important indicator of their status in the wider community. With the influx of Haitian refugees to New Orleans, after their 1809 expulsion from Cuba, and with a ragtag colony of French radicals, refugees, and outlaw corsairs taking shape in Barataria Bay, just below the city, Claiborne worried about the waning of Creole of color loyalties to the United States. The Louisiana Legislature ignored him: It repeatedly and very deliberately prevented free men of color from enlisting. Claiborne's letter to Jackson raises the stakes on this issue. It asks Jackson, the ranking U.S. military officer, to tender his opinion on the question of whether "all the free men of Colour in New Orleans, & its vicinity, being natives of Louisiana [and] represented to be about Six hundred might be organized, & received as a part of the Militia."[22] Claiborne explains that these men are of "good character" and "inured to the *climate* of Louisiana." He therefore inclines toward enlisting their service. Jackson replied just over a week later, on August 22, 1814, in favor of enlisting free men of color. In the end, state legislators would concede that, given the encroachment of the British, they needed to muster a "Militia for the service of the State of Louisiana, as well as for its defense." This militia would comprise "a certain portion of chosen men from among the free men of colour."[23] Mounting wartime pressure on local white militiamen led to the creation of not only this troop of "chosen" men of color, but also other nonwhite corps.

This would not happen, though, before local white men of influence had had their say. On September 21, 1814, Jackson makes his first direct reference to the recruitment address that would play a key role in the formation of the self-enlisting corps of free men of color (as opposed to the Legislature's "chosen" men of color). In a letter to Claiborne that found Jackson agitated by the shifting circumstances of the war, the general calls for the publication of the address. From his headquarters in Mobile, he writes:

> Our country has been invaded, and threatned with destruction. She wants Soldiers to fight her battles. The free men of colour in your city

[New Orleans] are inured to the Southern climate and would make
excellent Soldiers. They will not remain quiet spectors of the interesting contest. They must be either for, or against us—distrust them,
and you make them your enemies, place confidence in them, and you
engage them by Every dear and honorable tie to the interest of the
country who extends to them equal rights and privileges with white
men. I enclose you a copy of my address to them for publication, and
wish an experiment made for raising a Regt of them. They will be
officered by white men except the non commissioned officers, and
be placed upon the same footing with other volunteers for the war.
Should you succeed in raising a Regt Batallion or company advise me,
and I will send one of my aids to organize and pay them their Bounty
under the act of congress placing them on an equality with soldiers
procured by enlistment. No objections can be raised by the citizens of
N Orleans on account of their engagement, as they [the enlisted free
men of color] will be removed from amongst them [the white citizens
of New Orleans], if fears of their fidelity are entertained. I also enclose
you an address to the citizens of Louissiana, for publication.[24]

The letter concludes with a reference to the current state of the Choctaw
nation, as well as to the "overgrown pride of Britain."[25]

Claiborne's reply will be significant. Even here, though, in Jackson's letter,
there is cause to take issue with many antiracist and African American reprintings of Jackson's address. The mercenary pragmatism of Jackson's decision to
enlist free men of color tells against the high-minded sentiments later attributed
to him. Jackson appears to be, for example, immune to the ironies of his letter
to Claiborne. He suggests that enlisting free men of color will "engage them
by Every dear and honorable tie to the interests of the country who extends
to them equal rights and privileges with white men." He also states that "they
will be officered by white men except the non commissioned officers, and be
placed upon the same footing with other volunteers for the war." For Jackson,
the fact that African American men cannot serve as commissioned officers, as
they had done under Spain, does not register either as a hierarchical injustice
or as a logical contradiction to the statement that these men are on the "same
footing" as white men. Neither does he seem to think it odd that the wholesale
displacement of these soldiers from their home city should be undertaken at
the whim of the city's white citizens. Then there is that line about the other
enclosed address to the "citizens" of Louisiana. One might anticipate that the
difference reflected in the title of the two addresses, one to "inhabitants" and

the other to "citizens," tracks a distinction of the citizens of Louisiana (of whatever color) from the free men of color who were inhabitants of New Orleans. The content of these addresses suggests instead that Jackson simply had a difficult time countenancing the idea of a black U.S. citizen. Black citizens might exist in law, but in Jackson's parlance, and by virtue of it, all citizens were de facto white. At least some of the ironies of Jackson's letter make more sense if we assume Jackson's familiarity with the local history of black military recruitment and black uprising, as well as the more recent influx of refugees from Haiti. As Caryn Cossé Bell explains: "[A] sharp increase in the numbers of free people of color occurred between May, 1809, and January, 1810, when the Spanish government expelled thousands of Saint Domingue refugees from Cuba. Forced to seek asylum in New Orleans, over ten thousand white, free black, and slave exiles nearly doubled the size of the urban population."[26] Claiborne made the outline of these facts familiar to Jackson; he also noted the growth of the Barataria Bay encampment of corsairs, black and white French radicals, and radical republicans from Haiti.

The citizen-whites of New Orleans were, though, unmoved by Jackson's stated desire for a broadscale mustering of black troops. Thus those citizen-whites appear in full force in Claiborne's letter of reply, on October 17, 1814, regarding Jackson's two recently dispatched addresses: the one to the "free colored inhabitants of Louisiana" and the other to its "citizens." Claiborne's letter explains why the publication of both had been delayed. He tells Jackson that Jackson's letter containing both addresses was misdirected at Natchez. Notwithstanding this untimely delay, the address to Louisiana's citizens had now been published and was in "circulation." Not so with Jackson's communication to Louisiana's "free colored inhabitants." Claiborne explains that an influential group of "respectable [white] citizens" objected to the raising of a regiment of men of color from the city, an objection they had voiced many times since the Louisiana Purchase, out of a fear that to do so would be to "add to the force of the Enemy, and that nothing short of placing [free men of color] upon a footing with white citizens (which [Louisiana's] constitution forbids) could conciliate their affections." According to Claiborne, the only way that local white "Gentlemen of Influence" could foresee putting Jackson's plan into effect would be for Jackson not only to remove the black regiment from the state, as he had already promised to do, but also to provide a "guaranty, against the return of the [black] Regiment." These white "Gentlemen of Influence" feared that if "the Individuals [enlisted in the black regiment] were to settle in to Louisiana, with a Knowledge of the use of arms, & *that pride of Distinction*, which a soldiers pursuits so naturally inspires, they would prove dangerous." These citizen-whites might have been selectively remembering the charges brought against Pierre Bailly, a late eighteenth-century free man of color who served in the *pardo* militia under Spanish colonial control and achieved the rank of first lieutenant. A competitor later falsely accused him of conspiring with other free men of color and enslaved persons of African descent. Although Bailly was acquitted, this and other memories of real and imagined resistance lingered in the minds of the city's whites. In the event, the message of New Orleans's citizen-whites to their free men of color neighbors was clear: The citizen-whites would be willing to suffer free men of color to serve their homeland, but only if those free men of color agreed to alienate themselves permanently from any attachment to that homeland. Even Governor Claiborne recognized the folly of this proposal. "Such as are natives of Louisiana," he writes, "are much attached to their families & Homes, and I am inclined to think would not inlist during the war; But such as have emigrated, from St. Domingo & Cuba, may most probably be desirous to Join the army."[27] This is one among many episodes in the miserable history of racialized enlistment. It also marks a significant origin for the racist sentiment described in William Lloyd Garrison's 1831 "Address to the People of Color," the one that suggested the rootlessness of African Americans caused them to lack *amor patriae*. In this peculiar world, the only way for free men of color to prove their *amor patriae* would be to betray it, a betrayal that could then be used to prove their lack of *amor patriae*.

According to a letter from Claiborne on November 4, 1814, Jackson's address to the "free colored inhabitants of Louisiana" was finally published as a broadside at Jackson's insistence. Although no extant copy of the broadside has been located, Jackson's letterbook draft of the first address reads as follows:

> To the Free coloured Inhabitants of Louisiania
> Through a mistaken policy, my brave fellow Citizens, you have heretofore been deprived of a participation in the Glorious struggle for National rights, in which our Country is engaged.—This shall no longer exist, as sons of freedom, you are now called upon to defend our most estimable blessing. As Americans, your Country looks with confidence to her adopted Children, for a valorous support, as a partial return for the advantages enjoyed under her mild and equitable government. As fathers, husbands, and Brothers, you are summoned to rally around the standard of the Eagle, to defend all which is dear in existance.

Your intelligent minds are not to be led away by false representations. Your love of honor would cause you to despise the man who should attempt to deceive you. I shall not attempt it. In the sincerity of a Soldier, and the language of truth, I address you.

Your Country, altho' calling for your exertions does not wish you to engage in her cause, without amply remunerating you for the services rendered.

To every noble hearted generous brave freeman of color volunteering to serve during the present contest with Great Britain, and no longer, there will be the same bounty in Money & land, now received by the white soldiers of the United States viz $124.00 in Cash and 160 acres of Land. The Non Com. Officers and privates will also be entitled to the same monthly pay and daily rations, and clothing furnished to every American Soldier. On enrolling yourselves, the General will select Officers for your government from among your white fellow Citizens. Your Non Comm. Officers will be appointed from among yourselves. Due regard will be paid to the feelings of freemen, and Soldiers. You will not, by being associated with other men not the same Couler, be exposed to improper comparisons or unjust sarcasm. As a distinct, independant Battallion or Regiment, pursuing the path of glory, you will undivided receive the applause, reward, and gratitude, of your Countrymen.

To assure you of the sincerity of my intentions and my anxiety to engage your invaluable services to our Country I have communicated with the Executive of Lo[uisiana] who is fully informed as to the manner, of Enrollment, and will give you your necessary information on the subject of this address.[28]

This is the last documentary record of Jackson's address before it turns up in *Niles' Weekly Register*. It also differs in significant ways from later reprintings of Jackson's addresses.

There are many ways to parse Jackson's draft address so as to deflate any sense that it unequivocally affirms much of anything about African American men, but I want to focus on its references to debt and repayment. This focus will illuminate the specific work undertaken by antebellum antiracists who resisted the troubling notion of the human that is in fact embedded in Jackson's phrasing. At least twice in the letterbook version, Jackson evokes a transactional selfhood that undercuts the (bad-faith) equalitarian tone strained at elsewhere in the address. This language of transactional selfhood emphasizes black men's debt to the nation-state. This language appears first in the reference to military service as a "partial return for the advantages enjoyed under [the United States'] mild and equitable government," and second in Jackson's reference to "amply remunerating you for the services rendered." The second reference seems the more benign of the two, until it is read in light of the first. For the first reference reveals both of them for what they are: veiled threats to withdraw America's "mild and equitable government" and replace it with something harsher. This is anything but a soldier's appeal to equals, whatever Jackson might have said to the contrary. The first reference suggests, moreover, that free black men have been treated equitably by the state; as a result, those free men of color owe the state a debt that is equivalent to the price of their lives. The equal treatment that should follow from a radical notion of natural rights wherein the human resides in unowned fleshliness (and in nothing more) gets subtracted from the black man. Jackson thus rejects the view captured in a passage of Works Progress Administration testimony that Saidiya Hartman summarizes as follows: "The flesh, existence defined at its most elemental level, alone entitled one to liberty."[29] According to Jackson, free men of color in New Orleans instead owe a debt to the United States, because the United States has extended certain rights and privileges to them through its "mild and equitable government." It is not that black men have agreed to mix the natural rights inherent to their flesh with the natural rights of other (white) men to form a democratic state. White men have at their will and pleasure suffered black men the enjoyment of temporary privileges rather than responding to their rights. The facts are therefore clear. Rights that are no more than a gift trailing the debt that all gifts carry with them can always be retracted. Even when they are not, the gift of right is always presented to a debtor.

This logic of debt would have been particularly galling to New Orleans's free men of color. A number of them owed their freedom to a predatory system of debt and repayment enacted under the eighteenth-century Spanish colonial regime. *Las Siete Partidas*, the Spanish slave code, allowed for *coartación*, or self-purchase for the purpose of manumission. According to Bell, this "measure permitted slaves to accumulate personal funds by selling their extra labor to their masters or other people in need of their services. This source of income enabled slaves to purchase their freedom. An accompanying measure required the slaveholder to set a fair purchase price. If the slave considered the cost of self-purchase excessive, the bondsman could appeal to Spanish authorities for the imposition of a just value."[30] A fair number of the free men of color living in New Orleans in the 1810s were descendants of

eighteenth-century free men of color who had purchased their own freedom
in precisely this way. In this sense, the state had already set the price of these
men's debt burden; they, or their ancestors, had moreover paid a "just" price
for their own and their descendants' freedom. The notion of a renewed debt
would have seemed a bitter pill indeed.

More generally, Jackson invokes the notion of "burdened individuality" that Hartman suggests developed from eighteenth-century anglophone
natural-rights theory. Addressing the compromised "emancipation" of Reconstruction, which involved a massive intensification of perversities inherent to
classic natural rights thinking, Hartman writes the following:

> Despite the invocation of the natural rights of man, the emphasis on
> the "gift" of freedom and the accompanying duties . . . implied not
> only that one had to labor in exchange for what were deemed natural
> and inalienable rights but also that the failure to do so might result in
> their revocation. In short, the liberty and equality conferred by eman-
> cipation instituted the debt and established the terms of its amortiza-
> tion. The tabulation of duty and responsibility resulted in a burdened
> individuality in which one enjoyed the obligations of freedom with-
> out its prerogatives. The import of this cannot be underestimated, for
> the literal and figurative accrual of debt recapitulated black servitude
> within the terms of an emancipatory narrative.[31]

In this influential reading of the debt peonage that descended upon the formerly enslaved during Reconstruction, emancipation is less a movement
from bondage to freedom than it is a renegotiation of the repayment terms
on a loan that comes with no access to its principal. Neither the formerly
enslaved nor even the always free are presented as litigants entitled to repara-
tive justice. They are understood to be mere beneficiaries of a patronage that
was premised on the alienation of rights whose rewards they were never
really permitted to enjoy in the first place. Where slavery had its clear and
transparent limitations in a purportedly revolutionary-democratic nation,
moreover, postbellum African Americans found reflected back at them
from every corner a debt for the white gift of having recast black flesh as an
absence to be remediated and a hole to be filled, rather than as that which
secures human right. As it appears in his letterbook, Jackson's draft address
foretells this shift and recalls the language of the Spanish slave code, both of
which reckon black people as straining at white credulity when they assume
their right rather than petition for it by way of payment in the form of cash,

labor, or life. Indeed, Claiborne's earlier letter to Jackson suggests that New Orleans's white gentlemen of influence want the city's free men of color willingly to suffer a doubled subtraction: Not only are free men of color understood to owe a debt to the state, one that can only be erased by the sacrifice of their lives (and perhaps not even then), but should those men somehow manage to escape death on the battlefield, they must undergo a different kind of death, a forced removal from their land of nativity and the surrender of their at least cultural *jus soli*.

It seems significant, then, that Jackson's letterbook draft of his "Address to the Free Colored Inhabitants of Louisiana" is the last time that the following line appears in this exact form: "As Americans, your Country looks with confidence to her adopted Children, for a valorous support, as a partial return for the advantages enjoyed under her mild and equitable government." In the *Niles' Weekly Register* reprinting, the phrase "as a partial return" has been replaced with "as a faithful return." By the time we arrive at the *Proceedings of the Colored National Convention* of 1853, the reprinted line concludes at "valorous support." By 1853 we are no longer in a territory where enlisting and sacrificing one's life in battle counts as only a "partial return" on one's debt to the state. In the 1853 *Proceedings*, the language of "return" and the implication of debt have disappeared.

Although unattributed, the intervening reprinting of Jackson's address that encouraged this rewriting-through-elision appears to have been the one found in William Yates's *Rights of Free Colored Men to Suffrage*, which was published fifteen years earlier in 1838. The convention's *Proceedings* reproduces nearly verbatim Yates's variant of Jackson's address. The *Proceedings* also appears to follow Yates's lead in excising the notion of transactional selfhood. Like the 1853 *Proceedings*, Yates's version of Jackson's recruitment address cancels the reference to a "return," either "partial" or "faithful," owed to the (white racist) state. Neither does Yates accept that the U.S. nation-state is constitutionally either white or racist. In this last stance, Yates anticipates the position that Douglass himself would adopt and which precipitated his break with Garrison. Both Yates and the Colored National Convention of 1853 subtract from Jackson's address to the free colored inhabitants of Louisiana language that assigns a debt burden to black men and a racist ontology to the U.S. nation-state.

Who is the author of this subtraction? Is it the white man, Yates, whose *Rights of Free Colored Men* appears to have supplied the copy-text for the convention's reprinting? Is it Douglass (or one of his co-agitationists in the national colored convention movement), who may have owned, accessed, and reprinted Yates's version of Jackson's address, with Yates appearing to have borrowed, in turn, Garrison's translation of Jackson's second address? If we accept the argument about the human offered in the convention's reprinting of Jackson's address, then that question must go unanswered. Even better, it should go unasked. Authorial attribution that assigns responsibility, and therefore creative agency, to a single individual follows the framework of transactional selfhood called into question by the textual subtraction just identified. That particular notion of transactional selfhood was clearly weighted against attributing anything to African Americans other than responsibility for draining value from the world. That notion of transactional selfhood will therefore never be capable of tallying what the Colored National Convention's textual subtraction added to the world, in terms of print and in respect to the meaning of the human.

It is often taken for granted that conventional modes of authorship and authority were unavailable to African Americans in this period. This absence of writerly authority is used to explain the many appended certifying documents, the several signatories, and the endless endorsements characteristic of antebellum African American publication. The attribution of collective authorship that characterizes the Colored National Convention's *Proceedings*, as well as the subtraction of debt at play in this document, suggests a different possibility. Lack of access to a possessive individualist relation to text(s) might have done more to support than it did to confound antebellum antiracism, African American practices of authorship, and a shifting of the conversation about the human away from notions of burdened individuality. The sense of authorship reflected in modern practices of authorial attribution emerges from a world that increasingly burdens the individual not only with debt but also with property. These men were practicing a different kind of world. Their subtraction of a subtraction rejects the view embedded in the Spanish slave code, in Jackson's addresses, and in burdened individuality. It opens a space for a different account of the human to make itself known. It opens a space for the entry of a stranger of a different kind.

CHAPTER TWO

Frederick Douglass's Stranger-With-Thee

Well, suh, you is a stranger ter me, en I is a stranger ter you, en we is bofe strangers ter one annuder, but 'f I 'uz in yo' place, I wouldn' buy dis vimya'd.

—Charles Chesnutt, "The Goophered Grapevine" (1887)

Frederick Douglass's persistent interest in the figure of the stranger over the fifteen years leading up to the Civil War revealed a mounting sense that antiracists needed to come to grips with the historical meaning and political promise of strangerhood. During this time his writing investigated what it meant to be a stranger in the United States; it also reinhabited and reinflected a stranger persona that governed much contemporaneous African American and antiracist writing. Ultimately, Douglass ended up setting conventional accounts of the stranger on their heads, rewriting ideas recognizable on the one hand from the Bible and on the other from intensifying popular accounts that figured the stranger as a symptom of modernity. The stranger persona emerging from these revisions and in Douglass's later writing would have a key role to play in his projected vision of political community. This later writing posits credible experiences of strangerhood as pathways to a democratic community of the human emerging not from identification, but rather from open-ended scenes of encounter. If Douglass figures strangerhood as an escape route from the dubious terrain of sympathetic identification and as a condition available to all comers, he is also careful to specify the rules of the game called strangerhood. The seemingly pragmatic protocols of his later writing reflect a sense that "one becomes an individual subject only in virtue of recognizing, and being recognized by, another subject" understood as "equal and also as separate."[1] Anticipating Nancy Fraser's recent work on the politics of recognition, Douglass also stipulates what Fraser calls "parity of participation" as a condition of encounter, and he points to certain rhetorical and institutional reforms necessary to realize this parity.[2]

In his second life narrative, as well as his antebellum journalism and "The Heroic Slave," Douglass cannily engages the Levitical account of the stranger that often organized the slavery debate and lay at the core of antislavery rhetoric.[3] Like much antislavery writing, Douglass ventriloquizes the Levitical stranger's claim on hospitality. However, his post-*Narrative* writing also demonstrates a keen awareness that dependence on hospitality is no way to live, and it acknowledges the mixed fortunes of the Levitical stranger. He consequently taps into a rising popular and literary sentiment that emphasized the stranger's modern ubiquity to make a renewed case for the universality of strangerhood. Douglass in this way redefines strangerhood as the condition of being human; as he does so, he also rejects the emphasis on strangers having a right to nothing more than hospitality. This was an important and historically apt gesture. Biblical and especially New Testament tales of the stranger often emphasize the universality of strangerhood, but this period's scientific and romantic racialism, as well as the false beneficence of white abolitionism, had interceded to conflate strangerhood with racial status. As we will see below, both pro- and antislavery writing had come to portray African Americans as congenital strangers, redefining white North Americans as hereditary hosts. Both sides of the debate in this way hijacked some of the most radically egalitarian tendencies of Christian doctrine and hitched them to the train of hierarchy. Douglass resurrects the Bible's universalizing account of strangerhood and revises it for a modern age, fashioning a stranger persona who requires much more (of his readers and of the world) than merely the premodern hospitality that Leviticus enjoins (and which sounds an awful lot like sympathy). His stranger persona insists upon a world in which we are all strangers and hosts at once, and it does so in a way that acknowledges the "fourth dimension" that Nancy Bentley has characterized as "a distinct zone of experience" adjunct to "a three-dimensional world that remains oblivious to it."[4]

This is not simply to argue that Douglass's writing came to insist that certain key experiences of race and slavery would remain beyond the reach of white readers, no matter how much those readers believed in their own capacity for sympathy. Nor is it to propose that Douglass reinvests in the body or affect as a locus of political knowledge. The former is a settled fact, and the latter is a point still being compellingly debated. My emphasis is on how Douglass's writing reaches for a form of strangerhood appreciably different from the self-alienating disembodiment in print that other models of citizenship suggested were the proper basis of political community and the benefit of the print public sphere. At key moments his writing suspends analogical practices of reading; interrupts the notion that anyone's experience may be substituted with or for the experience of another person; demands intersubjective recognition; and so brings into view a polis predicated on mutuality rather than either sympathy or disinterested personhood. Strangerhood emerges here as the last best alternative to republican universalism, as well as a place of respite from liberal individualism. Like the 1853 Colored National Convention's "Address . . . to the People of the United States," it unburdens burdened individuality. Douglass does so here by articulating a subject who is a function of relations to his necessary equals.[5] This is Douglass's subject of stranger-with-ness. On the evidence of this writing, the ground of equality is a mutual acknowledgment that what it means to be human is to be in a constant state of coming-into-being, rendering each of us always strangers to those we encounter: We are strange because the constant state of coming-into-being necessarily forbids identification, to the extent that identification requires a relation to a static imago rather than to an evolving personhood. Strangerhood properly engaged is therefore an encounter without end in which the parties to the encounter never reach a final moment of full mutual intelligibility but instead have the opportunity to participate in a mutuality of recognition predicated on emergent difference. This is an encounter that acknowledges the writ for democracy, to the extent it grants that no party will ever attain the perfect and transcendental knowledge of any other's needs that would obviate collective deliberation and debate. This encounter is itself fully democratic only if and when institutional conditions permit its universal availability, but even the simple reaching toward such an encounter itself makes clear when those conditions are (not) present.

In order to elaborate my claims about the rewards of stranger-with-ness vis-à-vis Douglass's writing, this chapter first identifies an intensifying sense among antebellum popular and elite writers that the emergent conditions of modernity were occasioning a radical expansion of the number of strangers in the world. This literary account of the rise of the stranger gets translated into later influential sociological and historical treatments of the antebellum United States and the wider conditions of modernity. It has as a result dominated later perceptions of what it meant to be a stranger during this period. This literary and later critical focus on the quantitative rise of the stranger has had the peculiar effect of homogenizing the account of strangerhood in the nineteenth-century United States, preempting extended examination of the qualitative differences among the circulating characterizations of the stranger and the material impact of those differences. Although there were several competing discourses of strangerhood during this period, the overriding focus on the stranger as an exponentially increasing byproduct of urbanization has obscured them. Two of the most important emerged in the Bible debate over slavery, and so the second section of this chapter accordingly sketches the outline of this debate, focusing on the mixed fortunes of the Levitical stranger. Pro- and antislavery writers often staged their contest on the grounds of biblical accounts of the stranger: The former focused on the notorious "children of strangers" passage as a justification for racial slavery, while the latter emphasized the stranger's right to hospitality. Neither side seemed capable of imagining a multiracial world in which everyone was stranger and host at once. The third and final section of the chapter treats Douglass's engagement with the slavery debate's vision of the stranger, as well as his revision of the stranger persona and of strangerhood. For Douglass, the growing identification of modernity with the expansion of strangerhood provided an occasion to re-universalize strangerhood and so to go beyond both the pro- and antislavery accounts of the stranger. Douglass's new universal strangerhood sacrificed the rewards of hospitality, but it did so in order to pursue a new mode of engagement whose demands would be commensurate with its rewards.

As the argument of this chapter unfolds, a tension develops between what seems to be a simultaneously ontological and historical vision of strangerhood. At certain moments, that is, it may appear as though the mode of strangerhood Douglass pursues calcifies into its own set of static rules and protocols in a way that reifies strangerhood. Although the open-ended encounter associated with stranger-with-ness does generally emerge in Douglass as a normatively desirable one, the tendency toward depicting strangerhood as a fixed and static experience is more a quirk of critical description than it is a necessary feature of strangerhood itself. Strangerhood as it is posited in Douglass's writing and as it is discussed here must be understood as a contingent formation subject to revision, dissolution, failure, and inefficacy. As will be seen over the course of this book, whether an experience of strangerhood bends in the direction of stranger-with-ness or suspect-strangerhood depends on context. If Douglass as a result takes care with the rules of strangerhood, we also emerge with the sense that those rules must develop at the site of encounter, and with the agreement of those involved, rather than prior to that site's articulation.

In the chapter that follows this one, I play out what I see to be the main implication of this openness to a revision of the rules that does not deny their necessity. As I describe here, and as I discuss in greater detail in the next and later chapters, Douglass joins other African American writers in identifying a thin but essential line of distinction separating a practice of stranger-with-ness that encourages stranger-becoming from the suspect-stranger-making that renders strangers merely suspect. As Douglass's writing also indicates, there is room to move and to be moved across this line. One of his lifelong projects is figuring out how to remain on the right side of this line, both in his own moment and in later ones, by way of rhetorical and institutional praxis. Another of his projects is figuring out how to make sure that others have the chance to do the same. The rules of the game are important ones, but they never exist beyond the purview of human decision-making. Douglass asks his readers to attend to their roles in the making of those decisions.

Strangerhood and American Modernity

The significance of Douglass's engagement with the stranger persona comes into focus only in relation to his many interlocutors.[6] This is to say that understanding what was at stake in Douglass's account of strangerhood requires a broad view of the period's conversation around not belonging. *My Bondage and My Freedom* opens onto that widened vista of concern at several moments, including this one recounting Douglass's time in New York just after his escape from the South:

> New York, seventeen years ago, was less a place of safety for a runaway slave than now, and all know how unsafe it now is, under the new fugitive slave bill. I was much troubled. I had very little money—enough to buy me a few loaves of bread, but not enough to pay board, outside a lumber yard. I saw the wisdom of keeping away from the ship-yards, for if Master Hugh pursued me, he would naturally expect to find me looking for work among the calkers. For a time, every door seemed closed against me. A sense of my loneliness and helplessness crept over me, and covered me with something bordering on despair. In the midst of thousands of my fellow-men, and yet a perfect stranger! In the midst of human brothers, and yet more fearful of them than of hungry wolves! I was without home, without friends, without work, without money, and without any definite knowledge of which way to go, or where to look for succor.[7]

This passage explicitly impresses the figure of the stranger into service, and it is significant because it captures the overlay of premodern and modern notions of strangerhood that characterized the period and informs Douglass's writing, his politics, and his rhetorical and institutional interventions.

The urban location of the scene triggers images of the many seeming strangers that U.S. and European writers had come to depict as harbingers of modernity. It recalls the plot of *The Orphan Stranger: A Tale for the Lyceum Fair* (1839), for example, a children's book tracing the fortunes of an orphaned French girl fending for herself in the closed society of colonial New England. It equally invites comparisons to Benjamin Franklin's *Autobiography* (1791): "I had very little money enough to buy me a few loaves of bread"; Nathaniel Hawthorne's "My Kinsman, Major Molineux" (1832): "For a time, every door seemed closed against me"; Edgar Allan Poe's "The Man of the Crowd" (1840): "In the midst of thousands of my fellowmen, and yet a perfect stranger"; and Herman Melville's *Moby-Dick* (1851): "A sense of my loneliness and helplessness crept over me, and covered me with something bordering on despair." *My Bondage and My Freedom* would in this sense appear to index the historical experience of strangerhood described in these iconic texts and theorized in Karen Haltunnen's landmark inquiry, *Confidence Men and Painted Women: A Study of Middle-Class Culture in America, 1830–1870.*

Haltunnen adopts a pervasive and enduring critical view centered on a comparison of premodern to modern relations to strangers. This view continues to form the background of contemporary discussions of strangerhood across a range of fields and disciplines. She writes that in

> the small towns of colonial America strangers were the exception rather than the rule. Most inhabitants knew the other members of their community, and the arrival of a stranger was a special event that initiated certain traditional responses. Ship captains often reported the names of newcomers; inhabitants were expected to inform the authorities whenever they gave lodgings to a stranger; and certain large towns appointed special officials to watch for unknown visitors. Only those strangers "known to be of an honest conversation and accepted by the major part of the Town" were to be accepted as residents.
>
> As the city gradually replaced the town as the dominant form of social organization, however, the stranger became not the exception but the rule. By the mid-eighteenth century in New England, population growth and geographic mobility were making official surveillance of strangers increasingly difficult; and by the early nineteenth

century, an urban explosion was propelling vast numbers of Americans into what urban sociologist Lyn Lofland has called the "world of strangers," whose inhabitants know nothing of the majority of their fellow residents.[8]

By this reckoning a quantitative expansion of the number of strangers in the world is traceable to population shifts, and it precipitates a shifting morality around the figure of the stranger. Seen from this view, *My Bondage and My Freedom* might be read as registering nothing less than the demographic realignments associated with urbanization (as do Franklin, Hawthorne, and Poe) and globalization (*The Orphan Stranger*, Melville). These demographic realignments meant that, as early as the eighteenth century, traditional modes of surveillance were more and more challenging to enforce, with urbanization finally making them impossible. In the end, the pervasive presence of strangers made their regulation untenable.

It is worth noting two limitations of this model. First, as Douglass's experience would suggest, the modes of surveillance that Haltunnen describes might have declined in many quarters, but they became not less but rather more common in relation to African Americans. Writing in New Orleans's *Weekly Picayune* for April 30, 1838, the paper's editor positively celebrates the fact that "no city in the whole Union ... contains so great a portion of strangers as New Orleans." This embrace of the stranger does not extend to those whom the editor three weeks later, on May 21, 1838, refers to as "strange negro[es]." As I discuss in detail in my final chapter, these free men and women of color from communities other than New Orleans, the editor proclaims, "must produce some other evidence of [their] liberty than [their] own testimony" if they are to avoid incarceration. These comments draw their authority from the Louisiana Legislature's recently renewed commitment to prohibiting the immigration of any new free people of color into the state, a commitment that in turn led to the city of New Orleans demanding that free people of color arriving on board ships from other locales be detained in the city's jails for the length of their stay or post a considerable bond.[9] On January 10, 1845, the *Weekly Picayune* reports:

> Some thirteen free men of color, who came here on board vessels from the free states of the Union, were yesterday placed in confinement by the Second Municipality police, in pursuance to the act forbidding free persons of color to come within the limits of the State. Such an impertinent interference with our internal laws as that of

which Massachusetts has been guilty but tends to increased vigilance on the part of our police in these matters.

Although this incarceration represents an acute localized form of surveillance, one visible in bonds printed and sold in New Orleans to secure the liberty of free men of color entering the city as sailors, the national fugitive slave laws effectively deputized all U.S. citizens as agents of surveillance in such a way that meant the practices of New Orleans were more representative than they were exceptional. These brief examples moreover suggest that the pervasive presence in cities like New Orleans of strangers from the rural parishes and counties, as well as from around the globe, did not lead to a collapse of the feeling that at least some strangers deserved surveillance and bodily seizure.

The second issue to address concerns the sense of a quantitative shift in the number of strangers in the world. Haltunnen defines the modes of surveillance that she names as "responses" to the status of people newly arrived to New England towns, but it seems clear that stranger regulation is better thought of as a tool for assigning stranger status rather than as a response to a preexisting condition. As Jeffrey Alexander explains, "The employment of the *language* of strangeness creates the strangeness of a status, not the other way around."[10] Practices of surveillance and stranger naming are the technical means of suspect-stranger-making. They permit a community to consign a new arrival (or a long-standing resident) to one particular variant of strangerhood, suspect-strangerhood, and thereby to secure his or her social standing in the (new) locale. The process of suspect-stranger-making involves the invention, proliferation, and application of categorical distinctions rather than merely the recognition of some ontological or circumstantial status. In the conventional account of the stranger and modernity, of course, the stranger functions as a constant that crosses the great divide separating the premodern from the modern and colony from nation. This fixed category of the stranger permits the quantitative comparison that signals the onset of modernity, but it also occludes the finely calibrated processes of stranger-making that took place. In conventional accounts of the stranger and modernity, the category of the stranger has no synchronic historicity; it is instead a cipher for the diachronic history of other things. The stranger becomes the y-axis in the line graph of modernity. In actual fact, though, the stranger as a category is anything but a singular qualitative constant at any point during this period. Different sorts of strangerhood, and therefore different sorts of strangers, were being made every single day.[11]

The genre of stranger that Haltunnen describes may be traced to this period's literature and is, from the perspective of the present, the one most recognizable as such: This stranger has no particular qualities save a relation to an unfamiliar and usually urbanizing environment, as well as a recently achieved ubiquity. This emergent sense of the stranger's ubiquity is a significant fact: It suggests that popular and elite writing was developing an account of strangerhood that conduced to universal extension. In other words, this writing was making it possible to imagine detaching strangerhood from racial status, to which both pro- and antislavery writers were attempting to conjoin it, and reattaching it to the condition of being human. When this writing made it tenable to view strangerhood as the definitive condition of being human, it opened up an opportunity for antiracists such as Douglass to change the conversation around slavery and African American claims on political equality. As Douglass and others would have recognized, and as the excerpts from the *Picayune* indicate, however, African Americans were not automatically included in the emerging account of strangerhood as a human condition consequent upon modernity, nor did they have uncontested access to the kind of strangerhood that facilitates stranger-becoming. They had been, and were continuing to be, defined predominantly as a wholly different kind of stranger recognizable from the Bible.

Children of Strangers

When Douglass characterizes himself as a stranger, he triggers memories of antebellum literature's urban stranger. He also invokes a term with special relevance to the debate over slavery.[12] One main touchstone for nineteenth-century anglophone readers would have been Leviticus 19:34, the King James version of which was best known to Americans. It reads, "*But* the stranger that dwelleth with you shall be unto you as one born among you, and thou shalt love him as thyself; for ye were strangers in the land of Egypt." Within the literal Reformed hermeneutic that characterized much of the white Protestant United States, this verse endorsed the republican universalism dominating white abolitionism. This analogical account of the stranger, in which each of us may be substituted for any one of us, thus organizes a slew of antislavery narratives, tracts, and sermons produced from the late eighteenth century up to the Civil War, and it underscored the substitutability of black for white and vice versa. In this sense it functioned as a doctrinal complement to the more familiar tears and terrors associated with the aesthetics of sympathy.

The most influential antislavery pamphlets and tracts elaborating the Bible's warrant against slavery drafted upon and extended this particular Levitical stranger's broad familiarity, reminding readers that hospitality to the stranger runs wide and deep in both the Old and the New Testaments. Furthermore, a long roster of fugitive slave narratives explicitly summons both the Bible's charitable discourse on strangerhood and the sense that the warrant for antislavery pivots on the substitutability of black for white. That roster includes some of the central examples of the genre, as well as many more marginal ones: *The Blind African Slave, or, Memoirs of Boyrereau Brinch, Nick-Named Jeffrey Brace* (1810), *The Refugee: Or the Narratives of Fugitive Slaves in Canada* (1856), Harriet Jacobs's *Incidents in the Life of a Slave Girl* (1861), and many others.[13]

Invoking the Levitical stranger was not without its hazards, however, for one of the period's most influential proslavery arguments draws on a different moment in Leviticus and a very different account of just what strangerhood invites. Where antislavery forces argued for human substitutability by way of the figure of the stranger, proslavery theorists present the stranger as a site of insurmountable and irreconcilable difference. According to the most ardent proslavery theorists, the African's stranger status and the difference it registered permitted racial slavery. As they explain, Leviticus 25:44–45 commands: "Both thy bondmen, and thy bondmaids, which thou shalt have, *shall be* of the heathen that are round about you; of them shall ye buy bondmen and bondmaids. Moreover of the children of the strangers that do sojourn among you, of them shall ye buy, and of their families that *are* with you, which they begat in your land: and they shall be your possession." As the antislavery advocate the Reverend La Roy Sunderland suggests in his pamphlet *The Testimony of God Against Slavery*, which went through multiple editions: "This is the great proof-text of the slave-holder, to which he always retreats as his final strong hold."[14] As might be expected, then, not only proslavery writers but also antislavery ones frequently structured their arguments around a climactic exegesis of the children of strangers passage.

To proslavery theorists, the meaning of this passage was clear.[15] Adopting the highly literalist letter-over-spirit approach that had until this point dominated American scriptural analysis, the Reverend Thornton Stringfellow takes up the question of the stranger and slavery in his *Brief Examination of Scripture Testimony on the Institution of Slavery*, which was first published in 1841 and then republished many times. After an extensive review of antislavery objections to the peculiar institution, he rebuts these objections one by one, turning finally to the children of strangers passage, promising to make "good to the letter" on his commitment to demonstrate the Bible's endorsement of slavery. Stringfellow intones: "I ask any candid man, if the words of this institution could be more explicit? It is from God himself; it authorizes that people, to whom he had become *king and law-giver*, to purchase men and women as property; to hold them and their posterity in bondage; and to will them to their children as a possession forever; and more, it allows *foreign slaveholders* to *settle* and *live among them*; to *breed slaves* and *sell them*."[16] Antislavery theorists such as Theodore Dwight Weld would characterize such "candid" assessments of biblical chapter and verse as a form of eisegesis, or the imposition of meaning by fiat, as opposed to exegesis, which aimed to elucidate that which was immanent to the Bible. These same antislavery theorists would have a difficult time maintaining quite such a "candid" level of discussion, and they often appeared to be the ones engaged in arabesques of eisegesis. Breaching *sola scriptura* norms for the sake of their antislavery politics, figures such as Weld and George Bourne participated in a de facto shift in hermeneutical priorities that endorsed the supplementation and reinterpretation of the King James Bible. This shift was directly tied to the question of strangerhood. Bourne's *A Condensed Anti-Slavery Bible Argument* (1845), for example, contests the King James version of this passage by impugning its translators. Bourne writes:

> Preparatory to a critical examination of the celebrated statute contained in Lev. xxv. 44–46, it will be necessary to correct the common English translation of it, the same being the falsest translation I ever saw. The exact literal translation of it is as follows: verse 44—"And thy man servant, and thy maiden, which shall be to thee (shall be) from the nations which surround you. From them shall ye procure (the) man servant and the maiden."
>
> Verse 45. "And also from the sons of the foreigners, the strangers among you, from them shall ye procure—and from their children which (are) among you, which they brought forth into your land, and (they) shall be to you for a possession."[17]

Bourne next elaborates several finer points of Hebrew semantics and concludes with a short screed condemning King James's translators. "The true meaning of these words," Bourne writes:

> was ... perverted in the common translation, because since there were no words in the Hebrew language answering to our English

word "slave," "slaveholder," "slavery," &c., King James' translators, in imitation of the Catholic priests who first forged these perversions, falsely dressed up their English version of this statute, so as to resemble the modern Christian practice of negro slavery as nearly as possible—that species of slavery having at the period of their translation, under the sanction of these and similar perversions of the Scriptures, become very extensive, respectable, and popular, in several Christian countries, especially in their tropical territories. Like the false priests and Pharisees of old, these translators, in connection with many other corruptionists of their time, and with still more now existing, thus falsified the true word of God to gratify a corrupt public sentiment, and please their principal patrons for the sake of worldly popularity.[18]

Bourne accuses these translators of justifying the practices of the day rather than hewing to God's revealed truth, a significant gesture that breaks with the period's dominant biblical hermeneutic, which viewed the Bible as infallible and as God's direct untranslated word. As Mark Noll, a historian of religion, explains, the reigning assumption was that "people could see clearly and without ambiguity what the Bible said."[19] Breaching this *sola scriptura* norm, Bourne supplements and reinterprets the King James Bible. Nor was he alone in doing so. As Noll argues, the *sola scriptura* emphasis that had characterized American Protestantism since the mid-eighteenth century was a major casualty of the slavery debate: "The theological crisis signaled by antithetical interpretations of Scripture centered on the adequacy of the Bible itself. Although the United States had become one of the most ostensibly Christian societies on the face of the earth, the Civil War's division of the country's ardent Bible believers called into question the reputation of the Bible as an omnicompetent, infallible authority for life now and forever."[20]

As the quotation from *My Bondage and My Freedom* regarding Douglass's time in New York would indicate, these theological debates over the Levitical stranger intersected in popular discourse with the more secular sense of the stranger as a symptom of modernity. Douglass exploits this intersection. His recourse to the stranger persona redeploys the Bible's particularly resonant language in such a way as to confuse the growing sense of strangerhood as a universal modern condition with the Bible's own universalizing premodern account of strangerhood. Out of this confusion emerges a stranger neither sacred nor secular but political in nature: In Douglass's writing and his practice, the decline of the *sola scriptura* model opens onto normative political philosophy.

The Strangeness of Politics

It often seems that there were only two equally dissatisfying kinds of antiracist thinking in the nineteenth-century United States. There was the Garrisonian approach, which called for the embrace of an anachronistic civic republicanism that claimed to acknowledge the universality of the human but which in practice excluded all that looked particular from the perspective of propertied white men: women, people of color, the poor. Then there was the liberal individualism that took root in the Jacksonian period and that encouraged a withdrawal from the practice of deliberative democracy. It is reasonable to trace both of these tendencies in Douglass's writing and thought. There is a strong case to be made, for instance, that *My Bondage and My Freedom* resuscitates the strategies of sentimental identification allied with both the period's most liberal individualist and its most republican tendencies. Nineteenth-century readers conversant with the slave narrative's dominant formal conventions might have expected this second of Douglass's autobiographies to offer a detailed account of the clear and simple facts of Douglass's enslavement, escape, and subsequent life as a free man.[21] Douglass nevertheless refuses this expectation of full disclosure. When describing the physical violence done to enslaved African Americans, Douglass often stops short of a full revelation of these atrocities. He deflects the reader's attention at the last moment, dropping the curtain just as a violent scene reaches its climax and then remarking that certain things are in excess of words. Concerning the brutality of slave "discipline" in the South, Douglass writes that "language has no power to convey a just sense of its awful criminality."[22] He remarks that he has willingly "relieve[d]" his "kind reader" of certain "heart-sickening details" of the South's "dark crimes without a name."[23] We learn that his childhood experience of slavery produced recurring "feelings to which [he] can give no adequate expression."[24]

William Andrews's *To Tell a Free Story* would suggest that this play of revelation and opacity constitutes a central stylistic achievement of the first century of African American autobiography, but that it also may have done more to extend sympathy's life than it did to reset the terms of debate.[25] According to Andrews, the mature fugitive slave narrative first alienates the reader and then encourages her to substitute herself for the enslaved. "What the fugitive slave needed," Andrews explains, "was a mode of autobiographical discourse that subtly reoriented a reader's response to his text away from a distanced perspective and toward one that authorized appropriation." Anticipating more recent accounts of sentimentality, Andrews continues: "Through such a mode of discourse, a revolution . . . could begin in black autobiography. . . .

Understanding, that is, the transference of the reader into the psychic life of the narrator, could be facilitated in texts that had once been read only for explanation, i.e., the empirical verification, description, and analysis of some feature of objective reality (like slavery)."[26] Here the primary effect of the mature slave narrative is to collapse the distinction separating self from other. The now-familiar critique of sympathy would point out that this sympathetic transfer amounts to an erasure of the fugitive and his or her pain: When the reader imagines herself to be feeling a fugitive's pain, she is actually imagining what it would feel like to be herself in the same position. In seeking to bridge an unbridgeable gulf of experience, the reader narcissistically substitutes herself for the enslaved, and the enslaved person undergoes a form of politically charged erasure.[27]

Douglass is profoundly attuned to the sorry bargain of sympathy by analogy that frequently motivated petitions for details of his time in bondage. In the letter to James McCune Smith that prefaces *My Bondage and My Freedom*, Douglass remarks that he has "often refused to narrate [his] personal experience in public anti-slavery meetings, and in sympathizing circles, when urged to do so by [his] friends, with whose views and wishes, ordinarily, it were a pleasure to comply."[28] Indeed, across his later writings, Douglass struggles with the need to engage the dominant political vocabularies of the period while also reaching toward some alternative mode of being-with-strangers that does not hinge on sympathetic transfer. This alternative mode of being-with-strangers and the rhetorical shifts from which it will emerge come into focus in the following passage from a letter that Douglass wrote to his former master, Thomas Auld. First published in the *Liberator* on September 22, 1848, the letter reads:

> The morality of the act [of escape], I dispose of as follows: I am myself; you are yourself; we are two distinct persons, equal person[s]. What you are I am. You are a man, and so am I.—God created both, and made us separate beings. I am not by nature bound to you, or you to me. Nature does not make your existence depend upon me, or mine to depend upon yours. I cannot walk upon your legs, or you upon mine. I cannot breathe for you, or you for me; I must breathe for myself, and you for yourself. We are distinct persons, and are each equally provided with faculties necessary to our individual existence.[29]

As Douglass's address to Auld unfolds, rejecting substitutive identification takes shape as the first and last step on the road to becoming human. The primary emphasis is on preserving a distinction between self and other, an emphasis that might appear to preclude contingent personhood and being-with-strangers. Douglass's rejection of his dependency on Auld, in other words, appears to insist on Douglass's lack of commonality with him. Yet Douglass's deployment of a hybrid mode of address elsewhere in his writing will set the condition of possibility for a specific form of stranger relationality that acknowledges the plurality of human experience in such a way that makes it the condition of human commonality.

In *Publics and Counterpublics*, Michael Warner offers a key intervention that seeks to reset the terms dominating critical discussions of the stranger. Drawing from Georg Simmel's and Erving Goffman's works on these issues, Warner redirects our attention to how often strangerhood has been incorrectly figured as a subtraction—of agency, personhood, force, and specifiable content—in modern and contemporary discourse. He also writes:

> In modern society, a stranger is not as marvelously exotic as the wandering outsider would have been to an ancient, medieval, or early-modern town. In that earlier social order, or in contemporary analogues, a stranger is mysterious, a disturbing presence requiring resolution. In the context of a public, however, strangers can be treated as already belonging to our world. More: they *must* be. We are routinely oriented to them in common life. They are a normal feature of the social.
>
> Strangers in the ancient sense—foreign, alien, misplaced—might of course be placed to a degree by Christendom, the *ummah*, a guild, or an army, affiliations one might share with strangers, making them a bit less strange. Strangers placed by means of these affiliations are on a path to commonality. Publics orient us to strangers in a different way. They are no longer merely people whom one does not yet know; rather, an environment of strangerhood is the necessary premise of some of our most prized ways of being. Where otherwise strangers need to be on a path to commonality, in modern forms strangerhood is the necessary medium of commonality. The modern social imaginary does not make sense without strangers.[30]

With this passage, Warner rejects the sense that strangerhood must be an experience of atomistic alienation. He shows that strangerhood need not be, or be understood as, a predicate to some more binding form of familiarity that would in turn permit commonality and community. Strangerhood can be the first and last stop on the pathway to being-with-others. He suggests that strangerhood properly realized is a "medium of commonality," but this is a commonality of an unexpected kind. As Warner describes it, stranger-hood can facilitate communities signally different from those requiring, or at least pretending to require, the self-abstraction imagined to be a property of print culture and a requirement of civic republicanism. Warner's conceptual advance casts new light on a comment made by Andrews. Andrews suggests that the culmination of the slave narrative's development as a genre was the emergence of a more dialectical and ethically tenable version of identifica-tion, and he argues that "the standard rhetorical premise from which all the great slave narrators proceed" involves a tension between "distanciation" and "appropriation."[31] Warner demonstrates that strangerhood can involve a form of distanciation that permits commonality while forgoing appropria-tion. While strangerhood *can* be a "medium of commonality," however, it is equally important to recognize that, as I have argued here, it is not guaran-teed to be so. Strangerhood itself must be understood as taking more than one form. As Warner argues elsewhere in the same volume, felicitous modes of address, material conditions of circulation, and the capacity and desire to take up an instance of address have a significant bearing on what sort of stranger gets made—and made again over time. This becomes clear in the distinction between the suspect-stranger and the stranger-with.

If we have already seen suspect-stranger-making practices at play in the New Orleans newspaper, then stranger-with-ness appears perhaps most movingly offered in a letter that Douglass wrote to William Lloyd Garrison from Belfast and that appeared in *The Liberator* in 1846. The generosity of the letter has often gone unremarked, perhaps because it is a subtle and uncom-promising generosity. Given the fact that Douglass had not yet broken with Garrison, understanding the significance of what he would later admit to be his growing unease with his treatment by Garrison and his organization, and knowing the pivotal role his time in the United Kingdom played in Doug-lass's political transformation, the language here is striking:

> I have no end to serve, no creed to uphold, no government to defend; and as to nation, I belong to none. I have no protection at home, or resting-place abroad. The land of my birth welcomes me to her shores only as a slave, and spurns with contempt the idea of treating me dif-ferently. So that I am an outcast from the society of my childhood, and an outlaw in the land of my birth. "I am a stranger with thee, and a sojourner as all my fathers were."[32]

Following Caroline Levander's analysis of Garrison's use of direct address, it is possible to view the last line as an example of what Levander calls "sentiment's most traditional device to elicit sympathy," direct address, and thus as an attempt to bridge the gap of difference separating Douglass from his patron and Douglass from his (white) readers.[33] But we are in fact delivered here to different terrain. Quoting Psalm 39:12, Douglass adopts a form of oblique and divided address whose tripartite target is Garrison, God, and the implied reader of *The Liberator*: "I am a stranger with thee, and a sojourner as all my fathers were." Douglass's account of his own strangerhood initially channels the voice of the modern literary stranger with which we began and echoes at the same time the Bible's account of the Levitical stranger; this driving iteration of strangerhood next seems to mount toward a climactic account of Douglass's absolute alienation. In the end, however, the psalm functions as a coda that refigures what has come before: It indicates that our mutual humanity renders us permanent mutual strangers. As it turns out, moreover, strangerhood is the ground of our mutuality: "I am a stranger *with* thee." That "with" is vitally important. Reformulating the psalmist's address to God, Douglass identifies strangerhood as a shared human condition. For the Reverend Thornton Stringfellow, strangerhood invited enslavement; for his opponents, it warranted unilateral hospitality with no room for mutuality. Here it is the grounding condition of human life and therefore of political organization. Emphasizing our difference from even those who are most familiar to us, this oblique address entails a "conscious practice of drawing boundaries"[34] that permits stranger-becoming its opening. The stranger-with-ness Douglass proffers in this moment of generosity differs significantly from the more familiar scene of stranger witness appearing in Adam Smith's eighteenth-century account of human sympathy.[35]

In contrast to Smith's account of sympathy, which amounts to little more than uncorrupted witness and replacement, a community of the human forms, according to Douglass, around the endless assertion of an ineluctable barrier to absolute mutual intelligibility, with the barrier itself functioning as a hinge point for mutuality. Refusing to render any single African American's experience immediately transparent, this mode of address curtly rejects the anachronistic public sphere of civic republicanism espoused by many whites, which assumed that it was easy to identify a political subject with universally consistent experiences and needs but who was in fact a "provincial category that mistakes itself for a human universal."[36] It denies the democratic populism increasingly dominant in post-Jacksonian America, which figured race-based differences as insurmountable barriers to civic participation and

as the only form of particularity that mattered: In this sense, it imagines neither a universal *sensus communis* nor a racial one. It summons the Levitical
stranger and modernity's stranger; it then transubstantiates both of them to
generate a stranger who demands (and offers in return) neither charity nor
incarceration but instead recognition without end. Douglass gropes toward
an anti-universalist universalism in which to be like all others is to be similarly different, and he reaches toward a praxis of stranger-with-ness that
would be adequate to and reproductive of this condition. Bentley argues in
a related context that W. E. B. Du Bois develops an "extra-universalism, an
epistemology structured by the fact that reality exceeds what is taken to be
the ultimate horizon of the human."[37] In Douglass, strangerhood emerges as
neither a challenge to overcome nor a condition to dissolve, but as a polit-
ico-aesthetic project that underwrites the ongoing extension of the "ultimate
horizon of the human," a project that involves the abatement of suspect-
stranger-making and the cultivation of stranger-with-ness.

From the moment he signed with the Garrisonians, Douglass was put to
work on the North's abolitionist circuit. In one of *My Bondage and My Freedom*'s concluding chapters, Douglass reflects on this time as follows: "Now
what shall I say of this fourteen years' experience as a public advocate of the
cause of my enslaved brothers and sisters? The time is but as a speck, yet large
enough to justify a pause for retrospection—and a pause it must only be."[38]
During this pause, as is well known, Douglass recounts certain crucial incidents from his experience as a speaker, none of which lodges more firmly in
his consciousness than his growing disaffection with the Garrisonians' anachronistic republicanism and its corollary racism. He famously recalls that, at
first, he was "made to forget [his] skin was dark and [his] hair crisped."[39]
By degrees, however, his supposed allies began to demand that he not only
acknowledge but also trumpet these and other so-called facts of his blackness
and his enslavement. In an oft-quoted passage, Douglass writes, "During the
first three or four months, my speeches were almost exclusively made up of
narrations of my own personal experience as a slave. 'Let us have the facts,'
said the people. So also said Friend George Foster, who always wished to pin
me down to my simple narrative. 'Give us the facts,' said [another white aboli-
tionist], 'we will take care of the philosophy.' Just here arose some embarrassment."[40] When Douglass sought to extend his reach as a speaker by moving
from reciter of facts to a full-fledged political philosopher, he was met with
resistance from white abolitionists.

Even had these white abolitionists not directly objected to his transformation, Douglass would have found himself hamstrung by the formal protocols

that articulated the politics of this group. In Garrisonian abolitionist rhetoric, as was seen in the previous chapter, the category of the public emerged from an assertion of the public's responsibility for ending slavery. The public was in this sense united by a shared sense of responsibility, just as early American republicanism had emphasized the shared responsibility of the literally and economically enfranchised for the larger nation. This way of conceiving the public, and the modes of address it endorsed, necessarily excluded the enslaved, the formerly enslaved, and, according to Garrison's *Thoughts on African Colonization*, the always free African American. Founded in a framework of oversight and responsibility that claimed to speak for the universally human, this mode of address sought to constitute a category of persons to oversee and for whom one could be responsible. This mode of address established a public whose boundary was defined when the object of its charitable oversight came into being. In this sense, the Garrisonian mode of address was an unacknowledged tool for assigning a Levitical stranger status that warranted (at best) charitable benefaction while making "parity of participation" permanently impossible.[41] A different mode of address was required. Douglass was one of many who would together give it voice.

CHAPTER THREE

Les Apôtres de la Littérature
and *Les Cenelles*

Nature no longer displays the power of the community, it no longer
works on behalf of politics. This is not only because the Revolution is
over and the poet has come back from it. It is not enough to put an end to
the Revolution. One must put an end to it with writing, make the cloud
that accompanies poetic utterance solitary, separate it from the course of
the army of clouds that swing on the horizon, as all glory and empires do.
In this separation the path of lyrical enunciation is won.

> —Jacques Rancière, "From Wordsworth to Mandelstam: The Transports
> of Liberty," in *The Flesh of Words*

Couplets improvisés chez le Sociétaire de Béranger, qui, le lendemain de
mon arrivé, voulurent bien m'admettre comme visiteur parmi eux. . . .
Cette société tient ses séances, rue Condé 71, les lundis et jeudis de
chaque semaine. On est admis comme visiteur.

[Verses improvised in the society, *Les Sociétaires de Béranger*, which
kindly admitted me as a visiting member the day after I arrived. . . . The
society holds weekly meetings, on Mondays and Thursdays, at 71 rue
Condé. One is admitted as a visitor.]

> —François Destrade, *Chansons patriotiques, par le citoyen Destrade,
> ouvrier imprimeur* (1852, New Orleans)[1]

In the fall of 1867, one of New Orleans's celebrated black authors, Joanni Questy, published a short, nostalgic fiction titled "Monsieur Paul" in *La Tribune de la Nouvelle-Orléans*, a paper popular with a broad range of francophone New Orleanians. As Louisiana approached a late nineteenth-century renaissance of francophone literature, *La Tribune* and other news-papers, such as *L'Abeille de la Nouvelle-Orléans*, arbitrated the question of how literary aesthetics relate to politics by way of their editorial decisions. These included the reprinting and the original publication of certain stories, poems, and critical essays. For his part, Questy advocated a turn away from the earlier, mannered French romanticism that had dominated the city's francophone literary culture for most of the century. He sought to inaugu-rate a new literary realism. In the post scriptum to "Monsieur Paul," Questy describes this new realism as emerging from willing encounters with the street, with the ballroom, and with everyone and everywhere in between. Such encounters would permit attentive records of the detailed everyday. The literature resulting from them would therefore appeal "à toutes les classes de lecteurs," to all readers, from draymen to capitalists and heads of state. Questy's sense of a literary mission specific to New Orleans, relevant to all its people, and pertinent to humanity in general had in this sense two main specifications: Literature must issue from all forms of experience, the elevated to the lowly. It must also speak to the broad collection of human-kind from which it issued. The second requirement departs from many of the more familiar anglophone romanticisms-of-the-people, whose concern for "the people" tended to be restricted to the question of whether they were earthy enough to merit poetic depiction.

Many of Questy's Creole of color peers shared his desire for a new real-ism. This stance marked a departure from their earlier aesthetic manifestos and poetry, including the important collection *Les Cenelles: Choix de poé-sies indigènes* (1845). Published in New Orleans the same year that Freder-ick Douglass's *Narrative* appeared in New England, *Les Cenelles* is the first anthology of African American literature. Despite its chronological coinci-dence with Douglass's *Narrative*, though, *Les Cenelles* has failed to generate the same level of African Americanist enthusiasm as Douglass's text. There are several reasons for the traditionally temperate response to *Les Cenel-les*. The *Les Cenelles* poets are perceived to have absorbed the white racist norms of the period, and their poetry tends to be inattentive to the experi-ences of the enslaved. This is depicted as unsurprising: In addition to being accommodating of white people, some of New Orleans's *gens de couleur libres* owned slaves. Added to this is the *Les Cenelles* coterie's reputation for gender politics that were not much better than those of the white male planters who visited New Orleans to engage in the system of *plaçage*.

These facts invite heightened scrutiny. As will be seen in the final chapter of this book, the volume's inattention to the experience of the enslaved almost certainly has as much to do with Louisiana legislation prohibiting incendiary discussion of racial equality, whether those discussions appeared in imported or local publications, as it does with the more obvious demerits of these men and their culture. The question of what it meant for black people and *gens de couleur libres* in New Orleans to own one another was also complex. Finally, the exchange economy signaled in the volume's title troubles, as I will show in just a moment, the common notion that *Les Cenelles* is about an exchange of women between men that mirrors the city's broader gender politics. Michel Fabre nevertheless questions "why so few of these works offer a critique of the social and racial system" that defined antebellum New Orleans.[2] The translators of the only English-language version of the full volume use their introduction to depict *Les Cenelles* as French romanticism gone wrong: Stripped of any political significance, the poetry is described as sentimental and prevaricating. It is also understood as inadequately grounded in the experience of the common people and the enslaved. This is understood to follow from the *Les Cenelles* poets' access to early, advanced, and often expensive education at home and in Paris, which meant that they were often better educated than many of their white peers in New Orleans. One of the most famous, Victor Séjour, whose frequently anthologized story "Le Mulâtre" was first published in *La Revue des Colonies* in 1837, was a favored son of New Orleans who went on to become a dramatist popular in nineteenth-century Paris.

This access to education, financial wherewithal, and proximity to whites have ensured that the *Les Cenelles* poets are not typically thought of as poets of the (black) people. It is therefore notable to see Questy importing an older French romantic ethos of a poetry of the street into the post scriptum of "Monsieur Paul" and recasting it as a new realism. The story, set in 1859, is a nostalgic account of a period just before the Civil War when conversations touched on Lamartine, Béranger, and Hugues Félicité Robert de Lammenais. Though the story itself documents a time when Creole gentlemen settled their differences by well-fought duels, Questy's post scriptum nevertheless argues for a less courtly form of writing appropriate to the current age. When he calls for "les apôtres de la littérature française en Louisiane" to enact an apostleship germane to the time and place, "les apôtres," or apostles, become a pivotal feature of this new aesthetics. Where other New Orleanians

had chosen to embrace *un silence stérile*, Questy's own apostles for literature
would need to reach far and wide for their audience and subject matter:

> [P]our relever leurs autels qui s'écroulent, pour vaincre l'insensibilité,
> l'indifférence des métrophobes endurcis, les apôtres de la littérature
> française en Louisiane, au lieu de se complaire dans un silence sté-
> rile ou dans les hauteurs de quelque vague empyrée, n'auraient qu'à
> vivre dans notre bruit, autour de nous et avec nous; ils n'auraient qu'à
> descendre dans nos rues où presque chaque jour amène son drame,
> sa comédie, sa catastrophe: les tempêtes des passions, les caprices de
> la fortune, les fantaisies excentriques du hasard ou les combinaisons
> inattendues de la Providence leur fourniraient une suite de tableaux
> d'une variété infinite; ils n'auraient plus qu'à en faire un choix judi-
> cieux; et ces tableaux, relevés du coloris d'un habile pinceau, auraient
> le double avantage de plaire irrésistiblement à toutes les classes de
> lecteurs,—depuis le drayman qui sait lire jusqu'au gros capitaliste qui
> le sait à peine, depuis le moindre fonctionnaire public jusqu'au chef
> suprême de l'État,—et d'opérer en même temps, une réaction impor-
> tante en faveur du goût artistique en Louisiane.

> [Whether to shore up their crumbling altars or to overcome the cal-
> lous indifference of hardened metrophobics, those evangelizing
> French literature in Louisiana need only live amid our noise, around
> us and with us, rather than indulging themselves in barren silence
> or up on some undefined pedestal. They need only walk down our
> streets, which virtually every day see drama, comedy, tragedy: the
> outbursts of passion, the whims of fortune, the outlandish quirks of
> fate or the unpredictable schemes of Providence would all provide
> them with a series of infinitely diverse scenes—among which they
> would need only make a judicious choice. Such scenes, deftly and viv-
> idly sketched out, would be doubly advantageous—fascinating read-
> ers from all classes (from the literate drayman to the not-so-literate
> big capitalist, and from the lowliest of public servants to the supreme
> head of state) and at the same time catalyzing the promotion of artis-
> tic taste in Louisiana.][3]

Questy's ideal writers would not segregate themselves from the pains and
pleasures of daily life; they would embrace and catalogue the quotidian.
They would thereby speak to all New Orleanians, from the highest to the

lowest, from the most lettered to the least, as well as to humanity in general. The post scriptum concludes with an apology for Questy's failure to meet the expectations that he sets for himself and for others. He nevertheless remains convinced that the mission remains a true one. Attention to the real in all its manifestations, and a forthright encounter with the fullness of life, must replace a taste for the merely decorative and the rewards of the empyrean. The shift from the late romantic flavor of the 1845 poems in *Les Cenelles* to the more realist emphasis of Questy's 1867 story mirrors French and francophone literary history, in which these two aesthetic programs connect and overlap.

Questy's sense of having been part of a connected group of *amateurs* keeping the spirit of letters alive in New Orleans is nevertheless worth noting. For the object of apostolic witnessing undertaken by Questy's chosen *amateurs* was, it turns out, a version of literature in which literature makes all human experience available to all humans, but only by way of writing produced and held in common. Questy's group of *amateurs*, which in fact did exist in nineteenth-century New Orleans, in this way discredits the common identification of hyper-individualistic self-creation with eighteenth- and nineteenth-century romantic lyric. They did so by attending to every individual writer's debt to the collective of which they were a part, while at the same time accepting the valuation of the individual in some form. In combining the two tendencies, theirs is persistently a poetry of stranger-with-ness and provides an alternative to a more familiar poetry of romantic stranger witness. Their poetry assumes a condition of plurality and is solicitous of it.

The *Les Cenelles* circle dates at least to the 1843 publication of the short-lived literary journal, *L'Album littéraire: Journal des jeunes gens, amateurs de littérature*. The *jeunes gens* who loved literature enough to publish *L'Album* spanned the spectrum of francophone male life in New Orleans. Many had been tutored by Armand Lanusse, the editor of *Les Cenelles*; Lanusse would also later head the Couvent School, which had been endowed by a formerly enslaved francophone woman, Madame Couvent, to educate children of color in New Orleans. In *L'Album littéraire*, the aesthetic manifestos held more in common with Herder than with Balzac, but the persistent presence of the literary "we" ties *L'Album littéraire* to *Les Cenelles* to Questy's post scriptum. As will be seen later in this chapter, this literary we is signaled in Lanusse's introduction to *Les Cenelles*, where he refers to the volume as the product of his "amis en poésie." For Questy's apostles, substitute Lanusse's friends and vice versa. Where Frederick Douglass eventually arrives at a place where he seeks stranger-with-ness, in other words, the *Les Cenelles* poets seem to have always already lived there. *Les Cenelles* in this way recalls but also challenges Rancière's assertion that "the path of lyrical enunciation is won" in the moment that the "cloud that accompanies poetic utterance" is made "solitary." As with the writings of Douglass and his companions in the colored convention movement, and as with most of Douglass's later writings, Questy's I issues from and addresses a we. The "army of clouds" remains an army without eclipsing the emergence of the I.

This emphasis on an I-to-we relation is important for understanding both the aesthetic project of *Les Cenelles* and its contribution to black vernacular political theory. Historians have proposed that *Les Cenelles* offers a strong critique of the period's social and racial norms, despite literary-critical assertions to the contrary. Importantly, however, these historians suggest that the roots of the critique connect it to the republicanism of continental Europe by way of Haiti and even Mexico, an enforced genealogy that makes it difficult to trace the more specific contours of the *Les Cenelles* critique.[4] The genealogical view emphasizes borrowings in the writing of black francophone New Orleans from political-theoretical discourse emerging elsewhere, in turn presenting those borrowings and the New Orleans writing they inform as reducible to already-existing political republicanisms. The main visible contribution of the *Les Cenelles* poets is thus presented as an effort to accommodate republicanism to a local context without significantly reinventing either republicanism or the local context.

The supposed androcentrism of the writing of *Les Cenelles* would, moreover, appear to be a key factor confirming this view of New Orleans's *hommes de couleur libres* as practitioners of a derivative republicanism.[5] Like many white anglophone men of the period, the argument goes, New Orleans's francophone free men of color immersed themselves in humanistic idioms drawn from the classical tradition. They also took inspiration from eighteenth-century natural-rights discourse, as well as from a notion of disinterest that posited citizenship as male and propertied. Such a view of citizenship entailed a man leaving his women and slaves at home. Although it remains a matter of debate whether the logic of classical republicanism actually *required* the presence of women and slaves at home, it certainly did not prohibit the possession of other persons. Indeed, the background presence of the home and its inhabitants was often characterized as the temporizing force stabilizing the republic. The more the citizen owned, the greater his capacity for disinterest. This was understood to be the case even when the inventory of property included given and proper names.

Their brief period of loyalty to the Confederacy and their publications in both integrated and black-only papers, together with their perceived misogyny and overeducation, therefore fuel the notion that most of the men who constituted Questy's apostolic body were recidivist republicans of a familiar kind. The result is a not very flattering portrait of them or their volume. The *Les Cenelles* poets are made to appear no different from most white men. Contextualizing their work in terms of the broader republican traditions encourages us to see them as averse to a version of equality more demanding than (or even simply different from) classical republicanism. Their desire for a local account of liberty turns out to be not only not radical, but little more than a provincial reenactment of metropolitan views. It is a view of liberty that follows from visits to France and extended periods of education there. It can be traced to the training these poets received at home in New Orleans, whether at the hands of their parents, from their Paris-educated tutors, or in schools for free children of color. It can be seen to follow as well from the felt benefits of property held in persons of African descent who were their slaves. Those same enslaved persons of African descent were also sometimes the wives and children of these men.

This chapter will argue against this bleak portrait. It will propose that their interest in preserving and extending an I-to-we relation exceeds other republican frameworks, whether Haitian, French, Mexican, early American, or classical. Moreover, I will suggest that *Les Cenelles'* significant and original contribution to African American vernacular political and aesthetic theory is obscured by the tendency to cast its authors as either French or American, antislavery or slaveholding, indigenous or transnational. Their poetry mirrors the work of anglophone African American men writing and publishing in the North; it also echoes Béranger, Lamartine, and de Lammenais. In this way it develops a political-aesthetic idiom "indigenous" to the context of New Orleans, but one that has ramifications for all humans. It does these things by venturing a version of lyric that does not reproduce the privatized self-enclosure that will come to be associated with lyric utterance. Like Douglass and his colleagues in the North, the *Les Cenelles* poets engage practices of citation, revision, and address that disaggregate the sense of self without destroying it. An over-individuated sense of self was not on their agenda, in other words, but self-creation remained a primary figurative and political concern. Their use of the formal gesture perhaps most often discussed in accounts of lyric—apostrophe—makes this concern known. For the *Les Cenelles* poets, the relation of apostrophe to apostleship is a tight one. As I explain in more detail below, the apostle's words, especially the apostrophic words of the apostle, aim to expand rather than contract the circle of belonging without destroying the presence of the I. The successful apostle preserves a singular relation to his point of inspired departure. Typically this point of origin is an encounter with the divine, but in *Les Cenelles* it is a relation to a literary coterie in which women were understood to be key players.[6] Apostolic address furthermore permits this singular relation to open onto the world extending beyond the I. An apostle can never be a *pure* singularity: He must remain always alone and tethered to others.

Les Poésies Indigènes

It is significant that the bilingualism, and occasional French monolingualism, of New Orleans's *hommes de couleur libres* gave them access to the writing of the French republican tradition. It is no less important that this tradition did not decide in full the content or political consequences of African American men's writing in francophone New Orleans. The word *indigènes* as it functions in the subtitle of *Les Cenelles* is a key example of the latter: As I will suggest, that word, *indigènes*, highlights the difficulty of identifying this poetry as the product of a single national-cultural tradition, whether French, U.S., Haitian, or any other. To contemporary students of nineteenth-century African American anglophone writing, the word *indigènes* will seem anachronistic. The cultural nativism the word appears to signify does not significantly appeal to anglophone African Americans until the advent of the protomodernism of the late nineteenth century found in work by writers such as Paul Laurence Dunbar and Charles Chesnutt. Importantly, this later taste for the "indigenous" departs from the notion of *indigène* signaled here. Here, the *Les Cenelles* poets use this word to contest the increasingly commonplace and nationalistic white anglophone American claim to indigenousness on behalf of white European settlers. Indebted to and often emerging from white Native American political parties, as well as from Know-Nothing thinking, claims for the indigenousness of European white people in America dominated many anglophone papers during this period. They also turn up in New Orleans's francophone papers, albeit in a different form to be considered in just a moment. Other major European colonial communities in the eighteenth- and nineteenth-century New World witnessed similar arguments over national entitlement. It is not surprising to see it happening in New Orleans.

If their indigenousness is a nativity of these writers' own making, then *Les Cenelles* has much in common, I am suggesting, with anglophone volumes launching calls for a specifically American literature that would be indigenous to the United States without requiring the presence of autochthons. In *Les Cenelles*, in other words, francophone writing does not cede its place in the American national tradition: The *Les Cenelles* poets claim a title to that tradition more definitive than anything that Walt Whitman, William Cullen Bryant, or Henry Wadsworth Longfellow could hope to produce. In staking their claim to North American indigenousness, however, the *Les Cenelles* poets also place the patterns of social relations characteristic of local Creole life at the center of their notion of New World civilization, a gesture that differs significantly from the more familiar anglophone North American settler nativisms. The *Les Cenelles* poets engage in U.S. cultural nationalism, but their practices of composing, collecting, and anthologizing poetry lay claim as well to earlier and different places in addition to their "native" New World context without releasing either the Old or the New World from their grasp: *Les Cenelles* hybridizes the figures, formats, and forms of the French *chansonniers* with those of Rufus Griswold's influential anthologies of anglophone American poetry and prose from the same period. In so doing, it locates the origins of this poetry in these men's American homes, in the streets of New Orleans, *and* in the thoroughfares of Paris. *Les Cenelles* in this way encourages the coming-into-being of a self that emerges from layered citations to scenes of being-with-strangers extending along and across time and space, in this process doing more than many other modern volumes to acknowledge its people and its places. It practices dividuated lyric preservation at the same time that it pursues individual coming-into-being.[7] It is dedicated to an experience of stranger-with-ness that facilitates stranger-becoming.

The transnational origins of the volume have nevertheless tended to be of more interest to critics and historians than its indigenous ones. The city's free Creoles of color are most typically thought of as a cosmopolitan crowd whose identification with the United States was tenuous at best. Often the children of enslaved women of African descent and men of the white planter class who frequented New Orleans to engage in the system of *plaçage*, they were inheritors of property and francophiles to a person. The young men of this class were either schooled in Paris or educated by Parisian schoolmasters in New Orleans, forming a separate class in the city. Neither white nor black, they claimed certain privileges as their own. With the arrival of the American administration in Louisiana in the first decades of the nineteenth century, their privileges declined to reach a nadir in the 1840s and 1850s. From the perspective of this twice-told tale, whose origins include volumes such as Rodolphe Desdunes's popular history, *Nos hommes et notre histoire* (1911), U.S. nationalism did not feature prominently in how the city's *gens de couleur libres* imagined and inhabited the world. Henry Louis Gates Jr. has written of this volume: "*Les Cenelles* argues for a political effect—that is, the end of racism—by publishing apolitical poems, poems which share as silent second texts the poetry written by Frenchmen three thousand miles away. We are like the French—so, treat us like Frenchmen."[8] In this account, as in more recent arguments that emphasize this writing's French republican, Catholic universalist, and romantic humanist origins, the United States plays a bit part in how these writers conceive their politics and their selfhood.

The indigenousness referenced in the subtitle is nevertheless crucial to understanding the shape and meaning of this volume, as well as its nationalism, notwithstanding Règine Latortue and Gleason Adams's decision to delete it from the title of their translated edition. For present purposes the signification of the word as a botanical designation characterizing native flora is especially germane. The main title of the collection, *Les Cenelles,* directly cites the indigenous flora of the bayous, river bottom, and swampland that circled and threaded through antebellum New Orleans. Although "*Les Cenelles*" has sometimes been translated as "*The Holly Berries*," it in fact refers to the mayhaw plant. As the historian Jerah Johnson explains, mayhaws played a central role in the heterosexual courting rituals of New Orleans's free Creoles of color. Creole men of color ventured out in mayhaw-berry-gathering parties, and parties of Creole women of color then invited those men to join them in their kitchens as they turned mayhaw berries into mayhaw preserves. According to Johnson, the history of the mayhaw therefore helps to explain the volume's dedication to the "beautiful women of Louisiana."[9] In addition to citing a specific place and the social practices of its people, I would argue, the title of the volume also posits that *Les Cenelles* will not be fully realized until the members of "*le beau sexe louisianais*" have transformed the volume into something more than what is presented to them, much as they did with the mayhaw berries delivered to them in their kitchens. The central economy of gift exchange shadowing this volume and its contents is therefore not one of women between men. It is one of gifts circulating between men and women—and back again. Given the long and complicated history of black female property ownership in New Orleans, as well as the ways that white property often passed into Creole of color hands by way of Creole of color women, this exchange economy has at least as much significance as the relation of black men to white men, and *plaçage* in New Orleans.

In the New World context, of course, the "indigenous" has a vexed relationship with the national: The European colonizers of North America worked hard and with some success to disarticulate the modern nation-state, and the United States in particular, from the threatening sense that a nation's justification hinged on its population's indigenousness. The mayhaw's connection to U.S. nationalism emerges more clearly, though, when *Les Cenelles'* dialogue with antebellum anglophone poets such as William Cullen Bryant is acknowledged. Bryant famously uses indigenous North American flora to suggest that his own literary project is a nationally specific venture. In "The Painted Cup," "The Yellow Violet," "The Prairie," and other similar poems, he figures the landscape of North America as largely empty of human civilization. It is instead a terrain of virgin flora that only a new and specifically U.S. national literature can capably document. His poetry thus does not claim merely to reflect an already-existing nation. It proposes to conjure that nation into being by confusing the indigenous qualities of the flora with the defining qualities of the (white) American frontiersman and his poetry, all of which are made visible by erasing evidence of what had come before. The title *Les Cenelles* and the subtitle *Choix de poésies indigènes* strike a similar note, but they also relocate America's origins to southeast Louisiana. Where Bryant associates American flora and the United States with countryside stripped of human presence, moreover, the title *Les Cenelles,* as I have just suggested, cites indigenous flora associated with practices of affiliation specific to free Creoles of color. The title's reference to an indigenous plant that played a central role in the social world of Creoles of color identifies the practice of affiliation that defined Creole of color life as an appropriate indigenous precedent to and for the nation: In *Les Cenelles*, the indigenous is fully social rather than romantically presocial or savage. Lanusse furthermore asks his readers to translate the social practices of New Orleans's Creoles of color into a broader context. He frames Creole of color modes of affiliation as the indigenous and therefore preferred model for practices of U.S. nation formation. These are circuits that include women as agents rather than as simply objects of exchange.

Though it might at first seem like a stretch to suggest that the *Les Cenelles* poets were positing their social practices as a model for the nation, *Les Cenelles* was actually part of a broader emergent discourse coming from francophone New Orleanians who did not disidentify with the United States, but who laid claim to the nation and sought to shape its evolving sense of itself. In venues such as the column titled "Littérature indigène," published in one of New Orleans's "white" francophone newspapers, *La Réforme* (a newspaper to which *hommes de couleur libres* also contributed), Creoles of many shades responded to the city's growing anglophone American Know-Nothing nativism by routing a claim to the nation through their account of the indigenously American, which turns out to be francophone Louisiana. Although the *Les Cenelles* poets and their white francophone compatriots did set out to define a *littérature indigène* that contested anglophone American literary nationalism, in other words, they did not do so in order to separate from America.

The reading of the term *indigène* and of *Les Cenelles* that I will offer in just a moment, which will suggest that both this term and the title articulate a Creole U.S. cultural nationalism that seeks to fashion the universal out of an accumulation of local-particulars, has little critical currency vis-à-vis *Les Cenelles*. This may follow in part from the reluctance of collectors and editors to permit the *Les Cenelles* poets their claim on the forms of sociality associated with the nation. For example, Edward Larocque Tinker's extensive collection of Louisiana, much of which is housed at the American Antiquarian Society, includes a book sleeve that Tinker created for his copy of *Les Cenelles*. In a woodcut image that he designed for the *Les Cenelles* book sleeve and a pamphlet that he wrote about the volume, Tinker adopted the familiar tropes of nativist modernism. These tropes obscure the volume's link to Louisiana's indigenous flora by reattaching the term *indigène* to the poets themselves and reframing them as African natives—or, in other words, as the *indigènes* referenced in the subtitle. From the perspective that Tinker offers with his book sleeve, these poems lay no claim on the U.S. nation, despite the title's placement of this poetry at the center of an indigenously American tradition. Where the original reference to the indigenous mayhaw defines New Orleans's Creole of color community, and the cultural expression of their scenes of sociality, as a vital source of U.S. national-indigenous culture, Tinker redraws the circle to detach these poets from the United States and reattach them to a non-U.S. African diaspora.

The editors of a 2003 Tintamarre edition of *Les Cenelles* undertake a similar reframing, but they dislocate the *Les Cenelles* poets in a different direction. The contemporary series in which the edition is included, Les Cahiers du Tintamarre, reprints works from the francophone New World. The editors of the series write of its authors: "Américanisés par le hasard, ces colons, esclaves et réfugiés n'ont pas abandonné leur culture en mettant pied sur le sol louisianais. Au contraire, ils nous ont laissé, dans leurs journaux, leurs livres, leurs manuscrits et leurs chansons, un registre riche et varié de leur vie au nouveau monde" ["Americanised by chance, these settlers, slaves and refugees did not leave their culture behind the day they set foot in Louisiana. On the contrary, they left behind a wealth of diaries, books, manuscripts and songs giving a rich and diverse depiction of their lives in the new world"]. The divided loyalties registered, here, between understanding these colonials, slaves, and refugees as francophone or as French reappear a few lines later:

> Nous avons respecté la ponctuation ainsi que l'orthographe—sauf pour les réclamant des accents et les fautes évidentes. La question de guillemetage se révélait plus épineuse, là où il n'y avait souvent que des guillemets anglais dans des textes qui se voulaient—français! En effet, nous avons essayé de leur rendre toute leur francité en remplaçant les guillemets anglais par leurs analogues français et en les insérant au besoin.

> |We kept the punctuation and spellings as they were, with the exception of accented capitals and obvious mistakes. Quotation mark usage turned out to be a thornier issue: often, English-style quotation marks were all there was to be found in writings that purported to be . . . French! In an attempt, therefore, to render them as wholly French as they were intended to be, we substituted or added, as appropriate, French quotation marks throughout.][10]

When it comes to representing the speaking voice, only *francité* will do. In order for it to be intelligible, the Creole voice must be either American or French. There is no other option, and it is an either-or choice. Repeatedly and in regards to many different specific categorical distinctions, though, the *Les Cenelles* poets traverse this distinction. For them the intense specificity of indigenous flora limited to a defined habitus permeates the *socius*, the local, the regional, the national, the transnational, and the human. Intensely specific local phenomena seed a cumulative, additive, summative notion of the human that remains inconclusive and open to the new.

Apostleship, Apostrophe, and the Other Lyric(s)

Although apostrophe has long been the go-to literary figure for discussions of lyric and the politics of poetry, its potential to function as a form of apostolic invitation and to contribute to this cumulative notion of the human has gone unacknowledged. *The New Princeton Encyclopedia of Poetry and Poetics* offers this definition of apostrophe: "A figure of speech which consists of addressing an absent or dead person, a thing, or an abstract idea as if it were alive or present."[11] One clear indication that apostrophe is in effect is the presence of the "O": "O, muse"; "O, Wild West Wind," and so on. Apostrophe can target objects of adoration and respect, recipients of desire and loathing. In an influential reading, Jonathan Culler argues that apostrophe has moreover two significant imaginative effects. First, it animates its inanimate or absent object(s) of address. In familiar anglophone examples, such as Shelley's "Ode to the West Wind," the object of address achieves a subjective ontology that it otherwise lacks. What was previously mute and inactive becomes potentially active and as capable of responsive speech. As Culler writes, "[T]he function of apostrophe [is] to make the objects of the universe potentially responsive forces. . . . The apostrophizing poet identifies his universe as a world of sentient forces."[12] Culler's apostrophizing poet arrogates to himself the right of world making and the ability to transform objects into subjects. Second, apostrophe works in a counterintuitive way to animate the voice of the poem and in turn to empower the poet. In this reading, the voice of the poem, from which the figure of apostrophe emanates, has no preexistent force of its own. The poem's voice requires an answer from the world in order for it to achieve some measure of subjective coherence. For Culler, then, "apostrophe is a device which the poetic voice uses to establish with an object a relationship which helps to constitute him. The object is treated as a subject, an *I* which implies a certain type of *you* in its turn. One who successfully invokes nature is one to whom nature might, in its turn, speak."[13] The poetic voice achieves its significance by establishing a relation to the world of the inanimate that animates both the voice of the poem and its inanimate addressee.

It is not news that when apostrophe is taken up in specific contexts, it has a political charge. It is therefore of interest to see *Les Cenelles* littered with many, sundry, and often seemingly misjudged examples of it and related figures of address. To find apostrophe emerging from New Orleans's community of free people of color is to discover a literature making broad claims for itself and its authors. These poems claim the right to address the inanimate and thereby to animate the world. They also engage in a process of self-animation. If Culler is right that apostrophe is the primary figure of self-sufficiency, then these poems are proclaiming the self-sufficiency of New Orleans's free people of color. Even more important than this surface gesture toward self-sufficiency, however, is the way that this poetry simultaneously obviates the kind of self-sufficiency associated with burdened individuality, while raising the possibility of something like plurality.

This turning away from one version of self-sufficiency and toward another, a self-sufficiency of stranger-with-ness, is not obvious on a first reading of this poetry. A more established view would focus on the fact that apostrophe collapses the distinction between self and other upon which a politics of plurality must depend. For Virginia Walker Jackson, for example, apostrophe encourages a narcissistic confusion of self and other, particularly if it comes in the anodyne format of the postromantic codex collection of poetry that strips away all contextualizing references. Its anonymizing of any given poem makes it easy for the reader to identify with the apostrophizing voice, encouraging a problematic substitutive identification. A reading based on that established view might argue the following about these lines from Camille Thierry's poem "Toi," which was not included among the poems he published in *Les Cenelles* but which dates from the same period:

> Tu ne murmuras point quand l'heure était venue,
> > L'heure de nos adieux . . .
> Tu t'envolas tranquille à travers chaque nue,
> > Comme un ange des cieux.
>
> Enfant, nous te suivrons au delà des nuages,
> > Où l'âme trouve un port,
> Où l'on n'entend jamais le grand bruit des orages,
> > Où l'ouragan s'endort!
>
> [When the time came, you muttered not a sound—
> > The time for our goodbyes . . .
> Calm, you flew off, like angel heaven-bound,
> > Over the shrouded skies.
>
> Follow I shall, child, past the clouds, to reach
> > A port of soul's safekeeping,
> Where never brawls the tempest's blare and screech,
> > And the hurricane lies sleeping.][14]

In a now-familiar account of lyric, the reader does not recognize herself as "toi" but rather as the "je" implied in the "nous" of line 5. The apostrophic address to "toi" is so private as to be privative. It refers to no specific addressee, and it appears to emanate from no specific place or time. The "je" here is therefore abstract enough to be perceived as any "je." Rather than Thierry or even the voice of the poem (the poem's "je") traveling to the heavens with the object of address, it is the reader who ends up taking that imaginative journey. The reader also makes that journey alone. The soul that "trouve un port" is the reader's own, and the "port" turns out to be the reader's soul itself. Although the figure of apostrophe appears to require the poem's "je" and its "toi" to travel toward each other and toward a moment of encounter, it actually encourages an inward turn on the part of the reader that enfolds both the agent and the object of address into the reader's emergent "je." The reader's "je" is reinforced, even born, but in the process the poem's "je" and its "toi" disappear.

A "third position" may nevertheless be read out of this "structure of address."[15] This third position would not be the voice of the poem or the position of the reading subject. It would be the stranger invited to participate in stranger-with-ness and in the stranger-becoming that ensues. It would recognize the expansive possibilities of stranger-with-ness limned in Douglass's "I am a stranger with thee." In "Apostrophe Reconsidered," J. Douglas Kneale charges Culler with a basic definitional error, and his observations are illuminating in this context. He suggests that Culler's influential discussion of apostrophe mistakes apostrophe for direct address in general. According to Kneale, apostrophe targets more than just one addressee. Apostrophe requires a turning aside from a primary object of address to a new and different addressee. As the etymology of the word "apostrophe" and its origins in the classical context of the Roman senate chamber would suggest, Kneale argues, apostrophe is a form of interrupted address with at least three witnesses and usually more: the agent of address, its original target, and its secondary target. Quoting Kneale: "By describing apostrophe as a turning from an original . . . addressee to a different addressee, from the proper or intended hearer to another, we emphasize the figure as a *movement* of voice, a translation or carrying over of address. This understanding is crucial if we are to distinguish simple direct address from the turning aside of address, from the rhetorical and temporal movement of apostrophe."[16] Kneale emphasizes the performative quality specific to apostrophe: in the moment of apostrophic address, the primary object of address is made secondary and placed at a remove, but it is not released.

Kneale's reading at first appears to disqualify many lines in *Les Cenelles* from counting as apostrophe, because they do not clearly turn away from a prior addressee. This is the case because several of these poems open by addressing muses, absent friends, and inanimate objects. Valcour B.'s "À Hermina" begins in this way:

Amour, écoute un amant qui t'implore,
O Cupidon, le plus puissant des dieux!

[Hear O God of Love a lover's prayer,
Cupid, most powerful god of all!]¹⁷

His "À Malvina" opens in this way:

Belle de grâce et belle de jeunesse,
O Malvina, tu parus à mes yeux

[Aglow with grace and youth, O Malvina
In all your beauty to my eyes you appeared]¹⁸

He even turns jokingly to address the hat of his beloved in these first lines, in the manner of a latter-day cavalier:

Chapeau chéri,
De celle que j'admire

[Cherished hat,
Of the one I admire]¹⁹

Louis Boise animates spring with these first lines:

Tendre Printemps, viens rendre à la Nature
Et ses trésors et ses puissants attraits.

[Tender Spring, render to Nature
Her treasures and her enchanting lures.]²⁰

In each of these cases, and in many others in *Les Cenelles*, it is natural to assume that there is no former addressee. Is it not impossible to interrupt an address that has not yet begun? Yet these are actually some of the most important instances of apostrophe in *Les Cenelles*, to the extent that they "turn aside" from, and therefore assume and confirm as present from the start, an actually-existing target of address in addition to the nominal addressee, but one the poem also refuses to seal in a specific place and time, instead inviting entry from any given place and time. In the light of Joanni Questy's notion of apostleship, which opened this chapter, such opening apostrophes look less self-enclosing than apostolic. The moments of stranded apostrophe opening these poems invite the reader to join with the two who are already there. They further implicitly acknowledge the needfulness of a reader, which is to say both the reader's needs and the need of a reader, with their invitation to join an apostolic body committed to witnessing for literature.

As much as it is a self-aggrandizing gesture, apostrophe can under the right conditions function as a decorous, generous invitation. Those circumstances must be pursued deliberately, and so these men did by way of their publishing, teaching, coterie meetings, participation in Béranger societies, and other activity. Both their poetry and their activity surrounding poetry assume the incompleteness of the agent and the target of address, their mutual lack of self-sufficiency; they also posit stranger-with-ness as the only form of being available to us, but one nevertheless worth having. Apostolic apostrophe opens everything and closes nothing, unless and until it is made to do so by institutional circumstance. Even then, it lies in wait, ready to open/be opened when the time is ripe. The time will only ever be ripe when a group of willing apostles has studied the rules of address that characterize this particular semiprivate room. Importantly, and as is signaled in François Destrade's acknowledgment of his debt to New Orleans's Béranger society (noted in this chapter's epigraph), as well as in the radical citationality of *Les Cenelles* to be discussed in just a moment, like every semiprivate room this one has a specific street address and ordered set of rules.

First and Last Words

The apostrophizing poets of New Orleans do something more than simply claim the right to animate their inanimate or absent objects of address, acquiring in the process a subjective significance of their own. They claim the right to participate in stranger-with-ness and the right to grant that privilege to others. These poets in this way reset the terms of encounter according to which New Orleans's Creole free people of color will make their case at home and abroad. These poets do not engage in a form of address that is much more familiar to those who read mainly in the anglophone African American literary tradition. This poetry does not engage in petition. It does not petition its reader for sympathy, nor does it petition a constitutionally exclusive legislature for the right simply to be human. In this sense, it is neither sentimental in the terms that have been said to define anglophone sentimentality, nor does it display the standard gestures often identified with lyric. It instead opens a space into which its authors and their readers can emerge together as a new kind of human. In this space of strangers-with-ness, any human's experience is specific, not immediately knowable, and still in the process of unfolding. When we factor in the institutional spaces of their poetry, as well as the documentation of those spaces in the poetry, it becomes clear how the *Les Cenelles* poets, or New Orleans's authentic apostles for literature, embraced the potentials of stranger-with-ness.

Their poems describe a line of demarcation separating each of us from all the rest of us, but they do so in a way that summons a scale of human affiliation predicated on the unexchangeability of any one human for another. Like Douglass's later writings, they work to foreclose the privative burdened individuality often presented as the alternative to social disenfranchisement but whose rewards amount to a form of debt. *Les Cenelles* positions the free person of color as a stranger whose specificity is his alone, but in so doing it also draws a circle of affiliation accessible to anyone willing to acknowledge that specificity as a shared condition of being human and, therefore, to become part of that stranger's we. This poetry's attention to the spaces of that we's articulation—rhetorical and material spaces alike—played a major role in their pursuit of stranger-with-ness.

In this context, the notion of apostrophe as apostleship complicates some familiar accounts of lyric. If lyric has the potential to compromise the author/voice of a poem and its reader in a wash of narcissistic cross-identification, then for Michael Warner, this is one reason why lyric address and public address are at odds. If public address seeks to draw a wide circle of affiliation, then it is also predicated on being self-consciously addressed to strangers and marked as such. However, as Warner also indicates, a fully licensed citizen in modern society is neither more nor less than a stranger-in-relation, someone granted the privileges of what Erving Goffman calls "civil inattention." This form of oblique recognition, Goffman suggests, enables modern civic life.[21] *Les Cenelles* does less to encourage understanding, or sympathy, or identification than it does to acquire strangerhood and preserve it. *Les Cenelles* permits a moment of civil inattention: This is arguably the most that any one of us could hope for, for it permits vibrant stranger-with-ness.

It is therefore worth repeating that if this stranger is different from all others, as more conventional idioms of individualism imagine is the case, his difference derives from and demands his sociality. In *Les Cenelles*, one does not retreat to a pond to discover one's individuality. One preserves the bonds of sociality formed in one's writing circle. Indeed, *Les Cenelles* retards the dissolution of the generative third position of the stranger-with by enfolding within itself a residue of sociality. Jackson argues that modern readings of lyric as such hinge on the emptiness of a book form, the poetry collection, which encourages a delusory sense of real poetry as being addressed to no one in particular and from no one in particular. One of her central critical gestures is to reattach poems to their historical addressees.

It is significant that *Les Cenelles* does much of that work itself. It provides the given names of specific addressees in poems such as "À Hermina," "À mademoiselle Coelina," or À Elora." There are also poems such as Valcour B.'s "Épître à Constant Lépouzé, en recevant un volume de ses poésies," as well as "L'ouvrier louisianais (Imité de Béranger), à mon ami Armand Lanusse." In addition to these explicit addressees and dedicatees, members of this circle are cited and honored in other ways. Armand Lanusse's epigraph to his poem "Le prêtre et la jeune fille" comes from Alfred Mercier, a fellow New Orleanian whose writing was in circulation in the city during this period. Lanusse's "Besoin d'écrire" is dedicated "à mon ami, Nelson D." And so forth. This literalization of address makes it difficult to imagine these poems (or the others in this volume) as the product of a self in conversation with itself. A reader might wish to occupy the position of the lyric reader who overhears a solitary self, but instead must finally admit to listening in company with the dozen or so others addressed, named, and honored in *Les Cenelles*. Here the reader listens "dans une société."

Introducing his poem "La foi, l'espérance et la charité," Pierre Dalcour writes:

Dans une société, où l'on jouait aux Jeux innocents, il fut ordonné à un jeune homme, pour racheter son gage, de faire une déclaration d'amour à la dame de son choix. Il s'avança aussitôt auprès d'une jeune personne qui passait pour être un peu dévote, et s'en acquitta ainsi.

[At a gathering where they were playing *Jeux innocents* (innocent games), a young man, in order to redeem a wager, was ordered to make a declaration of love to a lady of his choice. He immediately approached a young lady who had the reputation of being rather devout, and acquitted himself of his duty in this manner.][22]

Les Cenelles encourages us to imagine in detail the actuality of the scene as the site of origin for the poem that follows. In a similar gesture, Dalcour subtitles another poem, "Caractère," with this account of the origin of the poem: "Mot donné par mon ami Armand L." ["Word proposed by my friend Armand L."].[23] Dalcour thus identifies the poem that follows as the product of an exchange between two people who retain the specificity of their names:

Moi qui fais des vers par caprice,
Aujourd'hui je suis condamné
Par un ami, Dieu, quel supplice!
A rimer sur un mot donné.
     Allons, ma muse,
     Un peu de ruse,
Il faut m'aider à sortir de ce pas;
     Vite, on me presse,
     Quelle détresse!

[I who write verses for pleasure
Today I am condemned
By a friend, God, what torture!
To rhyme upon a given word.
     Let's go, my muse
     A little ruse
You must help me to get out of this;
     Quickly, the pressure is on,
     What distress!][24]

The title, the subheading, and the poem locate this work in a scene of Creole of color sociality. Although an indefinite article opens the title of Lanusse's poem "Un frère au tombeau de son frère," the parenthetical addition to the title of "(25 Septembre 1836)" offsets that indefiniteness of person and place.

The thick citationality of *Les Cenelles* documents as well relations that exceed this particular New Orleans circle. Many of the poems in *Les Cenelles* are headed by the name of *l'air* to which they should be sung. In this respect, *Les Cenelles* recalls the European tradition of the *chansonnier*, which played a central role in the public life of poetry. These volumes found lyrics, and the tunes to which they were to be sung, appearing "alongside other songs and other forms of verbal exchange—jokes, riddles, rumors, and *bons mots*." The *chansonniers* permitted eighteenth- and nineteenth-century Parisians, in particular, to "constantly compos[e] new words to old tunes. The lyrics often referred to current events, and as events evolved, anonymous wits added new verses. The songs therefore provide a running commentary on

public affairs, and there are so many of them that one can see how the lyrics exchanged [in private] fit into song cycles that carried messages through
all the streets of Paris."[25] The *Les Cenelles* poets would have known of this
tradition from their visits to Paris. If they somehow did not, they might
have learned of it from *Le Chansonnier des Grâces, almanach chantant, pour
l'année 1809, dédié aux dames* (1809), which was collected and published
in New Orleans by Alexis Daudet. As with *Le Chansonnier des Grâces*, the
"air" that is to accompany many of the poems in *Les Cenelles* is specified.
Often those airs are from Béranger, whose fame precipitated the formation
of Béranger societies across France and in New Orleans, as the epigraph to
this chapter would indicate.

It is not only that the volume, *Les Cenelles: Choix de poésies indigènes*,
discourages the notion of lyric as inherently hermetic. It mobilizes apostrophe as apostleship in a way that de-isolates without destroying the lyric
voice present in a poem such as Camille Thierry's "Toi." Thus Lanusse's
introduction to *Les Cenelles* includes an epigraph from Félicité de Lamennais: "Toute conviction sincère mérite le respect, et la conscience de
l'homme est un sanctuaire sacré pour l'homme, un asile où Dieu seul a
le droit de pênitrer [*sic*] comme juge" ["Every sincere conviction deserves
respect, and a man's conscience is his hallowed sanctuary, a haven where
God alone has the right to enter and judge"].[26] In their translation of *Les
Cenelles*, Latortue and Adams render the first lines of Lanusse's introduction as follows. The original reads: "Afin de prévenir les personnes dans les
mains desqelles ce livre pourra tomber en faveur de ceux d'entre nos amis
en poésie qui ont répondu franchement à notre appel et qui ont daigné
contribuer à la production de ce volume, nous pensons qu'il nous suffira
d'exposer dans cette introduction, d'une manière brève et précise, les motifs
qui nous ont fait entreprendre la publication de ce recueil." The Latortue and Adams translation reads: "In order favorably to predispose the
reader toward the poets who have contributed voluntarily to this volume,
we believe that a brief, precise exposition of the reasons for its existence
might be helpful."[27] As Latortue and Adams understand them, these lines
constitute an address to "the reader" that puts the lyric writing subject's
abstract "asile" before "the reader" in a way that would permit "the reader"
to imagine his own "asile" to be one and the same with that of "l'homme."
In the original French, however, the lines that open this volume equally
stand in a tempering relation to the epigraph. Rather than addressing "the
reader," those lines reference instead "les personnes dans les mains des-
quelles ce livre pourra tomber." Instead of the solitary reader we have "les

personnes." Instead of "poets" we have the dividuated "ceux d'entre nos amis en poésie." Where the translation emphasizes the relation of "the reader" to an individuated collection of "poets," the original highlights the semiprivate room constructed through a collaboration among "ceux d'entre nos amis en poésie," "les personnes," and "ce livre." Poignant expressions of individual selfhood emerge in "ce livre," but they also demand, preserve, and extend a tightly woven social matrix irreducible to "ce livre." The lyric self of *Les Cenelles* thus always comes with a citation to its we, as well as an invitation to join that we in an experience of stranger-with-ness. This citationality is one of the potentials of not only "ce livre," but of any "livre." This way of collecting poetry extends an invitation to join in the work of constructing a self without denying the sociality that makes such efforts possible.

Pour Chanter

Even forgetting the scenes of sociality documented in *Les Cenelles*, other of its poems instructively illuminate the error of imagining that the poem as self-in-conversation-with-itself is a scene of one to which the reader is invited only as a singular self-serving witness. Two poems from the collection, both of which focus on a physically absent lover, emphasize how poetic utterance may permit the presentation of a self to others in such a way that the point is not to replace the other but to declare one's allegiance to that other and to hear such declarations in return. It is also clear in these two poems that the proper medium for such declarations of stranger-with-ness is a form of apostolic apostrophe. The first of these two poems, "Chant d'amour," opens the volume. Written by Pierre Dalcour, the poem is dated November 1844. Recalling the volume's dedication to the fair ladies of Louisiana, it exists in dialogue with a short strain of the second poem, from G. Lemoine, that functions as the volume's epigraph: "Le nom de celle que j'aime, / Je le cache dans mon Coeur; / Nul ne le sait que moi-même, / C'est mon secret, mon Bonheur" ["The name of my beloved / Is hidden in my heart; / No one knows it but me, / It is my secret, my joy"].[28] This epigraph appears to place the reader in the presence of a self overhead in conversation with itself, a self interested mainly in trumpeting its possession of a secret, and therefore a chamber for holding that secret, to the wider world in a way that emphasizes poetry as a place to put one's privacy on display without actually ceding that privacy to dissolution. Yet the space in which this particular self converses with itself includes in fact at least three: "cell que j'aime," "je," and the reader. The list of those present increases to four in "Chant d'amour"; the poem also refigures the office of poetry as permitting the poet not to sing of his own privacy, but rather "pour chanter la beauté que j'adore." This poem imagines a singing that is not only a *singing-about*, but also a *singing-to* and a *singing-with*. The song is therefore not the occasion for a radically privatized self-creation. Nor is the song the moment in which the speaking subject's ontology is achieved at the expense of others who are subordinated to mere witnessing. The song is a medium for engaging those separated by the constraints of space and time. The poem opens as follows:

> Pour chanter la beauté que j'adore, ô ma lyre,
>   Seconde mes efforts!
> De tes sons les plus doux, sur l'aile du zéphyr,
>   Porte-lui les accords!
>
> A la vague qui vient mourir sur le rivage,
>   Aux oiseaux dans les airs,
> A la brise du soir caressant le feuillage,
>   Emprunte tes concerts.
>
> Recueille de la nuit ces mille sons étranges,
>   Mais doux, harmonieux,
> Qui font que l'âme croit ouïr la voix des anges
>   Qui chantent dans les cieux!
>
> Si ma bouche jamais, près d'elle, n'osa faire
>   L'aveu de mon ardeur,
> O ma lyre, aujourd'hui, dis-lui donc ce mystère,
>   Ce secret de mon coeur.
>
> Puisse de tes accords la suave harmonie
>   S'exhaler doucement,
> Comme un concert lointain, comme une symphonie
>   Dans un écho mourant! . . .
>
> [To sing of the beauty I adore, O' my lyre
>   Promote my efforts!
> Of your sweetest sounds, on the wings of the zephyr
>   Bring her the harmony

From the wave which expires on the shore,
    From the birds in the heavens,
From the twilight breeze which caresses the foliage,
    Borrow your concerts.

Gather from the night these thousand sounds, as strange
    As they are soft and melodious,
Which makes the soul seemingly hear the voice of angels
    Singing in paradise.

If near her, my lips never dared
    Confess my love,
O' my lyre, today, tell her this mystery,
    The secret of my heart.

May your chords sweetly send forth
    The pleasant harmony
Like a distant concert, like a symphony
    In a dying echo! . . .][29]

In Lemoine's lines, the poet's primary goal is to speak out loud about what he will not speak: Poetry is nothing more than an opportunity to lend coherence to one's selfhood through an act of performative speech. There the thing performed is not love but rather the capacity for love; the crucial declaration is the declaration that his heart is present, subordinate to the subject's will, and full of secrets unknown to you. The possession of the name of the beloved becomes an occasion for self-possession, a self-possession predicated on the possessed remaining absent from view. This is republicanism gone awry: an *oikos* secreted within the body of the poet. By contrast, Dalcour's account of his beloved results in a reaching toward the beloved that requires transit through an animated lyre, borrows from the natural world around, and ultimately makes clear the distance of the beloved from the poet's body. Rather than emphasizing the possession of a secret love as an (arguably) narcissistic self-possession, this is a reaching toward the beloved in a way that prioritizes the acknowledgment of the beloved: The only point of the secret love for the beloved is to share it with the beloved. Indeed, as the poem continues, Dalcour emphasizes the extent to which the necessary distance from the beloved cannot be overcome by the possession of some interior secret. That necessary distance, once extended by circumstance into an untenable one, results in the

terrified dissolution of the self. The moment of radical disconnection associated with the self-enclosing gestures of the lyric utterance results here in a
form of pained madness:

> Quand de la nuit l'ombre s'avance
> Et, telle qu'un nuage immense,
> Descend sur la terre en silénce,
> Quant tout repose sous les cieux,
> Heure de douce rêverie,
> Parfois son image chérie
> Semble être présente à mes yeux!
>
> Je vois sa taille de sylphide,
> Son front pur, sa grâce candide,
> Ses lèvres de corail humide,
> Ses yeux noirs remplis de langueur;
> Et je sens la vive étincelle
> Qui, s'échappant de sa prunelle,
> Soudain vient embraser mon Coeur!
> . . . .
>
> Mais hélas! bientôt ce mirage
> Qui réfléchissait son image,
> S'enfuit comme un léger nuage
> Que chasse un vent impétueux!
> Ou telle, au lever de l'aurore,
> On voit l'ombre qui s'évapore
> Aux premiers rayons lumineux!
>
> Alors, mais en vain, je m'écrie:
> Reviens, ô douce rêverie,
> Ombre décevante et chérie
> Reviens une dernière fois!
> Hélas! quand ma bouche l'appelle
> Je n'entends que l'écho fidèle
> Qui réponde au loin à ma voix!—
>
> [When approaches the shadow of night,
> And, like an immense cloud,

Descends in silence upon the earth,
When all is still under the skies,
Hour of sweet reverie,
Sometimes her cherished image
Seems to appear to me!

I see her sylphlike waist,
Her pure brow, her simple grace,
Her lips of humid coral,
Her dark languid eyes;
And I feel the ardent spark
Which, escaping from those eyes,
Suddenly sets my heart ablaze!

. . . .

But alas! Soon this mirage
Which reflected her image
Flies away like a light cloud
Chased away by an impetuous wind!
Or like, at the break of dawn,
Is seen the evaporating shadow
With the arrival of the sun's rosy-streaked rays.

But then in vain I scream:
Return to me, sweet reverie,
Deceiving and cherished shadow
Return to me one last time!
Alas! When my lips call out
I hear only the loyal echo
Answering remotely to my voice.]

As the poem describes it, the moment of greatest coherence of the self comes at the moment when an at-least fantasized additional subject stands present to the primary voice. Neither is this really a prizing of a narcissistic reflection of the self in that additional subject. The beloved is a kind of ghost whose opacity makes any simple form of identification or self-creation both impossible and a seeming travesty of human being. When even the fantasized additional subject is made absent, the primary voice is left with nothing other than a relatively faithful echo that nevertheless seems to be slowly diminishing in its capacity to provide an organizing container for the original speaker. As the voice returns to itself it is no longer itself, and in this sense the original voice is revealed already to be a stranger to itself. The madness that accompanies the returning voice suggests that absent stranger-with-ness, which remedies what is otherwise mere isolation, an unhinging dissolution of the self ensues.

In one of the most interesting moments of the poem, we are allowed a view of what happens when this dissolution comes to pass. After the voice of the poem commands "Ranime-toi ma lyre!" ["Rise up once more, my lyre"], it introduces the possibility that there might have been not only a fourth animate presence in the room, but a fifth one as well: the voice of the poem, the waxing and waning presence of the beloved, the lyre, the reader, and the Virgin:

> Soit que l'astre du jour inonde de lumière
>> Et la terre et les cieux,
> Soit que sur nous du soir le voile de mystère
>> Tombe silencieux;
>
> Vierge, c'est toujours toi qui vis dans ma pensée,
>> Qui fais battre mon coeur,
> Qui ramènes l'espoir en mon âme affaissée
>> Sous le faix du malheur.
>
> C'est toi qui m'apparais, ô beauté que j'adore,
>> La nuit, dans mon sommeil,
> Quand le jour luit c'est toi que mon oeil cherche encore
>> A l'heure du réveil.
>
> [Whether the sun inundates
>> Both the earth and the skies,
> Whether the mysterious veil of night
>> Falls silently upon us;
>
> Virgin, you are constantly in my thoughts,
>> Making my heart beat;
> You always rekindle hope in my soul, sinking
>> Under the weight of misfortune.

Beauty that I adore, you appear to me
    At night, in my sleep
When the day breaks, my eyes still searching for you
    At the moment of my wakening.]

The confused casting is essential: Is it that the voice of the poem was not referring to a beloved in the same sense as G. Lemoine and had replaced the notion of the beloved with the Virgin? Or is it that the Virgin was there all along? It seems more likely that the latter is the case: The relation of being-with-ness once shared with the beloved must, in the moment of the departure of the beloved, be reallocated to an experience of being-with-ness shared with the Virgin. In this version of lyric utterance, there is no soul that is not already present and available only by way of a being-with others, whether the Virgin or Jesus or the beloved; the moment that all other beings cease to be in the vicinity of the self, the self ceases to be as well. There is no access to life as a pure singularity. There is only stranger-with-ness, suspect-stranger-hood, or some other way of being a stranger-in-relation.

CHAPTER FOUR

The Abundant Black Past

These words [of the workers] had to be removed from their status as evidence or symptoms of a social reality to show them as writing and thinking at work on the construction of a different social world. That is why [*Proletarian Nights*] renounced any explanatory distance. It instead sought to create the sensitive fabric required to make this upturning of the order that keeps times and discourses in their place resound in our own present. That is why severe theorists and historians deemed it to be literature.

—Jacques Rancière, preface to the new English edition
of *Proletarian Nights* (2012)

Not a single person is missing.

—Edward P. Jones, *The Known World*

In his preface to the new English edition of *Proletarian Nights: The Workers' Dream in Nineteenth-Century France* (2012), Jacques Rancière proposes that in order to engage the past in a politicized fashion, one must ignore its pastness as such. This is because extant distinctions separating past from present replicate a larger failing of intellectual work that claims to ally itself with the oppressed. The primary offense against the proletariat on the part of "mandarin" intellectuals, he argues, is to reinscribe ad nauseum the self-credentialing belief that some unspecified difference separates the compromised intellectual formations of those "below" from the "science" generated by the intellectuals who stand "above." His history of class struggle includes a long and tawdry tale of self-nominated scientists seeking to speak for and on behalf of those whom the scientists characterize as ideologically blinded to their proper roles as revolutionary agents of History. Rancière summarizes the force and direction of his argument as follows: "The equality of intelligences remains the most untimely of thoughts it is possible to nourish about the social order."[1]

Rancière's signature notion of the equality of intelligences inaugurates his early break with his teacher Louis Althusser, but, more important, it interrogates the role of self-designated intellectuals in the unfolding of human equality. In *Proletarian Nights*, Rancière prosecutes the case that the self-declared intellectual class has obstructed the otherwise open-throated voice of what can be heuristically called the people. If this obstructing is a problem in general, he suggests, it is an especially acute one when it comes to the fraught distinction separating past historical actors from present ones. Too often intellectual work on the past takes for granted the superiority of current knowledge when measured against knowledge generated in the past. "If only they knew then what we know now," in other words, represents a pernicious manifestation of a position that rejects the equality of intelligences across time. For the spatial hierarchy of above and below, substitute the seemingly benign chronological pairing of present and past. As an antidote to this hierarchical rendering of present and past, Rancière offered something—call it a link to the past formulated as a "sensitive fabric" of writing—that certain "severe theorists and historians" who took issue with his book would criticize as "literature." These severe critics denigrated *Proletarian Nights* as literature for trying to do the seemingly impossible: allow past "times" and past "discourses" of the proletariat to "resound in our own present."[2] Rancière's literature sought to accord past knowledges and past peoples a fundamental equality with the present.

Recalling Rancière's injunction to respect the equality of intelligences across time, it is easy to see how, in writing about the nineteenth century, it is tempting to stretch "our" present to accommodate what has been thought of as the increasingly distant past. If I take this risk of trying to forget the distance in time and circumstance separating me from the people and the places I study, however, in order to embrace the idea of the past's equality with the present, I find myself struggling with the sense of breaching a trust I agreed to some time ago. I recall the axiomatic view that mediation guarantees the failed transmission of direct experience. I hear the warnings pointing out the danger of identifying with the past and with historical subjectivities radically different from my own. I recall the cautions against imagining that a twenty-first-century white man might be equipped to communicate the experience of being a nineteenth-century black one. It is easy enough to dismiss these concerns as a dated commitment to poststructuralist verities. They are also key tenets of the intellectual legacies that define African American literary studies in its current formation.

If Rancière is right, though, all of these reservations around mediation and identification should be understood as the predictable attempts of a mandarin intellectual to guard against his fundamental equality with the past. For Rancière, the self-appointed scientist class that is his target has justified its reign by arguing that the complexity of ideology requires professional thinkers to clarify and guide the thinking of the proletariat. This emphasis on ideology's complexity and on the lack of self-awareness on the part of the proletariat is a mercenary ambit that conceals what the proletariat has thought, said, and written—often more than one time. In Rancière's reformulated framework, therefore, if intellectuals are to have any role at all, it will not be that of the exegete or the leader of the unwashed. Intellectuals will need to make themselves scarce and function as a medium of proletarian comment if they are to function at all. To reformulate this argument to accommodate the immediate context, the role of the intellectual in relation to nineteenth-century African America will not be interpreter, analyst, or agent of recovery. It will be to provide the medium, the sensitive fabric, that Rancière imagines, and the intellectual will do so only as needed. The concerns over mediation and identification turn out to be a screen against contending with the more serious work of figuring out how to do justice to a past intelligence that is equal to the present. This serious work involves an effort to recognize peoples and persons in the past without fetishizing their alterity in relation to the present.

If one takes this view to be a guiding one, there remains one unacknowledged wrinkle to Rancière's argument that is consequential for weaving a sensitive enough fabric. As with other Marxian understandings of history, one curious effect of Rancière's injunction to respect the equality of intelligences across time is to highlight the state of coming-into-being that defines people in the past. Rancière's injunction to respect the equality of intelligences across time, as well as his insistence on creating a sensitive fabric of writing, is predicated on a sense that the past is not completely unavailable to us. Nor are we to it. The past is not in a position of radical alterity in relation to the present; instead, the meaning and significance of the past, and the intelligibility of past peoples and past persons, take shape in relation to a continuously unfolding present that is equal and available to it. The phenomenological circumstances that constitute the past include events in the present that assign meaning in retrospect to that subject's actions and agency in life. The life of a black New Orleanian who struggled for civil rights in Reconstruction Louisiana meant something different in the moment *Plessy v. Ferguson* was decided from what it did when the Civil Rights Act of 1964 was signed into law. That life meant something different still when Hurricane Katrina rearranged the city of New Orleans's demographics. The past is always in a state of transformation. Its significance is always dynamically determined by the unfolding of a present that is its equal.

What might this kind of past require of the living if those living are to respect the equality of the past's intelligences and its openness to the future? What do the presently living owe to the unfinished past? What sorts of transmissions must the sensitive fabric known as literature accommodate? In a recent exchange with Axel Honneth concerning the politics of redistribution and recognition, Nancy Fraser explains that, in political philosophy, recognition "designates an ideal reciprocal relationship between subjects in which each sees the other as its equal and also as separate from it." This relation between subjects, she continues, "is deemed constitutive for subjectivity; one becomes an individual subject only in virtue of recognizing, and being recognized by, another subject. Thus, 'recognition' implies the Hegelian thesis . . . that social relations are prior to individuals and intersubjectivity is prior to subjectivity."[3] Summarizing the long and complex genealogy of a pivotal political concept in a few short sentences, Fraser points to the central role of mutual recognition in the construction of a just and healthy society comprising adequately realized political subjects. In a related study, she embeds this account of recognition in a global framework. She offers that traditional geographical boundaries, especially national ones, work to include and exclude persons and peoples from frameworks that permit the pursuit of justice as well as recognition. As she explains: "Far from being of marginal significance, frame-setting is among the most consequential of political decisions. Constituting members and non-members in a single stroke, this decision effectively excludes the latter from the universe of those entitled to consideration within the community in matters of . . . recognition."[4] The key issue here is the importance of thinking carefully about who is "entitled to consideration within the community in matters of . . . recognition." If we take seriously Rancière's challenge, then the right to recognition will extend to all of those included within the expanded frame demanded by the equality of intelligences across time. This is to say that the living owe recognition to and require it from living others, but they also owe recognition to and require it from those who died long ago but whose significance is still in the making. How would recognition work in this context? If the meaning of the past is only ever understandable through its relation to a permanently unfolding present, then the past is always in a process of becoming: What is it then that is already out there to be recognized?

If the living owe a debt of recognition to past persons, then these living owe this debt not to who those persons in the past were but to who they are still becoming: The critical-historical practice of recognition that Rancière's critics impugned as literature must accommodate itself to the fact that past historical actors are tethered to the present. This practice must address itself not to the persons those living imagine the dead to have been; it must acknowledge the evolving figures the dead continue to be. The fact that these persons and peoples in the past are strangers to the living, the impossibility of the living ever knowing them in full, does not derive from the past's silence or its absence from some record. The strangeness of people in the past follows from the fact that there will be no moment in which the fate of people in the past has been sealed. The dead may not be living but they are never done with life. To imagine that you can tell the final story of the dead is to make the mistake of imagining that their story has already ended. Perhaps it makes more sense to approach them as the strangers they should always be allowed to remain than it does to imagine that you can secure the story of a person who was and is no more. What might one of these strangers in the past say to the present? Call me Ishmael, perhaps. In saying so, the dead would be offering something like the exacting but generous offer contained in Frederick Douglass's "I am a stranger with thee." In saying so, however, the target of address, the recipient of the demanding gift, would not be a former master or even an antebellum collaborationist. The target, the recipient, would be us.

A Stranger History

The only appropriate gift in return would be to write a stranger history. This raises the question: what would a stranger history look like? *The Known World* recounts the fortunes of an antebellum Virginia plantation owner named Henry Townsend who is a former slave. In his freedom, Townsend elects to purchase slaves of his own. For many readers this novel's topical interest lies in its relatively unfamiliar account of slaveholding among free people of color, while its stylistic appeal derives from the way that Jones combines acute realism with the expansive imagination of what Madhu Dubey terms "speculative fiction meets neoslave narrative."[5] For these readers Jones's novel unveils a troubling nineteenth-century world in which intraracial slavery is a key feature of African American life.[6] By this account Jones's novel offers a critique of the heroicizing procedures that arguably dominate African American academic history writing.[7] Such history would represent people of African descent as strictly the targets of enslavement rather than as also participants in the peculiar institution, all the while adopting the questionable and undertheorized recommendations of mainline liberal U.S. historiography. However, this novel's critique goes even deeper. Although it is true Jones's novel takes issue with the conventions of academic history, it argues for something rather different from most recent proposals to liberate African Americans from a more conventional academic approach to history telling. In doing so, the novel encourages a view of stranger history that would see the present engage the past as a site conducive to the totalizing gestures of grand historical narrative, but that would require a careful recalibration of the practice of history-telling designed to align respect for the right to opacity with the political obligation to tell a total history. As I will suggest below, these two goals are less at odds than might at first seem to be true.

As many other African American texts have done, Jones's novel calls into question the academic project of additive history writing associated with the recovery movements that have sometimes dominated African American writing about the past. This novel also differs from several seemingly like-minded recent and nineteenth-century efforts to reject this additive history project, many of which focus on the partiality and incompleteness of the archive. Jones's novel does not engage in the "turn away from history" that Dubey has suggested characterizes recent African American fictional encounters with the past. Nor does it embrace the micronarrative as a desideratum of African American history writing, the second of the two major and related practices said to indicate black dissatisfaction with the project of mainstream history. Jones's novel in fact repudiates this emerging emphasis within African American intellectual and expressive culture on the importance of acknowledging the broken archive and embracing the partial narrative, as well as the related sense that History is a sorry bargain for the disenfranchised. *The Known World* lobbies instead for the rewards of totalizing history and thus pursues a history of totality that places the lives of (black) strangers-with at its center. This novel suggests that we must still seek to tell the history of totality, but it also argues that the only way to tell that history is through a considered encounter with the black past that respects the right to opacity of people in the past. This encounter would be modeled on and revise the nineteenth-century projects of total history that are traceable to Marx, Hegel, and, as we will see in just a moment, early African American history writing. According to *The Known World*, I am suggesting, engagement with the history of African American strangers-with is a necessary and sufficient condition of the total world history first identified in the nineteenth century as a resource for the struggle against injustice. It is moreover what a stranger history looks like.

Through a series of interpolated tales about flawed surveyors, cowardly census-takers, careerist historians, and drunken mapmakers, Jones's novel cues us to consider what is at first glance a series of very traditional questions about African America. It asks us to ponder first whether the absences and obfuscations inherent to slavery's institutional and economic archives constitute a permanent obstacle to telling the total history of black life.[8] If these absences and obfuscations do in fact confound conventional research protocols and narratological methods, the novel furthermore asks, then what would an efficacious black history look like? What formal practices would it necessitate? What would be its defining features? Nineteenth- and twentieth-century African American historiography, history, and historical fiction have long sought to answer precisely these questions. John Ernest, Stephen G. Hall, and Marnie Hughes-Warrington have shown, for example, how a specifically black historiography extends at least as far back as the nineteenth century. Tracing the rise of African American history writing in a "pre-professional mode," their accounts echo Dubey's recent claim about African American speculative fiction's relation to the past, as well as Susan Donaldson's framing of contemporary African American historical fictions of the American South as a species of historical theorizing. As I will explain in more detail below, Dubey's black historical fiction thinks metacritically in a fashion that echoes what Ernest argues was an early African American understanding of history writing as a critical intervention rather than a merely documentary realism, while Donaldson argues that African American historical fiction of the American South thinks through alternative approaches to writing the African American past.

These studies together would identify an intellectual communion connecting the speculative histories and historiographic essays written by nineteenth-century African Americans to the metafictional strategies of late twentieth- and twenty-first-century African American historical fiction. They further indicate that this metacritical and historiographical black tradition highlights absences, elisions, and breaks in the archive. Recalling Phillip Brian Harper's influential work on the origins of the decentered postmodern subject, as well as the emphasis noted in Chapter 2 of this study on reading the stranger as a site of absence, Ernest's and Donaldson's focus encourages us to understand the long-standing African American interest in the incomplete archive as in some sense postmodernist before and after the fact.[9] These critics and historians propose that the structured contradictions and elisions that dominate the African American experience of slavery and structural racism, as well as their archives, anticipate the world that would come to be known as postmodern. They suggest moreover that this world registers in both the form and content of African American history writing. The legacies of racial slavery and antiblack racism precipitate "nothing so much," Donaldson argues, "as those micronarratives that Jean-François Lyotard sees as emerging from the debris of master narratives shattered under the pressures of postmodernity."[10]

The Known World asks us to reintroduce the issue of historical totality into this conversation. It recalls that universal history has persistently appealed to African American writers and thinkers, in the antebellum moment and through to the present.[11] A commitment to totalizing history is generally absent from emergent critiques of African American progressive historiography, including those I have just described: The postmodern as a period and postmodernism as a critical stance, which African American history writing and historical fiction are said to mirror, preclude the turn to master narratives that any theory of historical totality requires. Nineteenth-century African American writing's perceived emphasis on rejecting totalizing historical accounts would further suggest that African American postmodern historical metafiction represents not a break with but an extension of nineteenth-century African American historical thinking. The *longue durée* of racial slavery ends up registering as a composite of piecemeal micronarratives, and it precludes any dialectical account of historical totality.[12] The natal alienation associated with the black stranger translates to a more general sense of History's (and therefore historical) impossibility.

At least some of these histories and historical fictions offer something different. They take up the challenge of producing an anti-reifying history of totality such as Lukács describes in *History and Class Consciousness*, while at the same time they seek to revise our sense of what a history of totality looks like, emphasizing the centrality of strangers-in-relation to such a history.[13] In this way they translate the lessons of antebellum stranger humanism into the idioms of historiography. Lukács's key contribution in "Reification and the Consciousness of the Proletariat" is to show how contradictions, absences, and elisions come into view only at the moment that an impulse to render a picture of totality is already at play. This insight reveals that micronarratives always exist in the context of the pursuit of a larger master narrative. By this logic the persistent African American questioning of history's absences and opacities follows from an impulse toward producing a history of totality, rather than being a sign of its rejection. According to Lukács, moreover, capitalist logic seeks to preclude the sort of synoptic vision that draws into focus the disjuncture among what on the ground look like highly rational laws but that, from a different perspective, resolve into a congeries of productively incoherent contingent practices. Reification names the process of conceptual and experiential segmentation that commodity fetishism permits, that eventually impresses itself on all features of daily life under capitalism, and that obscures the overall logic of capital. An account of history such as Marxism offers both identifies and dissolves that segmentation, Lukács argues, allowing the whole of history to come into view. This view of totality abstracts from particular local details, but it does not ignore them. It abstracts from details to reveal those modes of human interrelationship that commodity fetishism obscures. If Marx famously suggests that commodity fetishism turns a relationship among people into a relationship among things, then Lukács demonstrates how accounts of totality can revisualize relationships among people who have misunderstood themselves as things.[14] Although such accounts of totality permit neither sympathetic identification nor disinterested personhood, they do license and even require something much more central to political life: an understanding of the past as a scene of strangers-in-relation who remain tethered to the present.

Lukács's observations provide a framework for making the case that an ongoing African American attempt to revise the sense of how to produce a history of totality has been, much like African American attempts to refigure strangerhood into a generative condition, and for related reasons, overcharacterized as a wholesale rejection of that project. In order to make this claim, I will next offer a more developed characterization on an emerging consensus regarding the status of nineteenth-century African American historiography and history writing, focusing in particular on the influential work of John Ernest and Stephen G. Hall. I will then address in more detail Dubey's analysis of the recent turn away from realism in African American literature, as well as her sense of what this turn tells us about African American historical thinking. This permits me to identify certain continuities and discontinuities connecting African American history writing to African American historical fiction. Returning to Jones's novel, I will propose that it offers a compelling account of how to acknowledge the problems of the injured archive and produce a history of totality without dishonoring the archive's injuries. I will also consider Douglass's "The Heroic Slave" (1853) in the light of Lukács's account in *The Historical Novel* of properly anti-reifying historical fictions, pursuing the question of what Douglass's obvious debts to Sir Walter Scott might mean for his account of history. My conclusion draws a few axioms from Jones's novel and Douglass's novella, the most important of which concerns the relations connecting the history of stranger-with-ness to the broken archive to accounts of totality. Jones's novel and Douglass's novella suggest that the challenges of the broken archive do not preclude the creation of a total history, if we accept that a history of totality will always be no more than a history of strangers-in-relation, where the extension of relation has both synchronic and diachronic dimensions. Indeed Douglass and Jones remind us that accounts of totality typically assume an incomplete or unfinished archive. The hybrid modes of intellectual inquiry common to these accounts are a considered response to that state of incompleteness. In this sense these texts permit us to remember, at this moment of increased preoccupation with the archive in general; deletions from the African American archive, in particular; and the condition of limited access to the African American stranger, under any circumstances, that the empirical project of engaging with a documentary archive is quite different from the Hegelian, Marxist, and early African American approaches to total history. One might go so far as to say that a history of totality is the only kind of history possible in an unjust world that attempts to evacuate the many from the archive in service of the avarice of a few. In the end, these texts illuminate not only why it might be important to continue to pursue a master narrative, but also how to revise its form and content such that it does justice to the history of African American strangers-in-relation and in turn to the history of the world.

History, Historiography, and Literary Realism

In *Liberation Historiography: African American Writers and the Challenge of History, 1794–1861*, John Ernest offers a comprehensive account of how early African American history writing reconceived the office of the historian in relation to emerging white ideologies of history. He also tracks how African American historians and historical writers responded to the particular needs and demands of the African American experience vis-à-vis the problems of writing history. As he demonstrates in his introduction, Ernest is particularly concerned to show how African American historical writing

early on detected a fundamental limitation of the sorts of historical practice introduced as the mainstream during this period. Mainstream American
and European historical writing came at this moment to favor comprehensive and "totalizing historical narrative[s]" that subordinated the spread of
detail inherent to the archive to a coherent linear narrative of cause, effect,
and transformation.[15] African American historical writing took a very different approach, Ernest argues, because early black historians understood
that white supremacist ideology dictated that a Bancroft or a Parkman would
never adequately address the contributions of African Americans to the
emergence of the United States. White supremacist ideology also constituted
the main "cultural dynami[c] that shaped and limited the preservation of the
records of African American experience."[16] In other words, white supremacist
ideology determined in advance that African American historical experience
would be rendered inaccessible by excluding from the archives those documents suited to forming the backbone of a synthetic account of the African
American past.

In addition to this clear and present exclusion of African Americans from
the documentary trail of evidence, except as entries in chattel bookkeeping or
the emerging scriptive technologies of the American judicial system, African
American writers of history faced an additional burden. According to Ernest,
these writers were forced to contend with the fact that there was something
unspeakably sublime about the African American experience under slavery.
Adopting a critical vocabulary drawn from discussions of the challenge of
representation in a post-Holocaust moment, Ernest argues that these writers
were developing a mode of depicting an "unrecoverable past" and that this
past was "unrecoverable" not because of archival exclusions alone.[17] It was also
unrecoverable because it "resisted representation": "Beyond [their] necessary
responses to racist historiography," Ernest proposes, "African Americans faced
the troubling problem of representing a history that—in its fragmentation and
especially in the depth of its moral complexity—resisted representation. How
does one tell the story of the Middle Passage, or of slavery?"[18] Here the emphasis shifts from the nature of the archive to the nature of the story secreted in
the archive. Even if a full documentary record of the Middle Passage had been
at their fingertips, African American historians would have been faced with a
task of narration made impossible by the very nature of the black experience
rather than by any particular problem of the archive.

Faced with the compounded issue of the broken archive and the sublime
terror of slavery, African Americans adopted, Ernest continues, a very particular historiographic stance. During the pre-professional period of African

American historical writing, which both Ernest and Hall open to new scrutiny, these African American historians developed a metacritical account of
history. Their method met the "specifically textual challenge of creating an
approach to historical representation that could promote the development
of a unified African American community."[19] This alternative approach to
historical writing shifted the focus away from the details of history, many
of which had been made unavailable by white archival procedures, and
toward the very problem of writing history in a white supremacist world. In
other words, African American historical writing emerged as a substantively
metacritical and historiographical practice in the earliest stages of its formation: As Hall argues: "[B]lack writers constructed black history largely as a
metahistorical narrative that simultaneously transcended and reinterpreted
mainstream historical narratives."[20] As when Frederick Douglass opens his
one piece of fictional writing, "The Heroic Slave," with a meditation on the
elusive "marks" and "traces" of the slave named Madison Washington found
in the chattel records of the state of Virginia, African American history writing during this period repeatedly turned to the question of its own enforced
impossibility. This early emphasis on the inadequacies of the documentary
archive has shaped the practice of writing about the African American past
into the present moment. As Hall explains, "Scholars today often privilege
nontextual manifestations of black culture as the dominant modes of early
African American historical expression. Studying oral, vernacular, and com-
memorative culture and historical memory has become a prominent means
of examining the ways African Americans re-create their past."[21]

    We will return to Hall and Ernest in just a moment, but for now it seems
important to acknowledge that Hall's list of "oral, vernacular, and commem-
orative culture" might also include literature. The long and growing list of
African American literary texts that seek to provide a way into the African
American experience of the past suggests that African American literature
(past and present) understands itself and has been understood as an archive
of past experience rearticulated in the present moment. As Dubey explains,
this literature in many respects "confidently claim[s] to reveal the truth of
the past."[22] In a curious way, however, and notwithstanding Douglass's early
comments, the African American literary tradition has had, Dubey argues,
a longer road to travel to the metacritical impulse that Ernest and Hall suggest dates to nineteenth-century African American historical writing. Dubey
documents how African American fiction writing, in particular, long labored
under the demands of a social uplift model of realist fictionalizing that con-
strained the ability of these writers to open a space of imaginative possibility

for African American futures. In other words, with certain notable exceptions, such as Charles Chesnutt's conjure tales, African American fictionalizing was tasked with the same charge of certifying the truth of African
American life for white readers that had defined the fugitive slave narrative.
As Dubey explains: "Notwithstanding certain errant flashes of fantasy and
fabulism, the burden of realist representation began to ease off only by the
1970s, or the beginning of what is commonly termed the post–Civil Rights
period, which ... witnessed an outpouring of fiction that flouts the dic-
tates of realism."[23] Given the willingness of nineteenth-century historians to
point out the inadequacies of the archive and, therefore, the limitations of
any mode of realistic writing about the past, the general unwillingness of fiction writers to pursue similarly metacritical stances must be understood as a
legacy of what William Andrews has described as the novelization of voice
in African American literature, a process whose origins tie later novelistic
accounts of African American experience to the protocols of the fugitive
slave narrative, including its demand for authenticity and authentication, its
emphasis on certifiable detail, and its reluctance to abstract from the specific
and the empirically verifiable.

As Dubey documents, however, when realism's long-standing dominance
in African American fiction finally waned, it did so in significant and impact-
ful ways. Dubey suggests that

> recent novelists of slavery undo historical authority by exploiting an
> exorbitantly fictive imagination, the faculty that had to be devalued
> in order to shore up the disciplinary standing of history as "the cus-
> todian of realism." Refusing to regard the past of slavery as history,
> speculative novels suggest that the truth of this past is more fully
> grasped by way of an antirealist literary imagination that can flu-
> idly cross temporal boundaries and affectively immerse readers into
> the world of slavery. The turn away from history, then, becomes an
> immensely generative occasion for antirealist novels of slavery in the
> late twentieth century.[24]

Dubey's main point in the article from which this quotation is drawn is to
contest one emerging consensus about historical novels of slavery that dispense with the protocols of realism in favor of a more capacious account of
just what might be real. As she explains, one dominant view understands
these novels as reclaiming the historical past. According to this consensus
view, these novels of slavery, despite their dalliances with the speculative and

fantastic, nevertheless "confidently claim to reveal the truth of the past."[25] Dubey contests this reading, suggesting that these novels should be understood as altogether turning away from historical knowledge as a useful resource. She sees these speculative historical fictions of slavery as proposing that the inequities of the past have rendered the past a useless resource. From a methodological perspective, then, Dubey's main interest lies in defining more precisely the form that the African American turn away from history has taken and now takes.

In addition to illuminating certain continuities and discontinuities linking fictional and nonfictional African American accounts of the past, Dubey's analysis usefully recalls us to the fact that there are many different ways to turn away from history, and it encourages us to take her procedural question about these differences and run it back through the arc I began with—the one connecting Hall's and Ernest's nineteenth-century African American historical writing to Dubey's and Donaldson's late twentieth- and twenty-first-century African American speculative and historical fictions. If we do so, we can agree that across the broad expanse of theorizing and expression that constitutes this tradition, the compromised archive is a primary concern. We can also agree that across this broad expanse of writing, African American historians and African American writers have grappled with the partiality and incompleteness of the archive. What I want to ask now is whether it necessarily follows from these facts that the African American intellectual tradition around historical knowledge has given up on the idea of a vision of totality. In other words, have African American writers and historians conceded the idea of a total history to Hegel and Marx? Or have they simply been pointing to the added burdens and particular obstacles involved when universal or total history has to grapple with the history of African America? If the latter is the case, then how do we square the broken archive with the writing of a history of totality? Finally, what would such a total history have to do with African American strangers-in-relation?

Distributed History

African American historical fictions and nineteenth-century histories produce histories of totality more routinely than is imagined, to the extent that the partiality of clear concern to these writers comes into view as such in the context of their reaching toward totalization. Jones's novel in particular reminds us that one of the primary metacritical problems taken up by

African American historical writing is in fact how best to write a history of totality in a world of partial vision. Among other things, *The Known World* asks: What mode or modes of artistic practice can best replace reification with desirable forms of abstraction? What kind of thought understands how to transform the archive's details and its inadequacies into politically efficacious History? Those questions gather greatest force in *The Known World* in the *mappa mundi* section near the end of the novel. This section's emblematic account of an African American reaching toward a totalizing vision of history suggests both an obligation to the Lukácsian model and the necessity of certain signal revisions to it if black life is to figure in and figure as historical totality.

In this section, Louis, the brother-in-law of the now-deceased slaveholding former slave, Henry Townsend, writes a letter from Washington, D.C., to his widowed sister, Caldonia, describing his encounter with a formerly enslaved woman of African descent named Alice who escaped from the Townsend plantation. It is important to know that before her escape from the Townsend plantation, Alice is perceived as a madwoman who roams the plantation late at night. Recalling Faulkner's Benjy, she freely accesses the far corners of the county. One day she disappears. Louis's letter details an encounter with Alice in a D.C. boarding house and her unusual form of expressive culture. He explains that in a dining room off the main parlor of the boarding house hung two objects:

> People were viewing [first] an enormous wall hanging, a grand piece of art that is part tapestry, part painting, and part clay structure—all in one exquisite Creation, hanging silent and yet songful on the Eastern wall. It is, my Dear Caldonia, a kind of map of life of the County of Manchester, Virginia. But a "map" is such a poor word for such a wondrous thing. It is a map of life with every kind of life made with every kind of art man has ever thought to represent himself. Yes, clay, Yes, paint. Yes, cloth. There are no people on this "map," just all the houses and barns and roads and cemeteries and wells in our [hometown of] Manchester. It is what God sees when He looks down on Manchester.[26]

On the facing wall, Louis continues, hangs a second "Creation."

> This Creation may well be even more miraculous than the one of the County. This one is about your home, Caldonia. It is your plantation,

and again, it is what God sees when He looks down. There is nothing missing, not a cabin, not a barn, not a chicken, not a horse. Not a single person is missing. I suspect that if I were to count the blades of grass, the number would be correct as it was once when the creator of this work knew that world. . . . In this massive miracle on the Western wall, you, Caldonia, are standing before your house with Loretta, Zeddie and Bennett. As I said, all the cabins are there, and standing before them are the people who lived in them ere Alice, Priscilla and Jamie disappeared. Except for those three, every single person is there, standing and waiting as if for a painter and his easel to come along and capture them in the glory of the day. Each person's face, including yours, is raised up as though to look in the very eyes of God.[27]

Alice's two *mappa mundi* constitute an anti-reifying vision of totality that permits the nature of slavery to come fully into view as a relationship among persons, but they also push us to consider which media and how many specific formal practices might be required for the particular work of an anti-reifying African American encounter with the past to take place. This normative question recalls Lukács's desire in his study *The Historical Novel* to determine what form of novelistic writing would be adequate to telling the history of class struggle; it also demands a careful rethinking of Lukács's normative project.

In order to understand what sort of practice of total history Jones's novel envisions, one must first mark the fact that the novel describes not one but two "creations." The first creation, which resembles a county map, functions in the context of the novel as a critique of the mapmaking and surveying that go on elsewhere in the text. White surveyors are described as having limited skills that result in poorly constructed maps, but the novel suggests that Alice has walked each of the roads and byways rendered in her first creation. This critique cuts both ways, however, for the focal point of Alice's first map is illuminated in the moment we learn of its supplementation by the second map. We come to recognize from the presence of Alice's second creation that the first map does not prioritize that which would normally be used to clarify the meaning of roads, barns, wells, and byways, which is to say human beings and the relationships among them. The second map points to the absence of human forms from the first more familiar mapmaking project. As Louis's letter indicates, the world of slavery is depicted in the second map as a relationship among persons: "Every single person is there," he writes.

If these two maps go some way toward making clear that a vision of historical totality requires a map of the relationships among persons, as well as a map of the non-human world, the novel also identifies one additional formal element necessary to such a vision. It does so by virtue of including Jones's descriptions of these creations. Although the *mappi mundi* scene just described would seem to involve the unveiling of a key to the structure of the world that this novel describes, much in the way that certain editions of *Absalom! Absalom!* include Faulkner's genealogical and chronological key to the story, it is important to remember that in this moment Jones engages in ekphrasis, or the verbal description of (absent) visual art forms. Since Achilles' shield, ekphrasis has been associated with a desire to represent the totality of a historical moment and the inability to do so in the medium of language. Figures of ekphrasis in this sense connote that unaided writing is incapable of capturing the history of totality. Alice's creations might therefore be described as pointing to the novel's necessary failure fully to represent history—its reaching toward but never grasping a vision of totality. This could only be taken as a failure on the part of the novel, however, if we forget that the frustrated desire to represent the experience of slavery in language is a central feature of life inside the peculiar institution. Ekphrastic desire—if I could only see Alice's maps then I would fully comprehend this novel and the history it describes—regenerates one of the key features of African America: a longing for a bird's-eye view—a view of totality—in what is at first encounter (and often second and third encounter) a seemingly unmappable land not of one's choosing. In other words, Jones's novel has internalized the persistent sense within the black intellectual and expressive traditions that African diasporic culture has an obligation to document as it were the longing for perspective that characterizes the experience of enforced diaspora. With its ekphrastic description of maps, Jones's novel prompts an experience of perspectival desire that contributes to rather than confounds its history of totality. Jones's novel proceeds as though the history writer's procedures and formal practices must archive this desire for perspective as much as they capture the demographic patterns of the slaveholding South. Jones's novel also assumes that it is possible to do so. Rather than merely fetishize what is missing from the archive, a historian can and must document what it felt like not to know the known world without assuming the permanent inaccessibility of such knowledge. Of course the historian might also be required to reconsider history writing's formal practices. The history writer might in the end need to work in a variety of different representational modes in order to achieve the goal of a history of totality, which will always be a stranger history.

Although Douglass's "The Heroic Slave" does not involve the same attention to ekphrastic desire, it does indicate how, in the mid-nineteenth century, the historical romance as it descended from Sir Walter Scott and was refigured in the United States went some way toward achieving the total history pursued in *The Known World*. As Paul Christian Jones has argued, there is very good reason to read Douglass's novella as working in the tradition of Scott's historical romances. Christian Jones suggests that Douglass's novella reflects an engagement with and revision of the southern (U.S.) historical romance, often known as the plantation romance. Where Scott's historical novels focus on the fortunes of what Lukács identifies as an "average man, clearly not an ideologue," in order to see the fullness of history playing out around him, the southern historical romances imported the romantic hero into the historical novel.[28] Christian Jones suggests that that this importation of the romantic hero happens in "The Heroic Slave" as well, as the title might suggest. For Christian Jones this indicates Douglass's revision of the southern historical romance tradition, to the extent that Douglass refigures the romantic hero as a black man. From Christian Jones's perspective, then, the Lukácsian model would seem inapt. Where is our middle-of-the-road figure who permits us to see the shape and impact of warring historical forces? Lukács argues that "Scott's greatness lies in his capacity to give living human embodiment to historical-social types. The typically human terms in which great historical trends become tangible had never before been so superbly, straightforwardly and pregnantly portrayed. And above all, never before had this kind of portrayal been consciously set at the centre of the representation of reality."[29] He continues on to suggest the "compositional importance of the mediocre hero": "Scott always chooses as his principal figures such as may, through character and fortune, enter into human contact with both camps."[30] Douglass's hero, Madison Washington, could hardly be described as mediocre.

That description does apply, however, to two central figures in the novella: the friendly Quaker, Mr. Listwell, and Tom Grant, the formerly racist converted white sailor who recounts the story of the revolt aboard the ship *Creole*. Mr. Listwell has been read as a figure for the reader of the novella, the sympathetic white man or woman who imagines her- or himself in the role of aiding the fugitive slave by virtue of a proper mode of identification with his plight. Marianne Noble argues, for example, that we may understand

Mr. Listwell as a sign of Douglass's desire to make tangibly felt the possibility
of alternative forms of sympathy in which the sympathetic white becomes
as much listener as witness. Noble argues that Mr. Listwell suggests how,
for Douglass, "When the two members of a dialogue are generously willing to enter into the other's point of view, a deep communion is available,
even though full meanings and true selves are never present nor graspable."[31]
It is also possible, though, to see Mr. Listwell and Tom Grant as figures for
the mediocre historical hero that Lukács describes. In this sense we might
rethink Douglass's "The Heroic Slave" as attempting to produce a full picture
of the various warring historical forces at play in the Atlantic world, and particularly the United States, around the issue of slavery. In other words, Mr.
Listwell and Tom Grant permit the novella to stage a scenario in which a central figure "enter[s] into human contact with both camps." This is not quite
the bird's-eye view we saw being pursued in *The Known World*, but it does
allow for a restaging of the history of slavery as a story of strangers-in-relation translated into great historical forces. In other words, "The Heroic Slave"
rewrites the history of slavery as a story of relationships among people rather
than a story of things, while also doing justice to the broad historical significance and centrality to world history of those relationships that it portrays.

Total Visions

If Jones's novel and Douglass's novella in this sense suggest that a total history
of African America is achievable, then what about a total history that is written at the scale of totality? A different way of putting this is to ask whose world
we come to know in the process of reading *The Known World*. In *A Faithful Account of the Race: African American Historical Writing in Nineteenth-
Century America*, Stephen G. Hall suggests that African American historians
did develop, as Ernest argues, a historiographical stance alternative to mainline (white) U.S. and European historical writing. However, Hall focuses on
the way that, while white historians of the United States and Europe turned
increasingly to theories and practices based on a sense of national belonging,
African American writers expressed much greater interest in the parameters
of a "faithful account of the race" emerging from the study of the world as a
whole. According to Hall,

> By the 1830s, when white historians began to construct American his-
> tory in increasingly nationalistic ways, drawing on Romanticism to

construct ideal historical personalities and deriving crucial lessons from the immediate rather than the distant past, black writers, led by abolitionists trained in various clerical traditions, challenged this approach by trumpeting the authority of sacred, ancient, and modern history. In this way they preserved a more complex black subject who emerged from a review of *world* history rather than national history.[32]

Hall's point here is to draw a line of demarcation separating the practices of African American historians writing black history from those of the white European and U.S. historians that are much more familiar to most readers. The conceptual point, however, is equally important. Hall offers us the opportunity to see that, from a certain comparative perspective, it was the white European and U.S. historians who increasingly turned to the writing of what we might call national micronarratives. Although it is unlikely that Bancroft and Parkman would have admitted as much, it was really they who were writing partial narratives organized around an increasingly parochial view that would mistake the United States or Europe for the world. By contrast, according to Hall, "people of color throughout the nineteenth and early twentieth centuries viewed themselves in terms articulated by David Walker, as 'citizens of the world.'"[33] These same people of color, in their roles as intellectuals and historians, "used the intellectual culture of the nineteenth century, namely biblical, classical, and modern history . . . to frame a complex humanistic portrait of African American history that transcended the rise of the West with its attendant horrors of the Middle Passage and slavery and extended back to the 'first ages of man.'"[34] According to Hall, then, early national and antebellum African American historians proposed that the history of black people was the history of the world and vice versa. In this sense, they anticipated some of W. E. B. Du Bois's most memorable claims about the centrality of the color line to the modern world. *The Souls of Black Folk* opens: "This meaning is not without interest to you, Gentle Reader, for the problem of the Twentieth Century is the problem of the color line." A micronarrative this is not.

Hall, Jones, Douglass, and Du Bois remind us that African American history writing and historical fiction have not always dismissed the idea of a coherent vision of totality. They have at least as often argued for a better such vision capable of tracing what is from the perspective of a certain present seemingly impossible. If the traditions of African American historiography and African American speculative fiction described here are reconsidered in this light, we start to understand them as making a significant demand. These texts are not retreating into the domain of the micronarrative that writes a restricted history of the (black) nation. These texts pursue instead an account of totality that puts the experience and arrangements of blackness at the center of what it means to live this world. These texts also make the case that African American literature and African American history are and always have been world literature and world history, and not in a multiculturalist or additive sense. Precisely the reduction to topography, human relationships, and moral accounting that we see at force in *The Known World* and "The Heroic Slave" come into focus as a comprehensive mapping of human life under the conditions of modernity. In this total history, African American experience allows us to know this world: all of it. Or, really, all of the "we." In knowing this set of relations, we come to know the world of strangers, strangers who are constituted out of those relations.

What conclusions can be drawn from these observations? First, the long-standing African American interest in damage done to the archive should not be mistaken for a full-scale retreat from a vision of historical totality. To do so would be to conflate the identification of a problem with one particular approach to solving it. Second, Jones's novel understands the conceptualization and representation of totality as a project necessarily distributed across media, genres, and formal practices. This is a lesson taught and a practice engaged by African American writers, thinkers, and artists since at least Du Bois. This observation also draws into focus a potential limitation of the Lukácsian model, as well as an obstacle to thinking through totality as a concept. As my recourse to Lukács on the historical novel would indicate, it is easy to confuse the production of a totalizing vision of history with a linear narrative about the past. Although Lukács is useful and necessary here, it is also the case that he does not offer adequate tools for envisioning an account of totality that does not unfold as a linear narrative organized in fairly conventional terms. In this sense, he disallows a past that is neither linear nor particularly susceptible to being subsumed by linear narrative. This is particularly troubling because the great visions of totality are neither particularly linear nor particularly narrative. *Capital* is one of the most compelling such accounts, but its procedures are not those of linear narration. Anecdotes, algebraic equations, and reductions to principle all make an appearance, but it would be hard to describe them as adding up to something so straightforward as a narrative.

These texts encourage us to revisit the issue of totality, but as it relates to the history of slavery and African American life. In other words, totality as it has been figured in and through African American life. The expanding archive of slavery and the African diaspora consequent upon the preservation and recovery work undertaken over the last 150 years, as well as efforts of more recent vintage, will continue to generate micronarratives of many kinds. *The Known World* suggests, however, that the abundant black world of strangers-in-relation is a world that must be known in its totality if we are to know any world at all. If we are to know this world, micronarratives simply will not do.

CHAPTER FIVE

How to Read a Strangers Book

Each Proprietor may introduce strangers to the Atheneum, and such persons shall be entitled to admission afterwards, for the space of one month, upon having their names recorded with that of the person introducing them, who shall be responsible for their observing the regulations of the Institution.

—*Catalogue of the Library of the Nantucket Atheneum,*
with the By-Laws of the Institution (1841)

The Committee on the Condition of the Library of the Nantucket Atheneum laid its report before the annual meeting of the Atheneum shareholders on January 4, 1847. As the committee reported, it found itself in "peculiar and extraordinary circumstances." The previous year's condition report had described the Atheneum in glowing terms. It had been in a "very flourishing condition," and its "neat and commodious building" had contained "a large and increasing Library, documents of inestimable value pertaining to the early settlement of our island, a rare collection of Curiosities of Nature, and art, the works of man in his most barbarous as well as his most civilized state,—and Cabinets of Corrals, Minerals, Shells, &c." On the night of July 13, 1846, however, a "dreadful Fire, which also destroyed [a] large portion" of Nantucket, burned its Atheneum to the ground. In language both mournful and methodical, the committee tallies the losses: "From the Librarian," they write, "to whom we are indebted for all the information comprised in this report, we learn that 'at the commencement of the past year, the Library of the Atheneum contained 3200 volumes. Five years previous, the Books had been arranged and re-catalogued according to their subjects, and the subsequent purchases, though small, had steadily improved the character of each department.'" The report later betrays the committee's sense that the island's historical archive had been fatally compromised. The losses went beyond the Atheneum library's valuable, if mainly replaceable, books. They even extended beyond Nantucket, covering the whole of natural and human history. For the fire had destroyed not only the Atheneum's books and its archival papers, but also its growing collections in "Mineralogy, Icthyology, Ornithology, and Entimology," as well as "a great variety of arms, domestic utensils and other implements from Polynesian reports." The loss of the Polynesian items was a particular tragedy, since "the barbarous habits of the islanders [had] disappeared before the advancing light of civilization." In the committee's view, a hole had been rent in the collective fabric of human history.[1]

One item lost to the Great Fire, but omitted from the report, was the Atheneum Strangers Book. The Nantucket Atheneum provided for strangers to enter the building. So did the atheneums at Boston and Providence, which, like the Nantucket Atheneum, also developed tools for the proper management of strangers. Article XIII of the 1841 Nantucket Atheneum bylaws mandates, for example, that "strangers . . . hav[e] their names recorded with that of the person introducing them." These regulations led to the creation of a curious genre: the strangers book. The surviving strangers books from the Nantucket, Boston, and Providence atheneums follow the same basic format; similar volumes with more prosaic titles from other early American subscription libraries adhere to it as well. As the charters and bylaws of these various institutions required, the four-columned strangers books provide space for recording each stranger's date of introduction, or entry, to the institution; the stranger's name; the stranger's place of origin or residence; and the name of the introducing member. The entries tend to be written either in a consistent hand or in a limited number of hands, suggesting that the strangers books were kept by an institution's librarian or librarians. They do not appear to have been left openly available for signing. The strangers books in this respect marked a threshold equipped with two guardians: the book itself and the keeper of the book. As a result of Nantucket's Great Fire, we do not know whether Frederick Douglass was entered into the Atheneum Strangers Book during his first visit to Nantucket in 1841, or four years before the publication of the *Narrative* that would ensure his eventual fame. We do know that during this visit he spoke at the first annual Nantucket Anti-Slavery Convention. The convention was held at the Atheneum, and William Lloyd Garrison would later describe it as the moment when Douglass "rose and found his voice." Not too long after, the Atheneum would close its doors to people of color for almost two years.

In a different port city much farther south, one connected to Nantucket by the coastwise shipping trade, another book was being kept. Though its cover did not read "Strangers Book," as did the cover of the book at the Atheneum, this second book should be read as a strangers book, because the Atheneum Strangers Book and this second book had a single project in common: transforming observed facts into markers of suspect-stranger status and thereby making strangers suspect. The second book resembles the Atheneum Strangers Book in several ways. Its entries are also written in a limited number of hands, and it too emerged from a mandate requiring the registration of "Nommes des personnes," "Lieux de naissance," "Epoque d'arrivée," and, in the "Observations" column, a sponsor. This second book is at the same time more exhaustive than is the Atheneum Strangers Book. It supplies eight, rather than four, columns. The "Observations" column also includes a generous amount of space for notes. It differs as well in other aspects of its format. Where the library strangers books are kept in simple hand-ruled registers, with strangers entered by their date of introduction to the library, this second book was bound with precut and preprinted alphabetical tabs extending from the recto of each opening page of its twenty-six sections.

Embossed in gold on its cover, the title of the book reads "Register for Free Colored Persons Entitled to Remain in the State. Mayor's Office." The four additional columns of the Register are "Sexe et couleur," "Age," "Professions," and "Dates d'enregistrement." They follow the directives of an 1830 Louisiana law demanding that a specific group of people register with their parish judge. Amended in 1840 and 1843, the first two paragraphs of the original law read as follows:

> It shall be the duty of all free negroes, griffs, and mulattoes of the first degree, who came into this state after the adoption of the constitution thereof, and prior to the first day of January, 1825, within sixty days after the promulgation of this act, to enroll themselves in the office of the parish judge of the parish where they may be resident, or in the office of the mayor of the city of New Orleans; setting forth their age, sex, color, trade or calling, place of nativity and the time of their arrival in the state; for which enrolment the parish judge or mayor shall be entitled to demand and receive the sum of fifty cents.
>
> It shall be the duty of the said parish judges to transmit to the mayor of the city of New Orleans, before the first of July next, a copy certified by them of the book mentioned in the twelfth section of this act; and the mayor shall cause a general list to be made out, of all the

lists so transmitted to him from the several parishes of the state, and of the one which he shall himself have caused to be made; and it shall be his duty to keep in his office the said general list.[2]

The eight-columned artifact described above is one of several surviving volumes composing the "said general list" mandated by the Louisiana Legislature. It reflects the growing trend in the nineteenth-century United States toward increased regulation of free people of color, greater controls on their movements across state lines, and the deepening curtailment of their right of free passage. Although not all restrictions such as these were exclusive to people of color, some of them most decidedly were. Even those that did hold universally were differently consequential for people of color, as the story of the "strange negro" in New Orleans told below will demonstrate. Thirty-five years earlier Kant had declared a universal right to hospitality amounting to little more than the right of aliens to pass unharmed though a foreign state. The southern states of the United States were growing unwilling to extend even that minimal hospitality to their own nation's citizens. Laws restricting black people's freedom of movement would result in the printing and keeping of many instruments of regulation similar to this Register, including, for instance, the preprinted bonds that a white ship captain could purchase from a bond seller to secure the liberty of a free sailor of color traveling on the captain's ship through the port of New Orleans. These bonds were necessary once the Louisiana Legislature and New Orleans officials began to demand either a bond or imprisonment for free people of color onboard ships docked at New Orleans.

The Nantucket Atheneum Strangers Book, the Register of Free Colored Persons Entitled to Remain in the State [of Louisiana], and the project of attempting to make people into suspect-strangers that these two documents together share invite the following question: How do you read a strangers book? That question in turn begs this one: Can you tell a strangers book by its cover? As an answer to the first question, I am going to propose a more detailed account of the practice I am calling stranger history. This stranger history would encompass the adoption of a relation of address inherited from the stranger humanism of antebellum African American men's writing and their organizing practices. I am also going to argue that every book can be made to do the work of a strangers book, both the good work and the bad, whatever its cover might say. Every book therefore necessitates a stranger history. I will conclude with an argument for approaching history as such as a strangers book and for conceiving all history-telling as necessitating a practice of stranger history. The stranger history that I have in mind, and that I will develop in more detail in a moment, would respect the right to opacity of people in the past, while at the same time it would approach historical archives as much more than sites memorializing the loss of personhood, morally bankrupt forms of accounting, and the destruction of ties of belonging. This approach to the past would apply even—especially—in the case of archives deriving from the most embattled of human lives, and even in the case of those archives that would appear to reduce persons to things. In this respect, stranger history as a practice would model itself on antebellum African American stranger humanism, as well as on recent literary, artistic, and scholarly attempts to engage with the many archives of dehumanization. Stranger history would nevertheless also make clear that the pursuit of full access to any specific individual in the past is an ethical and a political error. The legitimate desires that often motivate such pursuits would be acknowledged, but stranger history would also insistently frame history-telling as the task of simultaneously clarifying the relationships among persons in the past and avoiding the misrepresentation of those relationships as having emerged from (or as having generated) fixed beings who are reducible to a single moment. It would furthermore attend to the relationships of persons in the present to one another, as well as their relationships to persons in the past, but it would do so without sealing any of those persons off from other moments and without reducing those persons to their place in a single established set of relationships. Stranger history would be a history of being-with-strangers as human being. Stranger history would also be always in the making, because stranger-becoming is always at work, even when practices of suspect-stranger-making are in the ascendant.

Like the nineteenth-century men who refigured Andrew Jackson's address to the free people of color of Louisiana, the stranger historian would take the humanness of African Americans as a given, rather than as something requiring documentation or even discussion. As I argued in Chapter 1, the terms established by antebellum African American stranger humanism stipulate that any African American is assumed always to have been in a state of transformation; it follows that the stranger historian can never claim to have accessed a settled black interiority in the past. This is not because black interiority was not or is not there. For the purposes of stranger history, this question is beside the point: Any given black interiority is unavailable for specification, because any given black interiority is forever in the process of becoming something different. Moreover, the necessity of specifying black interiority as such dissolves when the humanness of African Americans is not at issue. For the ethics, politics, and intellectual practices of stranger history, such specification serves no practical purpose. This approach to history does not alleviate the need to discuss blackness or the history of race. Every individual's state of transformation unfolds in a world made up of people who will have lived some relation to the fantasy of race. In this formulation of stranger history, however, the stranger historian's most pressing work would be to manage the facts that come into focus once the lessons of antebellum African American stranger humanism, and of more recent African American theories and practices of the archive, are taken as axiomatic. These lessons would include the recognition that both suspect-stranger-making and stranger-becoming are latent in any document of human culture. The goal of stranger history in this context would be to diagnose instances of the former, while encouraging the unfolding of the latter. Sometimes attending to race as a historical fantasy will stand front and center in this work; sometimes it will necessarily play a smaller but still present role. As a hard fact of history, race will not disappear.

The insights of antebellum African American stranger humanism prescribe that when we read a strangers book we take care not to decide in advance what sorts of strangers the book has made or has the capacity still to make. Patience and persistence are required in these matters. The writings of Frederick Douglass and the *Les Cenelles* poets can retard the application of suspect-stranger status and speed the process of stranger-becoming through their choice of specific idioms of address and participation. Strangerhood itself is not an objectionable thing, then, but the line distinguishing the suspect-stranger from the stranger-with who is engaged in a healthy scene of stranger-becoming is a crucial one to monitor. It is also essential to consider how that line gets drawn. A constantly shifting line, its travels map activity in the past and in the present. As the readings of the strangers books in this chapter attempt to make clear, it is possible to move, and to be moved, across the line of distinction separating different forms of strangerhood even *after* the initial event and the seeming consequences of an instance of stranger-making have been realized. History-telling is one of the things that make that movement happen; thoughtful and vigilant history-telling is therefore a necessity.

Violent acts of suspect-stranger-making circumscribe our notion of the human, indexing persons to the yardstick of a static and therefore inadequate reference point. As I will demonstrate below, strangers books seeking to reroute relationships among persons through a relation to an institution or institutions—the state, for example, or the library, or both—often pursue such circumscription. It remains possible to read even what might seem to be a purely objectionable strangers book against its grain. (It is in this way possible to participate in the drawing of the line of distinction between

suspect-strangerhood and stranger-becoming.) Even the most objectionable forms of stranger-making characteristically require the author(s) of a
strangers book to write a significant level of detail into its pages. Strangers
books as a result always end up cataloging relationships of care *and* relationships of liability, even when their stated aim is to reduce persons to things.
The archive is not short on data. Even when the relationship among persons
that a strangers book records is one of brutal liability, as is often the case,
those relationships that are noted are worth noting again (and again). If, as
in Alice's creation in *The Known World*, "every single person is there," then
every single person is also recorded in sufficient detail to testify to something requiring no testament, which is to say the humanness of the persons
recorded therein, as well as to imply the (good or bad) role(s) that any single
person played in the making of other strangers.

Strangers books always have the potential to tell the story of how a
stranger who is in the process of being made suspect was also engaged in
a form of becoming that exceeded determination by the powers of reduction. The presence of a strangers book for this reason always invites a work
of stranger history that witnesses the plurality of every person in the past;
acknowledges strangerhood as a human right; and specifies the conditions of
human relationality—now and/or in the past—that support(ed) or delay(ed)
achievements of plurality. Stranger history does this while admitting the
precarious nature of stranger-becoming even at the best of times: Stranger-
becoming is a contingent thing rather than a thing of guarantees.

The last stipulation of stranger history is this: One of the stranger historian's persistent aims must be to document the institutional, formal, and political structures that mediate the movement of address, as well as to document
those instances of address themselves. Stranger history would do this in such a
way as to recognize that every movement of address embraces the potential for
multiparty disclosure and multiparty recognition. It would also do so without
subsuming either the origin or the target of address into some larger covering
category, whether author, public, audience, collective, or even individual, for
these categories resolve a set of unfolding relations into a stable whole.

Every book is a strangers book if you know how to read it, and every
strangers book is open to deliberate acts of a stranger humanism that permits
stranger-becoming. As an approach to reading and a practice of stranger-
becoming, stranger history would acknowledge how relationships among
persons make for life. Every book can be read as a strangers book; every
stranger history can be told. A stranger history can even be told when (some
of) the strangers books that would seem to be its most logical source have

been lost. This is the lesson of the story of Frederick Douglass's first engagement at the Nantucket Atheneum, as I will explain when I return to it below. Texts such as the New Orleans Register, the Nantucket Atheneum Strangers Book, and even Douglass's *Narrative* are not sufficient to telling a stranger history. Neither is any single one of them necessary to it. Stranger history is as much an ethical act and a political activity as it is an archival procedure. Focusing on what is absent from the archive encourages a bad faith refusal of the simple truth that the possibilities of the archive will always outrun our capacity for acts of stranger history. The issue is not one of absence. The issue is how best to permit the present and the past their just shares of stranger-becoming. When Douglass remarks that he "cannot remember a single connected sentence" of his speech on Nantucket, therefore, this does not mean that there is nothing of consequence left for the stranger historian to say about that speech.

The Strange Negro in New Orleans

The arrival of the bark *Hazard* in New Orleans from Rhode Island in 1837 set off a chain of events that found a free man of color from Providence incarcerated in a New Orleans workhouse, set to work on the city's chain gang, and eventually sold at auction to pay the debts that his workhouse labors had (somehow) earned him. In the course of telling its version of these events, the storied New Orleans newspaper, the *Picayune*, defended the city's laws regulating free people of color, characterizing those laws as fair to the point of generosity. It also created a new category of person: the "strange negro." The events of the story of a strange negro, summarized in the *Weekly Picayune* of May 21, 1838, go undisputed by the paper. The ship *Hazard* sailed from Providence with a cook who was a free man of color and "a native of Providence." According to the Woonsocket (Rhode Island) *Patriot*, from which the *Picayune* gathered the details of the story, the *Hazard*'s coastwise passage was a hard one. By the time it drew up to New Orleans, it was "considered unseaworthy." When its captain decided to abandon the ship as unsafe, he left the cook from Providence to his own devices. One evening not long after the cook's arrival and abandonment in New Orleans, he made the mistake of being out past the firing of the gun that signaled to all people of color that they must by law make their way indoors. He also made the grave error of being found on the levee of the Mississippi River, a location known and described locally as the lounging place of "strangers." Despite the fact that he was merely out searching for work and later for a place to rest, the municipal police arrested this cook from Providence and sent him to prison for six weeks. Unable to pay his prison fees, he was remanded to the chain gang and then to the auction block.

Although the *Picayune* accepted the facts reported in the *Patriot*, it also rejected the latter's characterization because the *Patriot* was part of what it called "the northern Abolitionist prints." The *Picayune* states its view as follows:

> When he was called to account for parading in the streets, why did he not show his "free papers?" Had he none? . . . had he no "honorable discharge" to exhibit? These things would have satisfied our police, and he would have been discharged. For we can state with sincerity and truth, that there is no city that we have ever seen where free negroes have less cause of complaint than in New Orleans.—Their rights are respected, and their freedom is even rigidly guarded by our laws; but a strange negro must produce some other evidence of his liberty than his own testimony.

In a snide rebuttal to the *Patriot*'s claim that the only title to a human that would be worth acknowledging would have to be "signed by the Almighty," the *Picayune* continues: "We do not require [documents] 'signed by the Almighty.' The name of a legally appointed Recording Clerk, however, is required." For a black man to walk through the city is to "parad[e] in the streets"; laws designed to compromise the liberties of black people "rigidly guar[d] them." This type of prevarication is familiar. More significant is the line that reads "a strange negro must produce some other evidence of his liberty than his own testimony," which appears to suggest that a "strange negro" is a black person who does not, by some measure or another, belong in or to the city of New Orleans. The implication follows that black people who were not "strange" and who, by some measure or another, belonged were excused from giving evidence of their own liberty than their own testimony.

The heightened white paranoia about slave insurrection, abolitionism, and, more generally, black people in New Orleans at this time, which the *Picayune* liked to stoke, made it unlikely that any self-declared oath of liberty from a black person would have counted for much in the city. Indeed, the contents of the Register of Free Colored Persons Entitled to Remain in the State, and the 1830 law that mandated the Register, demonstrate that a black person's testimony regarding his or her own liberty counted for very little.

The column of the Register titled "Observations" is something of a miscellany, but its main purpose matched that of the Atheneum Strangers Book column recording the name of each stranger's introducing member or institution. It was a place to observe the registrant's identity by establishing her or his status in relation to a person, to an institution, or to both a person (or persons) and an institution (or institutions) other than him- or herself. As will be seen in just a moment, this act of observation effectively functioned as a practice of suspect-stranger-making, notwithstanding its pretensions to objective description. (It also betrayed the observationists' intentions, telling us much more about New Orleans and its people than was planned.)

In addition to those cited by the *Picayune*, there were many de facto and de jure practices of quotidian suspect-stranger-making in New Orleans that could have occasioned the arrest of the cook from Providence and started his slide down the slippery slope from free man of color to strange negro to enslaved person. Not only the 1830 law requiring the registration of free people of color who possessed the right to stay in the state, nor even the series of laws banning any new free people of color from entering the state, but also a full complement of laws of various kinds ensured that black people in New Orleans felt themselves addressed as suspect strangers whether these laws strictly speaking applied to them or not. Moreover, although certain of the laws were selective in terms of the black people whom they targeted, it was nevertheless the case that if you were in some way construable as black, a law would be found to fit the purpose of harassment. These included laws restricting the publishing activities of black people in Louisiana and preventing their military service, as well as de facto sumptuary codes, such as the practice of wearing *tignons*, held over from the time of Spanish colonial rule. Although the 1830 law that led to the creation of the Register did not apply to anyone who had settled in the state before the ratification of its Constitution, thus excluding many of the city's oldest black families from this requirement, other laws, such as those restricting black and antiracist publishing, were felt keenly by this group's members. In New Orleans, in other words, all "negroes" were being made into "strange negroes"; they were in this way being made into suspect-strangers. A family's or an individual's length of residence, their property-holding status, and their connections to the white community mattered less and less each day.

These suspect-stranger-making practices generated data that testify to the presence of something in addition to suspect-stranger-making: the experience of stranger-with-ness that determines the rate and direction of stranger-becoming. Both suspect-stranger-making and stranger-with-ness are present in each of the Register's many entries. The one for Marie Louise Dalila reads, for example, "DALILA (Marie Louise), negro, 60, seamstress, born Port au Prince, St. Domingue, freed 3 Apr. 1828 by Jean LAMBERT h.c.l. [*homme couleur libre*] by act passed by L. T. CAIRE, recommended by Mr. CADILLAN, registered 5 Aug. 1841." The entrants to the Nantucket Atheneum required only one sponsor, but Marie Louise Dalila is here supplied with three: Jean Lambert, the free man of color in Haiti; L. T. Caire, the New Orleans notary who certified her documents; and Mr. Cadillan, who "recommended" her to Mr. Caire and so vouchsafed for her reliability. In the case of a young woman named Elizabeth Cordelia, only two additional names were required: "CORDELIA (Elizabeth alias POPE), see Letter P [in the Register], negress, 18, washerwoman, born Louisville, Ky., arrived 1829, recorded upon an act of emancipation dated Louisville Ky. 11 June 1833 of her mother Betty POPE (from Js. GUTHREE Esq.), 5 ft. 4 in. 3/8, registered 4 Apr. 1846." The name of Cordelia's mother, when offered with a document certified by Senator James Guthree of Kentucky, was sufficient to the task of identification. In several entries, such as the one for Prosper Blair, the name of only one other person is recorded. In the case of Blair, though, the scanty documentation comes with a more fully elaborated story pointing to relationships extending farther afield than the Mississippi River basin or even the Caribbean: "BLAIR (Prosper), Indian (Note: Prosper BLAIR is registered here because he fears causing alarm because of his brown color, and he wants the witness of Jh. Paul COULON in his favor in order to conserve his liberty), 48, grocer, born Calcutta . . . , arrived 1822, Joseph Paul COULON, registered 13 Aug. 1840." In more than one entry a mother's own testimony is insufficient to certify her child's freedom and must be supplemented with some other form of witness: "ANSON (Austin), negro, 25, coachman, born New Orleans, freed by his mother 19 Aug. 1834, 5 ft. 5 in., certificate of Jh. GENOIS certifying his freedom, registered 11 July 1840."

The Register's entries invite comparison to the certifying documents bracketing the African American fugitive slave narratives, which create, according to John Sekora, a white envelope for a black message. They also recall the reduction to type, or typifying discourse, that Ian Baucom, following Mary Poovey, associates with eighteenth-century novels, finance capitalism, modern insurance, and slavery, as well as a similar reduction to type described by Susan Mizruchi in her account of the ties connecting sociology to late nineteenth- and early twentieth-century American writing. By this measure, the Register of Free Colored Persons participates in a pernicious project of suspect-stranger-making in which the plurality of a given person— her unfolding difference from herself and from others—is uninteresting to the state as represented by the Register. The Register was designed with the intention that it would testify to nothing other than a given black person's right to remain in Louisiana. To this degree, it reads any black person registered therein as comprising nothing more than one single and circumscribed right—the right to remain. By framing this right as an ascribed one, the Register also indicates the non-self-evidence of either this or any other right in relation to black people; in other words, it posits the non-self-evidence of the rights of the black people registered therein. The moment that a right moves from being assumed to being ascribed or documented, it is no longer self-evidently a right; it becomes a delegated privilege. Ultimately, the authorities delegating such a right arrogate all sovereignty to themselves by way of the act of delegation.

Yet these entries also highlight the shortsightedness of applying these measures alone to a strangers book. On the count of the white envelope, the testimony securing freedom comes from free white people, but it is also supplied by free men and women of color (Dalila); it comes from (presumably) formerly enslaved black women in relation to their children (Anson); and non-"black" freemen supply it in relation to other non-"black" freemen (Blair). There are many other unpredictable configurations. On the count of pursuing a reduction to type, the Register's demand for multiple layers of testimony—its refusal to take black people at their word—generates a detailed map of human relationships that makes it possible to mark out the place of individuals in a larger whole. Excepting a very few registered persons permitted to testify on their own behalf, who were perhaps known to the recording clerk, a second and often a third or fourth name certifies the identity of the person being registered. In this way, the strangers book that is the Register does more to establish the singularity of the person recorded therein than it does to reduce that person to a type. The singularity of the person—their plurality—derives, after all, from the relationships that permit and condition their stranger-becoming. In this unlikely location, the strangers books, where reduction to type, algebraic racial accounting, and the denial of self-evident human right seem to be the main projects, persons are not listed by name only; relationships among persons are prominently featured. In addition to those relationships already mentioned, the Register traces, for example, sibling connections, legally unrecognized marriages, and other unsanctioned kinship structures, such as those that collapse mother into owner, husband into freedom witness. Moreover, human relationships need not be sustaining in order to be consequential. Sometimes the relationships recorded in a strangers book constitute a moral crime, but they too require notation in the

present. History-telling in this mode would document with equal rigor relationships of care and of unforgivable abuse.

Scenes of being contingent upon others, in good ways and in bad, are
coupled in the Register with varying levels of naturalistic detail. Details of
things recorded on the bodies of the persons populating the Register are especially common. These descriptions appear to be fashioned with the intent of
one day using them to certify the identities of those enrolled in the Register.
They do so by way of cross-referencing bodily marks with patterns of human
relationship. The entry for Charles Butler, for example, reads as though cal-
culated to provide evidence in the future of exactly who he is: "BUTLER,
Chs. Thornton, mulatto, 27, barber, born Lafourche, free by certificate of
Y. LESNE, Rector of St. Anthony Chapel dated 22 Feb. 1844 and the affidavit
of L. FAURE dated 9 Mar. 1844, 5 ft. 6 in., one scar on the forehead over the
left eye, also a cross scar on the third joint fore finger left hand, crucifix in
India ink on the left arm, registered 9 Mar. 1844." The naturalistic description
associated with advertisements seeking the return of fugitive slaves played a
role even in securing the freedom of black people; this role was inextricable
from that played by Lesne and Faure.

The same documentary demand that emerged from the legally mandated
racism represented in these strangers books also did the work of confirming
what was otherwise an embarrassment to the racist state: Black people were
mothers and fathers, sons and daughters, sisters and brothers, lovers, freedom sponsors. Often those relationships were legally unsanctioned, but they
approached the force of common law in a state, Louisiana, where Latin colonial tradition made things more hospitable to statutory regulation. Neither
were those individual sons, daughters, friends, lovers, or freedom sponsors
reducible even in the Register to their function in an equation tying them to
the registering person and the state that required the registration: The disclo-
sures in these documents include signs of the coming-into-being of the persons noted in the Register as well, and in this way they imply a very specific
declension of what Marshal Sahlins calls mutuality of being. What caused
that scar on the "third joint fore finger left hand" of Charles Thornton Butler?
Was the "crucifix in India ink" the price of Rector Lesne's testimony? Or was
it intended to signify Butler's faith? Or to connote something else entirely?
Who inscribed that crucifix? And where? By way of questions such as these,
the line between data and disclosure can be crossed without shading over
into an abrogation of the right to opacity of a person in the past.

As these and other entries make clear, the testimony of a black person
regarding her or his own liberty was never enough to meet the standards

established by the state of Louisiana in its law of 1830 or in the several revisions to it. Every "negro" was being made into a "strange negro." Even those whose families had lived free in New Orleans for decades felt addressed by these laws. The elaborate apparatus of second-hand (and third- and fourth-hand) testimonial, certification, and physical cross-referencing engaged in by this book furthermore set a new standard of personhood for anyone who might be thought of as black. It dissolved the already waning convincingness of the testimony of black people before the state. It also rendered irrelevant, even impertinent, the self-certifying testimony of any single free person of color. Registering with the state involved more than just entering one's name into some book; it meant transferring responsibility for that name to other persons whose words and documents were made to coordinate with (and so to invest meaning in) a set of bodily marks. This was the opposite of self evidence; it was an attempt to render the justifiably opaque into the entirely mute.

This is not the only story that this strangers book can tell. The annotation of a few small marks on the body, coupled with the recording of human relationships, opens onto the unfolding of human plurality, of the historicity of a human life. Two possibilities lie latent in any strangers book: stranger-becoming or suspect-stranger-making. Which of these is most fully realized, and the pace and place at which that realization happens, follows, in part, from the relation of address taken up by those who read the strangers book. Approach it as a place of suspect-stranger-making, that is what it will be; approach it as a place of stranger-becoming, that is what it will be. Neither angle of approach is exactly right or completely wrong. Both are defining, but neither one is fully so. The lessons of antebellum African American stranger humanism also suggest, however, that one's angle of approach to a strangers book is more than a matter of individual volition. One's relation of address to strangers in the past derives in part from the (past and present) institutional conditions that make any such relation possible. Those conditions are never fixed or final. They include the fact that the New Orleans Public Library, where the Register of Free Colored Persons is now kept, was spared much of the destruction visited upon other parts of New Orleans during and especially after Hurricane Katrina. They also include the institutional training that is leading you, but not requiring you, to read these lines in the way that you now do, whether skeptically or sympathetically, inquiringly or antagonistically. As will be seen in just a moment, they include as well both the Nantucket Atheneum's lecture hall and the swept yard of the African Meeting House on Nantucket, where black children were learning their letters well before Frederick Douglass made his trip across Nantucket Sound.

The Strangers of Nantucket

As Frederick Douglass tells the story of his 1841 speech at the Nantucket Atheneum, it is the story of an absence. His first major speech before a racially
mixed crowd of abolitionists, it took place during the first Nantucket Anti-
Slavery Convention. "My speech on this occasion is about the only I ever
made," Douglass writes, "of which I do not remember a single connected
sentence."[3] Douglass's description of his trepidation when asked to take the
stage by William Lloyd Garrison precedes this line; it is followed by Douglass's account of Garrison's rousing speech. The only memorial Douglass
makes to his own speech is a statement of amnesia. Garrison's description of
Douglass's speech, included in his preface to Douglass's *Narrative*, is equally
unhelpful. Although Garrison characterizes Douglass's 1841 speech as the
moment when Douglass "rose and found his voice," as well as the moment
when he entered the "field of public usefulness" for the first time, Garrison
offers very little in the way of what Douglass actually said. (Neither does he
credit, as a form of publicly useful voice, Douglass's previous work speaking
and preaching to enslaved and free people of color.) If Douglass's presentation of his first Nantucket speech as an absence invites an assessment of
archival loss, then Nantucket's Great Fire of 1846 solicits a further imaginative layering of absence upon absence. The fire destroyed the Atheneum
building where Douglass spoke. It incinerated the minutes of the Atheneum
shareholders from prior to 1846; those minutes would have noted how it was
decided to permit the antislavery gathering to meet in the Atheneum building. (There are notices in the island's newspapers advertising in advance the
shareholders meeting where the issue was to be put to a vote. The consequences of the vote are also discussed. The decision was apparently reached
not without a fair amount of controversy.) The strangers book(s) from prior
to 1846, which the Atheneum bylaws required, are also missing. They per-
ished in the fire along with the "documents relating to the early settlement of
our island," the 3,200 "recently-catalogued" volumes, and the items brought
back from "Polynesian reports."

The long-standing reputation of the *Narrative of the Life of Frederick Douglass* as a founding text of the African American literary tradition, and the
fantasy of an enforced silence surmounted by that text, makes it tempting to
read this description as echoing more familiar scenes of archival absence that
followed from anti-black-literacy laws. The story of what is missing from the
archive on Nantucket is, nevertheless, much less interesting than the story of
what is there. Indeed, if Nantucket's archive lacks anything of consequence to

the larger story I have sought to tell here, it is something that nobody really has the right or capacity to know: As Glissant might suggest, Douglass's experience of that moment need not and perhaps cannot be shared. If Douglass refuses to provide us with even "a single connected sentence" drawn from his speech that night, however, there is more than enough data available to construct a stranger history of this moment. As a series of literary, historical, and archaeological projects on the island has revealed, the story of Nantucket is the story of a community of multilingual, highly literate black readers, writers, and teachers, as much as it is the story of Queequeg and Ishmael and Tashtego. Douglass spent time with this black community during his 1841 visit. From beginning to end, in other words, and not only with his turn to the colored convention movement, or his founding of the *North Star*, or any other of the famous moments of his many entries into print, Douglass's was an intellectual and political career conceived in and through relationships with lettered black people of many kinds. Although Douglass, his companions in the colored convention movement, and the *Les Cenelles* poets helped to strengthen the institutional structures that facilitated such connections, they alone cannot be credited with the invention of these structures, as they themselves likely would have confirmed. To do so would be to misrepresent the origin of the mode of address characterizing this and other, later and earlier invitations to write a stranger history as issuing from a single source. The thriving multiparty disclosure and witness that I have argued can successfully cultivate plurality did not issue from Douglass and his nearest friends alone, nor from Armand Lanusse and his nearest friends alone, nor from any single coterie alone. The stranger-with-ness that facilitates stranger-becoming was instead a persistent feature of African American print culture. In order to see how this is so, however, the story of Frederick Douglass on Nantucket must itself be made to call into question just what is meant by African American print culture as a category.

The story of Frederick Douglass's entry into print with which I wish to conclude is therefore a story not of books or of circulation or of copyright. It is a story of two buildings, one large and one small, on the island of Nantucket. The first of the two buildings, the original Nantucket Atheneum, was purchased and renovated in 1838. The Greek Revival additions to the building, which had formerly housed a Unitarian church, signaled a desire, common on the island at this point, to resuscitate early American republicanism. The lectures presented in Atheneum Hall were often spectacular rather than ennobling, including, among others, a show put on by a disabled man who lacked arms and performed the duties of a barber with his feet. Nevertheless, the Atheneum Hall, where Douglass spoke and where the antislavery convention met, signified still a commitment to a resurgent republican ideal. In the imagination of the island's elite, who had been reared on a cultural diet of early American republicanism, a speaker's appearance before his fellow citizens performed his status and at the same time recognized theirs. On the one hand, this endorsed a sense of substitutable personhood; on the other, it designated certain members of the community suspect-strangers in relation to the demos.[4] Although citizens might be equal to and therefore exchangeable with one another, such an equation did not factor in exchangeability with women, enslaved persons, foreigners, or unpropertied men. It permitted the displacement of the non-citizen but not exchangeability. The Atheneum's library reflected similar aims. Its collection followed in part from a commitment to nursing back to health the U.S. and international republic of letters. The Atheneum's bylaws, the many reports of its doings in Nantucket's newspapers and personal diaries, and the Atheneum library's policies make these loyalties clear.

The Atheneum was in this respect designed as a kind of homeopathic national antidote to the southern slaveholding society that Douglass anatomizes in *My Bondage and My Freedom*. There he attends in detail to the architectural, print cultural, and spatial arrangements that permit slavery to thrive. His focus is on the South's travestying of the divisions separating the public sphere, the private sphere, and the state. Slaveholding only thrives, he explains, where "public opinion," "public influence," and "public life" go missing. Where the state, society, and private life are indistinguishable, the regulatory functions of the public sphere, in particular, always wither and die. Forecasting W. E. B. Du Bois's memorable vision of life in the black belt, Douglass describes a South where the light of public opinion never shines. He argues that slavery's worst depredations go unpunished, because they never rise to the level of visibility enabled by the presence of a general public. The columns lining antebellum plantation verandas turn out to be fronting tricked-out medieval fortresses. "[T]here are certain secluded and out-of-the-way places, even in the state of Maryland," Douglass writes, "seldom visited by a single ray of healthy public sentiment." "Just such a secluded, dark, and out-of-the-way place," he continues, "is the 'home plantation' of Col. Edward Lloyd, on the Eastern Shore, Maryland." What marks this place as different, and what secures its aberrant practices, is its isolation: "It is far away from all the great thoroughfares, and is proximate to no town or village. There is neither school-house, nor town-house, in its neighborhood."[5] This isolation and self-sufficiency of Lloyd's plantation does not recall the *oikos* of classical antiquity. It represents instead a return to the Middle Ages:

"In its isolation, seclusion, and self-reliant independence, Col. Lloyd's plantation resembles what the baronial domains were, during the middle ages in
Europe. Grim, cold, and unapproachable by all genial influences from communities without, *there it stands*; full three hundred years behind the age, in
all that relates to humanity and morals."[6] Like Mark Twain's *A Connecticut
Yankee in King Arthur's Court* (1889), Douglass's *My Bondage and My Freedom* transports us to the nadir of a republicanism first fashioned in Greece
and Rome, resuscitated in the Renaissance, and revived again in the context
of the revolutionary nationalisms of the late eighteenth century. According to
Douglass, a properly functioning public is not a transhistorical given. Institutional and social arrangements join people in specific ways that permit them
to assert their authority. Physical spaces permit citizens to gather and delib-
eratively govern (a "town-house"); institutions of basic and cultural literacy
(a "school-house") are also required.

If Douglass echoes the Garrisonian interest in constructing a critical public, though, he will also, as I have already argued, refine this model in important ways. Douglass's biographers document that by the time he published
My Bondage and My Freedom he had grown weary of the Garrisonians. By the
measures of a more fully developed antebellum African American stranger
humanism, the fact that the Nantucket Atheneum echoed Garrisonian and
classical expectations of republicanism was precisely its problem. Founded as
a private lending library and reading room, it would eventually host lectures
and spectacles accessible to the wider community by way of purchased tick-
ets.[7] The Nantucket Anti-Slavery Convention that Douglass attended at the
Atheneum was the first to be held there; it appears to have been the last. If
the Atheneum was also one of many period institutions seeking to resuscitate
rational-critical debate, then such was its central failing: The secular-revival-
ist mentality of the time identified literate institutions as incubators of normative public opinion and as capable of articulating universal human needs
without fully factoring into account the consequences of something so basic
as lending policies and practices of admission. The Atheneum founders had
a republicanized version of the Liverpool Atheneum and Lyceum in mind as
one of their templates. It is noteworthy in this context that Douglass recalls
one of his first visits to such an institution as follows: "Soon after my arrival
in New Bedford, from the south, I had a strong desire to attend the Lyceum,
but was told, '*They don't allow niggers in here!*'"[8]

Established in 1834, the Atheneum resulted from the merger of the Nantucket Mechanics' Social Library and the Columbian Library Society, two
private associations, and it was committed to the notion that holding print

cultural institutions as private legal property was not inconsistent with its aims. It was instead necessary to them. As Betsy Tyler's concise history of the Atheneum explains, the

> first of the two, the Nantucket Mechanics' Social Library, was founded for general education in 1820 by David Joy, Charles G. Coffin, and five other well-educated, prosperous men; their original library consisted of twenty-six books. Although contemporary British mechanics' libraries were furnished with books focusing on scientific topics and featuring lectures and experiments for the benefit of tradesmen and artisans, the Nantucket library did not have a lecture series and was not of a scientific bent. It cost three dollars to join, with a quarterly fee of fifty cents, a fairly high rate that would have been prohibitive to the island's working classes.[9]

Tyler also explains that the Columbian Library Society was "organized in 1823 by, among others, . . . William Coffin, Jr., surveyor, mapmaker, and teacher."[10] As we will see, the surnames of Joy and Coffin are significant. As far as the building itself was concerned, following their purchase of the decommissioned Universalist Church, the founders "remodeled [it] to feature a library room, committee room, and museum room on the second floor, while the first floor—the original church sanctuary—was easily transformed into a lecture hall that could seat four hundred and fifty people." The final alteration was perhaps the most significant: "a Greek Revival style portico was added."[11]

The Atheneum's organizational structure reflected local economic and political history, as well as the sought-after republican renaissance registered in the aspirational addition of that portico. The Atheneum's growing collection of books, the activities of its resident artist and its librarian, its viewing cabinets, its museum, and its lecture hall were all administered by a committee of trustees. The Atheneum trustees were shareholders in the Atheneum, and they included a significant number of descendants of the island's "first proprietors," who were the original white settlers, Joy's and Coffin's among them, and who displaced the island's indigenous inhabitants when they purchased the island from a white Christian missionary in the seventeenth century. A second, much larger body of shareholders, from which the trustees were drawn and who were known as proprietors, held property in the Atheneum. As Tyler explains, they each paid ten dollars for a single share in the Atheneum, then paid an additional two-dollar fee each year. Their property rights licensed them to borrow books. They also permitted shareholders to vote on Atheneum matters of consequence, serve on its committees, attend its yearly meetings, and participate in its governance. Finally, these property rights gave shareholders the key privilege that necessitated the Atheneum Strangers Book: "Each Proprietor may introduce strangers to the Atheneum," according to the bylaws, "and such persons shall be entitled to admission afterwards for the space of one month, upon having their names recorded with that of the person introducing them, who shall be responsible for their observing the regulations of the Institution."[12] Islanders who neither held property in the Atheneum nor were granted stranger status by a proprietor did have a measure of access to the building, but it was significantly reduced. Borrowing privileges alone could be purchased for three dollars per year, but the greatest number of the island's population of ten thousand residents probably entered by paying the fifteen cents required to visit the Atheneum museum. These policies, and the presence of the Strangers Book, in particular, clarify how modes of surveillance that had been common to the colonial New England environment had been folded into the Atheneum's functioning. Before the 1830s, New England towns and villages frequently required innkeepers and residents to report any strangers present in the area, especially if those strangers had plans to lodge overnight. The records that were kept were the original strangers books; the atheneums at Nantucket, Providence, and Boston adapted their format and something of their function.

The records of other literate institutions on the island tell related stories of how such institutions were to become one of the most important places for the reinvention of practices of suspect stranger-making inherited from earlier periods. The many white islanders who were de facto excluded from shareholding in the Atheneum, by virtue of their economic status, and the island's black residents, who appear to have been excluded on these and other grounds, were cognizant of the reinvention that was taking place. Although some nonshareholding white locals no doubt attended the 1841 antislavery convention, others stood outside throwing rocks and rotten food through the windows. These attacks would have been motivated not only by the intense anti-abolitionist sentiment that followed the Garrisonians' perceived slighting of the Nantucket clergy,[13] but also by the fact that the island's population remained in economic thrall to a select few members of the island's first families, many of whom were involved with the Atheneum and with organizing the antislavery convention. Another of the island's literary societies, moreover, went through a period of intense transition in the 1830s.[14] After the membership passed resolutions allowing entrance for men under twenty-one years of age, admittance for women, and simple majority votes, many of the literary society's landed and wealthy founding members resigned their officerships and their memberships in protest. This (white men's) republic of letters apparently could not tolerate even that most mild-mannered of things: a white literary democracy.

A somewhat different story had been playing out for some time elsewhere on the island. The section of Nantucket known as New Guinea lay beyond the gate separating the town from its grazing lands, and it was home to most of the island's residents of African descent. According to Douglass's biographers, Douglass visited New Guinea that August night in 1841 after he, in Garrison's estimation, "rose and found his voice" at the Nantucket Atheneum. An agent for *The Colored American*, Edward Pompey, lived there, which would indicate that Douglass probably returned to the neighborhood again on at least one (or more) of his four subsequent trips to the island. On one of his trips to New Guinea, Douglass's hosts perhaps explained how in 1837, a young woman of African descent from Nantucket's New Guinea, whose name was Eunice Ross and who became a talented student of French, applied to attend the island's white public high school.[15] After an intense and bitterly divided town meeting, her application was summarily rejected. The conflict over the desegregation of Nantucket's public schools that followed Ross's application would last for ten years, until 1847, and covering the time when Douglass first "rose and found his voice." At that time nonwhite children were finally put on equal standing and given leave to attend the island's public schools. (According to the diary of one white Nantucketer, this seeming step forward into integration, which had already been mandated throughout the state by the Massachusetts legislature several years before, and which Nantucket was threatened with fines for contravening, was actually a return to an earlier and seemingly uncontroversial practice of integrated schooling on Nantucket prior to the 1820s.)[16] On one of his post-1845 trips, Douglass might also have been informed of how, between 1843 and 1845, the same Nantucket Atheneum where Douglass first entered the "field of public usefulness" had closed its doors to people of color.[17] No doubt he also noticed on one of his later trips to the Atheneum that by 1883 his name still was not to be found in the Nantucket Atheneum Library Catalogue. Perhaps this is why, when he returned to the island for the final time late in his life, he decided to offer a lecture titled "William the Silent."

Two years before black people were banned from the Atheneum and not long after Douglass's 1841 lecture, a group of men of African descent founded their own antislavery reading room over a dry-goods store. This reading room appears to have functioned as one of at least two meeting places for literate and any nonliterate black Nantucketers.[18] The other was the second and smaller of the two buildings on which this story of early African American print culture on Nantucket finally depends. The African Meeting House on Nantucket still stands at the corner of York and Pleasant, in what is now known as Five Points and was in the 1840s called New Guinea. The earliest record of the Meeting House appears in town documents certifying the sale of a plot of land. As Mary Beaudry and Ellen Berkland explain, the land was "legally obtained on March 26, 1825, from Jeffrey Summons, a successful black laborer who sold the parcel and a *standing structure . . .* for $10.50." Based on a variety of documents, Beaudry and Berkland surmise that the African Meeting House served a number of purposes. In 1834, the year that the Nantucket Atheneum was founded, one of the Meeting House's functions was as a dispensary for smallpox vaccinations for the black community.

In the late 1990s, the Meeting House was purchased by the Afro-American History Museum of Boston, and extensive renovations of the building, which had fallen into disrepair, were undertaken. Before those renovations got under way, a limited archaeological excavation of the Meeting House site was performed. One of the most striking findings of that excavation had to do not with the building, but with the ground around it. As Beaudry and Berkland explain, there is "a strong tradition of 'swept yards' in Africa and the rural American South, and archaeologists regularly find evidence of swept yards at slave quarters and freed slave sites in the southeast and in the Caribbean." They suggest though that "examples of swept yards [had] not been encountered in New England."[19] On Nantucket Beaudry and Berkland found clear evidence of a swept yard, including the telltale tamped earth and a raised walkway. For these archaeologists this "provide[s] clear evidence that black Nantucketers considered themselves to be African," or at least members of a larger African Atlantic diaspora. As they further explain, the tradition of the swept yard is a "way of organizing and maintaining communal space that results in a compact 'living floor' affording open space for a variety of activities." For example, items found and that were "possibly lost from women's workbaskets or workbags included a tiny turned bone cap with screw threads, possibly the lid for a pin poppet or needle case, and a deep-drawn machine-made copper alloy thimble of a form typical of the first half of the nineteenth century."[20] There was also an intriguing piece of glass "bear[ing] the embossed image of a periwigged male face" that had been flint-knapped and appears to have been an ad hoc tool used for "tasks such as sewing and minor cutting" as well as for women's healing kits.[21]

This varied evidence of what Beaudry and Berkland refer to in their study of the Meeting House as "communal activities" makes it tempting to characterize the Meeting House as a holistic space undisturbed by the written or the printed word. However, other facts about the African Meeting House on Nantucket tell against this picture. The bill of sale for the Meeting House included an entailment: Jeffrey Summons stipulated that the deal was contingent on the trustees of this building, which would be known not only as the African Meeting House, as it is now called, but also as the African School, promising to keep "a school house standing on the said land which is kept in good repair and a school to be kept in it forever."[22] Summons's demand helps to explain why, among the items discovered in the Meeting House excavation, there were included the following:

Marbles
The face of a porcelain doll
A doll's eye and its arm
Two rubber balls
Two harmonica parts
The tip of a small flagpole
A writing slate
Stylus fragments

One final item appeared as well: "a copper alloy tip from a writing pen."[23] This stranded "copper alloy tip from a writing pen" recalls another writing pen: the one that Frederick Douglass used to write his *Narrative*, which, he tells us, could have been laid in the gashes of his frost-cracked feet during his winters under slavery. Yet the copper alloy tip from the Nantucket writing pen does not function here as an imaginative passageway permitting the reader to travel through wounded skin into a flowing bloodstream and thereafter into a beating heart. The copper alloy tip from this Nantucket writing pen is much colder. It is also more demanding. The copper alloy tip from the Nantucket writing pen asks—permits, really—only one thing. It must be taken up in the writing of a stranger history that never abrogates the right to opacity of the child who first formed her letters with the tip of that lost Nantucket pen.

Stranger Literature

Across several of his influential anthologies of American literature, Rufus Griswold—a nineteenth-century anthologist, poet, and erstwhile editor of Edgar Allan Poe—offers conflicting measures for what is now called early American literature. In Griswold's *The Prose Writers of America*, for example, which first appeared in 1847 and later went into multiple editions, he offers a familiar and currently derided set of parameters for this corpus of writing. In his prefatory remarks, dated May 1847, Griswold explains that he has chosen not to include "the merely successful writers" who precede him. Although success might appear to be a bar high enough to warrant inclusion, he emphasizes that he has focused on writers who "have evinced unusual powers in controlling the national mind, or in forming ... the national character."[1] This emphasis on what has been nationally consequential echoes other moments in *Prose Writers*, as well as paratextual material in his earlier *The Poets and Poetry of America* (1842) and his *The Female Poets of America* (1848). In his several miniature screeds condemning the lack of international copyright, as well as the consequent flooding of the American market with cheap reprints, Griswold, for instance, explains the "difficulties and dangers" this poses to "American literature." "Injurious as it is to the foreign author," Griswold writes, "it is more so to the American [people,] whom it deprives of that nationality of feeling which is among the first and most powerful incentives to every kind of greatness."[2] In *The Poets and Poetry of America*, he similarly complains that America's "national tastes and feelings are fashioned by the subject of kings; and they will continue so to be, until [there is] an honest and politic system of RECIPROCAL COPYRIGHT."[3] Even in *The Female Poets of America*, which one might anticipate having changed the nature of this conversation, Griswold returns to the significance of these women writers for the national project. He cites the fact that several of the poets included in the volume had written from lives that

were "no holydays of leisure," but defined rather by everything from "practical duties" to the experience of slavery; he also responds to those carp-
ing "foreign critics" who propose that "our citizens are too much devoted
to business and politics to feel interest in pursuits which adorn but do not
profit."[4] To these critics, Griswold replies that these home-laboring women
writers may end up being the source of that which is most genuinely American and most correctly poetic: "Those who cherish a belief that the progress
of society in this country," he explains, "is destined to develop a school of
art, original and special, will perhaps find more decided indications of the
infusion of our domestic spirit and temper into literature, in the poetry of
our female authors, than in that of our men."[5] Even women poets are held
to the standard of national self-expression and national self-realization; the
surprise lies only in the fact that they live up to this standard.

Given his driving emphasis on the national character of an emergent
American literature, it is easy to overlook the extent to which Griswold's "literature" is itself a moving target. In fact, the national spirit, which Griswold
suggests is realized across a range of different kinds of writing, turns out to
be the main constant linking the various materials covered by his framework.
If Griswold is confident enough about what constitutes America, in other
words, he seems much less certain about what to call literature and what to
exclude from this categorical distinction. In this respect, Griswold is our near
contemporary, as much as he is a product of his moment.

Perhaps unsurprisingly, Griswold's indecision around the category of literature is most pronounced when it comes to prose. Anticipating the current
configuration of early American literary studies, as well as this field's historically manifest and currently latent anxieties concerning the adequacy of its
objects when measured against, say, Wordsworth or Donne, Griswold opts
for a policy of radical inclusion. "With Dr. Channing," he writes, "I consider
books of every description, whether devoted to the exact sciences, to mental
and ethical philosophy, to history and legislation, or to fiction and poetry,
as literature."[6] He will qualify this statement a few lines later, when he writes
that he has restricted himself to the "department of belles lettres." Even so, his
belles lettres is a capacious department indeed: it comprises history writing
(Prescott, Bancroft), the historical correspondence of the Revolutionary Age
(the letters of Washington, Adams, Franklin, Jefferson, Jay, Hamilton, and
"some of their compatriots"), oratory (Webster, Clay, Calhoun, and others),
political economy, jurisprudence, "archaeology, oriental, and classical learning," ethnography, mathematics, meteorology, chemistry, mineralogy, ornithology, entomology, zoology—and romantic fiction. Other than in certain

fleeting moments, what Griswold seems to lack here is any clear principle of exclusion save a vague sense of a nation-in-the-making.

Griswold is somewhat less catholic in his relation to American poetry in *Poets and Poetry of America*. There we get some inkling of the boundaries being drawn around what Griswold frames as a sort of catalogue raisonné of the American national spirit. He explains that all of the authors collected in his volume "have lived in the brief period which has elapsed since the establishment of the national government." He indicates further that "[a]lthough America has produced many eminent scholars and writers, we have yet but the beginning of a national literature."[7] It is a familiar-enough claim, and for a time (though perhaps not as long as is sometimes thought), it was the burden of anyone seeking to work in the pre-national literatures of North America. For Griswold, as for those who, back in the day, attended more closely to F. O. Matthiessen than they did to Perry Miller, "the early colonists were men of erudition, deeply versed in scholastic theology, and familiar with the best ancient literature; but they possessed neither the taste, the fancy, nor the feeling of the poet, and their elaborate metrical compositions are forgotten by all save the antiquary, and by him are regarded as among the least valuable of the relics of the first era of civilization in America."[8]

If Griswold seems to gesture here toward a logic of selection, attentive readers will nevertheless notice a familiar conflict of principles emerging in this context: On the one hand, we have a chronological justification for inclusion (i.e., these poets are American because they wrote after the establishment of a national government); on the other, we have a connoisseur's quasi-aesthetic arguments (taste, fancy, feeling, meter). There is at least one instance when Griswold seeks to settle the issue; this moment's syntactical looseness is perhaps the most telling of all his reachings toward classificatory coherence. Speaking of the "quaint and grotesque absurdities of Folger, Mather, and Wigglesworth," Griswold suggests that it would be unfair to compare these writings to "the productions of the first cultivators of the art in older nations; for literature—mental development—had here, in truth, no infancy."[9] Like any attempt to square a circle, Griswold's definitional exertions ultimately fail to satisfy. He suggests through a gesture of apposition that literature is—simply enough—equivalent to something called "mental development." What might count as "mental development" is left unsaid, and so the notoriously unhelpful voice of common sense is left to have its sententious say. Of course we know what literature is: mental development.

Even if he were to offer a capable definition of "mental development," however, and this again is the main point, we would be left with the radically underdefined ghostly presence called literature, which is conjured by virtue of Griswold's very inconsistency around definitions. A sign of the national spirit; a manifestation of "mental development"; ornithology; "good verse"; something in accord with Johann Joachim Winckelmann's standards: Griswold presents all of these in apposition to American literature, but no single one is acknowledged as potentially exclusive of any other. This is the power of apposition: It is associative rather than logical, permitting the accumulation of other appositions while forestalling any moment of reckoning in which exclusion becomes not only possible but logically (or politically or ethically) necessary. At the moment of one of its earliest instantiations as a nameable phenomenon, American literature can therefore find itself premised on a certainty around the nation that either precipitates or masks merely appositional approximations of what should count as literature. One consequence is that many of the things currently associated with a revanchist account of literary study—periodizations that mirror national historical trajectories, Johann Gottfried Herder's notions of the geographic differences inherent to national cultures, and so on—seem permissible and even necessary because an account of literature that would rely on a form of chronology in which literature itself is an event is rendered impossible. We don't know when literature started, because we do not know what it is; we can therefore possess no sense of the advent of early American literature as a historical event. We do have a fair sense of the moments when North American colonization, the Articles of Confederation, Shays' Rebellion, and the Monroe Doctrine appeared on the horizon. We might choose to move away from the conservative historian's event-based chronology and favor instead the long centuries approach, as many have recently done, but even in the turn to this model, which argues for reducing the status of the event in historical narrative, those events whose significance require recalibration and diminishment often demonstrate only a tenuous relation to literature.

In certain respects this is neither news nor a cause for alarm. Many would cite it as a key feature of the thriving state of early American literary studies as it now stands: This field has comparatively strong links to other fields such as history, a long-standing interdisciplinary character, and an openness to nonanglophone writing and nonscriptive forms of representation that some other critical traditions would do well to emulate. At the same time, Griswold's circumlocution summons one of the latent questions that literary studies, in general, and early American literary studies, in particular, has been reluctant to address in recent memory: What is literature? This is not the same question as the following questions, which are perhaps related and which I would suggest deserve some very unoriginal answers: What should we study, teach, preserve, and propagate? (To be determined in situ.) Does a given text have a place in a literary studies curriculum? (As above, the case must be argued.) Should American literary studies continue to add nonanglophone and nonscriptive texts to its canon? (Ditto.) I also want to state openly my recognition of the fact that the history of literary studies is no guide here, as well as my lack of any nostalgia for an earlier age. On the first count, anyone conversant with the history of literary criticism and theory recognizes the difficulty of doing justice to even the most influential attempts to define literature. On the second, almost nothing that I care about would be an acceptable object of study in earlier ages. Sneering dismissals of early African American writing that condemn its failure to live up to some underdefined notion of literariness more or less make the case that this is tricky terrain and that any attempt to enter it must be cautious. As Robyn Wiegman has argued, moreover, efforts to define and to circumscribe any object of study are often something other than what they seem.

All things considered, it might nevertheless still be a useful exercise to consider in passing what would follow—what new periodizations, archives, and reading practices—from seeking out an adequate and effective definition of literature on the terrain of early American literary studies as it intersects with African American literary studies. There are several reasons why this site of intersection might be especially productive for this undertaking. To begin with, antipathy to the project of categorical definition and to categorical exclusions has definitively shaped these two areas of inquiry. Among the founding premises of both areas of study is the notion that the hierarchical exclusions embedded in conventional—that is, mid-twentieth-century Anglo-American academic—notions of literature have made the significance of pre- and extra-American Renaissance North American expressive cultures more or less indiscernible. Both projects have at their heart a sense that the drive toward the specification of literature as such has been associated with canonizing projects antithetical to the kind of work that makes possible a rich, politicized, historically informed understanding of, say, Jupiter Hammon, Michael Wigglesworth, or even Anne Bradstreet. Just this suspicion around the exclusionary power of the category of literature, as well as the sometimes frustrating turn to the historian's event-based chronologies that have defined these fields, makes them much more likely to be able to formulate a significantly new version of a very old conversation. Rather than a case of the fox guarding the hens, we would have something more like the hens setting the fox a program of reform.

The precise shape this conversation might take will be hard to determine in advance, but one place to begin might be with the relation between literature and the category of the human. First, it is obvious to say that since at least the mid-eighteenth century, and likely before, one particular categorical understanding of literature has been premised on the notion of literature as a sign of the fully human. There are many ways of responding to this notion of literature, including the familiar post-Nietzschean suggestion that it permits an overvaluation of both literature and the human. Many have elected to dispense with both of these categories—the human and literature—precisely because of the seemingly circular and self-regarding logic of their embrace. We know what is human because it produces literature; we know what is literature because it expresses what is human. Very cozy.

However, it might also be productive to exploit this bind, as well as to make it differently productive, by, as I have attempted to do here, starting with the category of the human as it has been rendered in nonhegemonic cultures. From this point, one might elect to exclude from the category of literature anything that does not, to borrow Nancy Bentley's language one final time, "exten[d] the horizon of the human."[10] To do so would be to take up the challenge laid down by the scholars in African American and black diaspora studies discussed in this book, as well as the antebellum writers I have considered within it. Revisiting the category of the human from the perspective of its figuration in African diasporic and other "minor" cultures makes it clear that there is unfinished business to address.

To take up the challenge of this unfinished business would be to force the issue of what is at stake in refusing to exclude from the province of literature much of anything. Thinking Griswold's radically inclusive project alongside the critics and writers I have considered, for example, highlights the extent to which the insistence on a radically inclusive definition of literature, which extends into the period of slavery rather than following from the radical movements of the 1960s, permits the inclusion, dissemination, and reproduction *as literature* of texts that are themselves predicated at core on articulating their own principles of exclusion. It seems worth noting that Griswold's especially generous definition of literature licenses him to include within this category Samuel George Morton's *Crania Americana, An Inquiry into the Distinctive Characteristics of the Aboriginal Race of America* (1839–1849). Morton's contributions to the emergence of scientific racism have been analyzed and debated at length, often in the context of American literary studies, African American studies, and related antiracist projects. The capaciousness of these fields, like the capaciousness of Griswold's understanding of literature, has permitted the bringing to bear of a host of modes of textual analysis. It seems worth acknowledging, however, that the ultimate horizon of this critical analysis has been a reorientation of ideology that would disallow the racism that Morton's writings arguably permit. The procedures of these fields assume that one primary goal is to disallow the logic of exclusion embedded in Morton's *Crania Americana*.

Along the way, it has sometimes been assumed that in effecting this transformation, it would be possible to avoid formulating exclusions of any kind—despite the fact that delegitimizing and hence excluding from political representation the arguments of scientific racism was the point all along. This is to identify the conflation of exclusion, as a general principle, with antidemocratic exclusionary practices and logics, as well as the assumption that a full-throttle redefinition of literature that does not reproduce antidemocratic exclusions is impossible. If exclusion as a principle has been rejected in literary studies, and especially in American literary studies, then what Ellen Rooney calls the seductive reasoning of pluralism has often been allowed to organize the practices of the field.[11] A different approach to these issues might seek to recapture the category of literature, with its normative force; redefine it according to the stated desires of many nondominant peoples for a new understanding of the human, as well as the principles of the human articulated therein; and then set about the work of separating the literary wheat from the antihumanist chaff. In all honesty, I do not know how this would work. What I do know is that logics of exclusion are always at play; the task is to articulate a logic of exclusion both capaciousness enough and closed enough that it becomes possible to invent new names and new categorical distinctions sufficient to those other things that will no longer be literature but that will (likely) continue to warrant study, teaching, and preservation. If this appears to assume that, when the new definition of literature arrives on the scene, literature itself will be revealed to have taken place, it does not. It instead makes it possible to imagine a world—now or in the past or even in the future—in which literature has not yet happened.

NOTES

Introduction

1. Ellen Rooney, "A Semiprivate Room," *differences: A Journal of Feminist Cultural Studies* 13, no. 1 (Spring 2002).

2. Alexander G. Weheliye, "After Man," *American Literary History* 20, nos. 1 2 (Spring/Summer 2008): 321.

3. Jeannine DeLombard, *In the Shadow of the Gallows: Race, Crime, and American Civic Identity* (Philadelphia: University of Pennsylvania Press, 2012).

4. See also Stephen Michael Best, *The Fugitive's Properties: Law and the Poetics of Possession* (Chicago: University of Chicago Press, 2004).

5. Leon Jackson, "The Talking Book and the Talking Book Historian: African American Cultures of Print—the State of the Discipline," *Book History* 13 (2010).

6. Houston A. Baker, *Blues, Ideology, and Afro-American Literature: A Vernacular Theory* (Chicago: University of Chicago Press, 1984).

7. Frances Smith Foster, *Love and Marriage in Early African America* (Hanover, N.H.: University Press of New England, 2008).

8. Anthony Bogues, "And What About the Human?: Freedom, Human Emancipation, and the Radical Imagination," *boundary 2* 39, no. 3 (2012); Soyica Diggs Colbert, "'When I Die, I Won't Stay Dead': The Future of the Human in Suzan-Lori Parks's *The Death of the Last Black Man in the Whole Entire World*," *boundary 2* 39, no. 3 (2012); Sylvia Wynter, "Unsettling the Coloniality of Being/Power/Truth/Freedom: Towards the Human, After Man, Its Overrepresentation—an Argument," *CR: The New Centennial Review* 3, no. 3 (2003).

9. Paul Gilroy, *Against Race: Imagining Political Culture Beyond the Color Line* (Cambridge, Mass.: Harvard University Press, 2000), 13.

10. Also: Michael Warner, *Publics and Counterpublics* (New York: Zone, 2002), 76.

11. Édouard Glissant, *Poetics of Relation*, trans. Betsy Wing (Ann Arbor: University of Michigan Press, 1997), 190.

12. Ian Baucom, *Specters of the Atlantic: Finance Capital, Slavery and the Philosophy of History* (Durham, N.C.: Duke University Press, 2005).

13. Hannah Arendt, *The Human Condition*, 2nd ed. (Chicago: University of Chicago Press, 1998).

14. Nicole Waligora-Davis, *Sanctuary: African Americans and Empire* (New York: Oxford University Press, 2011).

15. Saidiya V. Hartman, *Scenes of Subjection: Terror, Slavery, and Self-Making in Nineteenth-Century America* (New York: Oxford University Press, 1997).

16. Nancy Fraser and Axel Honneth, *Redistribution or Recognition? A Political-Philosophical Exchange*, trans. Joel Golb, James Ingraham, and Christian Wilke (New York: Verso, 2003), 10, 229. By focusing on the importance of equal and separate to this formulation, my argument departs from John Stauffer's *The Black Hearts of Men: Radical Abolitionists and the Transformation of Race* (Cambridge, Mass.: Harvard University Press, 2001). Stauffer proposes that James McCune Smith, along with Douglass, thought that "whites had to understand what it was like to be black. They had to learn how to view the world as if they were black, shed their 'whiteness' as a sign of superiority, and renounce their belief in skin color as a marker of aptitude and social status. They had to acquire, in effect, a black heart." Although my argument is different in its emphasis from that of Stauffer, it relates more to the sense of how one arrives at the achievement he describes. It may very well have been the case that all four men who are the subject of Stauffer's accomplished study pursued a black heart. My suggestion is that Douglass's aesthetics indicate a sense that in order to "blu[r] and brea[k] down distinctions of race, religion, class, and gender," these men would first have to participate in the process of differentiation and recognition that I define here as strangerhood. The categorical distinctions that Stauffer names would need to be replaced with other more critically singular ones that were conceivable as a ground of commonality before "race, religion, class, and gender" could begin to dissolve from within. In addition to this difference of emphasis, I also trace something realized primarily at the level of formal practice rather than in the structures of friendship that Stauffer considers. Stauffer, *The Black Hearts of Men*, 1, 3.

17. Fraser and Honneth, *Redistribution or Recognition?*, 27–33.

18. Jacques Rancière, *The Politics of Aesthetics: The Distribution of the Sensible*, trans. Gabriel Rockhill (London: Continuum, 2006); Audre Lorde, "The Master's Tools Will Never Dismantle the Master's House," in *Sister Outsider: Essays and Speeches* (Berkeley, Calif.: Crossing Press, 2007).

19. On Douglass's moments of withholding, see Marianne Noble, "Sympathetic Listening in Frederick Douglass's 'The Heroic Slave' and *My Bondage and My Freedom*," *Studies in American Fiction* 34, no. 1 (Spring 2006); William L. Andrews, *To Tell a Free Story: The First Century of Afro-American Autobiography, 1760–1865* (Urbana: University of Illinois Press, 1986). On Douglass's interest in embodiment and perspectivalism, see Nick Bromell, "A 'Voice from the Enslaved': The Origins of Frederick Douglass's Political Philosophy," *American Literary History* 23, no. 4 (2011); Robert Fanuzzi, *Abolition's Public Sphere* (Minneapolis: University of Minnesota Press, 2003), xiii–xiv.

20. Stauffer suggests that this period saw a "major shift in cultural and intellectual history—one that moved beyond an understanding of 'character' as fixed and unchanging, based primarily on heredity and social status, toward a highly subjective notion of the self in a state of continuous flux. At the heart of this shift was an effort to reintegrate cultural dichotomies that had long been present in Western culture—those of black and

white, body and soul, sacred and profane, ideal and real, civilization and savagery, and masculine and feminine." Stauffer, *The Black Hearts of Men*, 6–7.

21. The standard studies of this issue now include Andrews, *To Tell a Free Story*; Robert B. Stepto, *From Behind the Veil: A Study of Afro-American Narrative* (Urbana: University of Illinois Press, 1979); Rafia Zafar, *We Wear the Mask: African Americans Write American Literature, 1760–1870* (New York: Columbia University Press, 1997).

22. Stauffer, *The Black Hearts of Men*, 48.

23. Ibid., 49.

24. Saidiya Hartman, *Lose Your Mother: A Journey Along the Atlantic Slave Route* (New York: Farrar, Straus and Giroux, 2007), 4.

25. Arendt, *The Human Condition*, 22–78.

26. As Giorgio Agamben suggests, "In the classical world . . . simple natural life is excluded from the *polis* in the strict sense, and remains confined—as merely reproductive life—to the sphere of the *oikos*, 'home.'" Agamben, *Homo Sacer: Sovereign Power and Bare Life*, trans. Daniel Heller-Roazen (Stanford, Calif.: Stanford University Press, 1998), 2. See also Elizabeth Maddock Dillon, *The Gender of Freedom: Fictions of Liberalism and the Literary Public Sphere* (Stanford, Calif.: Stanford University Press, 2004); Jürgen Habermas, *The Structural Transformation of the Public Sphere: An Inquiry into a Category of Bourgeois Society* (Cambridge, Mass.: MIT Press, 1989). Nancy Bentley usefully glosses Robert Reid-Pharr's reframing of this issue as it pertains to nineteenth-century African Americans. See Bentley, "The Fourth Dimension: Kinlessness and African American Narrative," *Critical Inquiry* 35, Winter (2009): 281. On mid-nineteenth-century accounts of subjectivity predicated on models of interiority, and the pursuit of "human(s) without humanism," see Christopher Castiglia, *Interior States: Institutional Consciousness and the Inner Life of Democracy in the Antebellum United States* (Durham, N.C.: Duke University Press, 2008).

27. Recent studies, such as Anthony Kaye's *Joining Places*, Dylan Penningroth's *The Claims of Kinfolk*, and Katherine Clay Bassard's and Joycelyn Moody's pivotal works on African American spiritual communities, take inspiration from established accounts of how nineteenth-century African America interrupted the genealogical isolation of social death associated with slavery and state-sanctioned racism. From Deborah McDowell's interrogation of Douglass's place in the African American literary canon, to Hazel Carby's attention to how black women refigured womanhood in the nineteenth century, to Hortense Spillers's and Valerie Smith's focus on the centrality of maternal figuration in black writing, to Frances Smith Foster's recovery and theorizing of black writing on love and marriage, the point has been repeatedly made: African American life understood exclusively as the story of triumphant individuals overcoming the enforced isolation of natal alienation (only to become that much more isolated in the carapace of individualism) is black life viewed through a narrowly androcentric aperture onto the past. See Katherine Clay Bassard, *Transforming Scriptures: African American Women Writers and the Bible* (Athens: University of Georgia Press, 2010); Anthony E. Kaye, *Joining Places: Slave Neighborhoods in the Old South* (Chapel Hill: University of North Carolina Press, 2007); Deborah E. McDowell, *"The Changing Same": Black Women's Literature,*

Criticism, and Theory (Bloomington: Indiana University Press, 1995); Joycelyn Moody, *Sentimental Confessions: Spiritual Narratives of Nineteenth-Century African American Women* (Athens: University of Georgia Press, 2001); Dylan C. Penningroth, *The Claims of Kinfolk: African American Property and Community in the Nineteenth-Century South* (Chapel Hill: University of North Carolina Press, 2003); Valerie Smith, *Self-Discovery and Authority in Afro-American Narrative* (Cambridge, Mass.: Harvard University Press, 1987); Valerie Smith, *Not Just Race, Not Just Gender: Black Feminist Readings* (New York: Routledge, 1998); Hortense J. Spillers, *Comparative American Identities: Race, Sex, and Nationality in the Modern Text* (New York: Routledge, 1991); Hortense J. Spillers, *Black, White, and in Color: Essays on American Literature and Culture* (Chicago: University of Chicago Press, 2003).

28. For the emergence of the police power, see Bryan Wagner, *Disturbing the Peace: Black Culture and the Police Power After Slavery* (Cambridge, Mass.: Harvard University Press, 2009). For an authoritative account of how African Americans were subject to surveillance in the register of print culture, see Jeannine DeLombard, *Slavery on Trial: Law, Abolitionism, and Print Culture* (Chapel Hill: University of North Carolina Press, 2007). The costs of abstract personhood under liberal democracy have been treated at length in a variety of studies. Some of the most influential in American literary studies include Russ Castronovo, *Necro Citizenship: Death, Eroticism, and the Public Sphere in the Nineteenth-Century United States* (Durham, N.C.: Duke University Press, 2001); Wai Chee Dimock, *Empire for Liberty: Melville and the Poetics of Individualism* (Princeton: Princeton University Press, 1989); Dana D. Nelson, *National Manhood: Capitalist Citizenship and the Imagined Fraternity of White Men* (Durham, N.C.: Duke University Press, 1998); and Christopher Newfield, *The Emerson Effect: Individualism and Submission in America* (Chicago: University of Chicago Press, 1996).

29. Hazel V. Carby, *Race Men* (Cambridge, Mass.: Harvard University Press, 1998).

30. See also Kenneth Warren's suggestion that much of what goes on in black writing before and after Jim Crow was rendered unintelligible by measuring all black writing as if it sought to answer to the needs of black people living under Jim Crow. See Warren, *What Was African American Literature?* (Cambridge, Mass.: Harvard University Press, 2011).

31. Barbara Johnson, *Persons and Things* (Cambridge, Mass.: Harvard University Press, 2008), 6 (emphasis in original).

32. Ibid, 9.

33. Meredith L. McGill, *American Literature and the Culture of Reprinting, 1834–1853* (Philadelphia: University of Pennsylvania Press, 2003).

Chapter 1

1. Translated by Amandine Lepers-Thornton.

2. Kwame Anthony Appiah, *Cosmopolitanism: Ethics in a World of Strangers* (New York: W. W. Norton, 2006), xviii.

3. Hartman, *Scenes of Subjection*.

4. Frederick Douglass and Philip Sheldon Foner, *The Life and Writings of Frederick Douglass* (New York: International Publishers, 1950).

5. McGill, *American Literature and the Culture of Reprinting*; David Paul Nord, *Communities of Journalism: A History of American Newspapers and Their Readers* (Urbana: University of Illinois Press, 2001).

6. Eve Kosofsky Sedgwick, *Tendencies* (Durham, N.C.: Duke University Press, 1993), 23; Frederick Douglass, *The Frederick Douglass Papers*, ed. John W. Blassingame et al. (New Haven: Yale University Press, 1979–2009), series III, vol. 1, 189.

7. On this issue, see Christopher Looby, *Voicing America: Language, Literary Form, and the Origins of the United States* (Chicago: University of Chicago Press, 1996).

8. Hans Robert Jauss, *Toward an Aesthetic of Reception* (Minneapolis: University of Minnesota Press, 1982); Talal Asad, *Formations of the Secular: Christianity, Islam, Modernity* (Stanford, Calif.: Stanford University Press, 2003), 34.

9. William Lloyd Garrison, *Thoughts on African Colonization: Or an Impartial Exhibition of the Doctrines, Principles and Purposes of the American Colonization Society. Together with the Resolutions, Addresses, and Remonstrances of the Free People of Color* (Boston: Garrison and Knapp, 1832), iii.

10. Ibid., I: 8.

11. Ibid., 12.

12. Ibid., 4.

13. Ibid., II: 10.

14. Ibid., 9.

15. The Colored National Convention's *Proceedings* mistakenly identifies Part II as the first part of Garrison's *Thoughts*.

16. Garrison, *Thoughts on African Colonization*, II: 4.

17. Ibid., 4–5.

18. William Yates, *Rights of Colored Men to Suffrage, Citizenship and Trial by Jury: Being a Book of Facts, Arguments and Authorities, Historical Notices and Sketches of Debates—with Notes* (Philadelphia: Merrihew and Gunn, 1838), iii–iv.

19. Ibid., 50 (emphasis in original).

20. Ibid.

21. Ibid., 50–51 (emphasis in original).

22. *The Papers of Andrew Jackson*, ed. Harold D. Moser et al., vol. III, 1814–15 (Knoxville: University of Tennessee Press, 1991), 116.

23. In Caryn Cossé Bell, *Revolution, Romanticism, and the Afro-Creole Protest Tradition in Louisiana, 1718–1868* (Baton Rouge: Louisiana State University Press, 1997), 48.

24. *The Papers of Andrew Jackson*, vol. III, 144.

25. Ibid., 145.

26. Bell, *Revolution, Romanticism, and the Afro-Creole Protest Tradition*, 37.

27. Ibid., 165.

28. Papers of Andrew Jackson [Microfilm], Library of Congress, 1967, roll 12.

29. Hartman, *Scenes of Subjection*, 5.

30. Bell, *Revolution, Romanticism, and the Afro-Creole Protest Tradition*, 18. See also Kimberly S. Hanger, *Bounded Lives, Bounded Places: Free Black Society in Colonial New Orleans, 1769–1803* (Durham, N.C.: Duke University Press, 1997).

31. Hartman, *Scenes of Subjection*, 133.

Chapter 2

1. Fraser and Honneth, *Redistribution or Recognition?*, 10.

2. Ibid., 27–33.

3. It has become standard to distinguish Douglass's *Narrative* from his later writing. See Bromell, "A 'Voice from the Enslaved,'" 698–99. See also Stauffer, *The Black Hearts of Men*, 45. Andrews argues that in Douglass's later autobiographies, as in African American life writing more generally, "[s]elfhood became increasingly identified with individuality. Prevailing norms for judging propriety in behavior, speech, and writing came to be judged according to the personal standards of some narrative 'other.' This other was a good deal less solicitous of the white reader's empathy and trust than earlier autobiographical personae had been. Instead of appealing to the reader's moral values and literary expectations, this other tried to alienate the reader from these kinds of supports, thus disorienting but also freeing him or her to participate in a new kind of social and psychological agenda for the reading of black autobiography." Andrews, *To Tell a Free Story*, 2. I follow these scholars in arguing that something significant changes after the 1845 *Narrative*. The specificity of my claim relates to the nature of that change.

4. Bentley, "The Fourth Dimension," 281. On the exchangeable nature of host and guest in classical culture, see David Simpson, *Romanticism and the Question of the Stranger* (Chicago: University of Chicago Press, 2013), 23.

5. Hartman, *Scenes of Subjection*, 115–24.

6. Michael Warner offers a succinct review of stranger personae in a discussion of the origins of publics and counterpublics: "In many ways, the unending process of redefinition [of what it means to be a public]—always difficult and always conflicted—can be strategic, conscious, even artful. Much of the art of writing, or of performing in other media, lies in the practical knowledge that there are always many different ways of addressing a public, that each decision of form, style, and procedure carries hazards and costs in the kind of public it can define. The temptation is to think of publics as something we make, through individual heroism and creative inspiration or through common goodwill. Much of the process, however, necessarily remains invisible to consciousness and to reflective agency. The making of a public requires conditions that range from the very general—such as the organization of media, ideologies of reading, institutions of circulation, text genres—to the particular rhetorics of texts." Warner, *Publics and Counterpublics*, 14. See also Andrews, *To Tell a Free Story*, 17.

7. Douglass, *Frederick Douglass Papers*, II: 2, 195.

8. Karen Halttunen, *Confidence Men and Painted Women: A Study of Middle-Class Culture in America, 1830–1870* (New Haven, Conn.: Yale University Press, 1982), 34–35.

9. Bell, *Revolution, Romanticism, and the Afro-Creole Protest Tradition*; Hanger, *Bounded Lives, Bounded Places*; Shirley Elizabeth Thompson, *Exiles at Home: The Struggle to Become American in Creole New Orleans* (Cambridge, Mass.: Harvard University Press, 2009).

10. Jeffrey Alexander, "Rethinking Strangeness: From Structures in Space to Discourses in Civil Society," *Thesis Eleven* (November 2004): 93.

11. Bentley's account of kinlessness suggests the complexity of the stranger statuses being disbursed during this period. Bentley proposes that "[b]y [Douglass's] own testimony, his brothers and sisters are in fact a distinct kind of stranger and thus kin and strangers at once. Yet there is no word for this species of kin relation. Douglass can only describe it by marking its distance from conventional denotations of proper usage, opening a gap or space of knowing for knowledge that lies outside normative definitions of kinship." Bentley, "The Fourth Dimension," 276. Douglass's perspective points as well to the distance of his relationship with his brothers and sisters from "normative definitions" of strangerhood.

12. Andrews would suggest that "autobiography answered a felt need for a rhetorical mode that would conduct the battle against racism and slavery on grounds other than those already occupied by pro- and antislavery polemics." Andrews, *To Tell a Free Story*, 5. I am proposing that when Douglass and other African American life writers summoned the language of strangerhood, their comments ended up being keyed to those very same polemics.

13. Although this list is far from comprehensive, the following texts explicitly summon the Bible's discourse on strangerhood at one or more points in their unfolding: *The Light and Truth of Slavery: Aaron's History* (Worcester, Mass.: n.p., 1843); Charles Ball and Thomas Fisher, *Fifty Years in Chains; or, the Life of an American Slave* (New York: H. Dayton, 1858); William Wells Brown, *Clotel, or, the President's Daughter: A Narrative of Slave Life in the United States* (Boston: Bedford/St. Martin's, 2000); William Craft and Ellen Craft, *Running a Thousand Miles for Freedom; or, the Escape of William and Ellen Craft from Slavery* (Miami: Mnemosyne, 1969); Benjamin Drew, *A North-Side View of Slavery: The Refugee; or, the Narratives of Fugitive Slaves in Canada Related by Themselves; with an Account of the History and Condition of the Colored Population of Upper Canada* (Boston: John P. Jewett, 1856); Ellwood Griest, *John and Mary; or, the Fugitive Slaves, a Tale of South-Eastern Pennsylvania* (Lancaster, Pa.: Inquirer Printing and Publishing Company, 1873); Josiah Henson and Harriet Beecher Stowe, *Truth Stranger Than Fiction: Father Henson's Story of His Own Life* (Boston: John P. Jewett, 1858); Harriet A. Jacobs, *Incidents in the Life of a Slave Girl* (Boston: Pub. for the author, 1861); Daniel H. Peterson, *The Looking-Glass: Being a True Report and Narrative of the Life, Travels and Labors of the Rev. Daniel H. Peterson, a Colored Clergyman; Embracing a Period of Time from the Year 1812 to 1854, and Including His Visit to Western Africa* (New York: Wright, 1854); Benjamin F. Prentiss and Boyrereau Brinch, *The Blind African Slave, or, Memoirs of Boyrereau Brinch Nick-Named Jeffrey Brace* (St. Albans, Vt.: Harry Whitney, 1810); Mary Prince, *The History of Mary Prince, a West India Slave*, 3rd ed. (n.p., 1831); Peter Randolph, *From Slave Cabin to the Pulpit* (Boston: J. H. Earle, 1893); Moses Roper and Thomas Price, *A Narrative of the Adventures and*

Escape of Moses Roper, from American Slavery, 4th ed. (London: Harvey and Darton, 1840); Thomas Smallwood and Richard Almonte, *A Narrative of Thomas Smallwood (Coloured Man)* (Toronto: Mercury, 2000); Bethany Veney, *The Narrative of Bethany Veney, a Slave Woman* (Worcester, Mass.: n.p., 1889).

14. La Roy Sunderland, *The Testimony of God Against Slavery, or a Collection of Passages from the Bible, Which Show the Sin of Holding Property in Man* (Boston: Webster and Southard, 1835), 25.

15. As David Brion Davis explains, the proslavery interpretation of the children of strangers passage was not limited to Protestants. Feeling compelled to weigh in on the issue of slavery, while offering no official Jewish position on the question of slavery, several rabbinical scholars offered assessments that endorsed the proslavery view of Leviticus. Davis, *Slavery and Human Progress* (New York: Oxford University Press, 1984), 82–101.

16. Thornton Stringfellow, *A Brief Examination of Scripture Testimony on the Institution of Slavery, in an Essay* (Richmond, Va.: Religious Herald, 1841), 8 (emphasis in original).

17. George Bourne, *A Condensed Anti-Slavery Bible Argument* (New York: S. W. Benedict, 1845), 46.

18. Ibid., 47.

19. Mark A. Noll, *America's God: From Jonathan Edwards to Abraham Lincoln* (New York: Oxford University Press, 2002), 381.

20. Ibid., 397.

21. The slave narrative's burdensome relation to facticity has been amply documented. Andrews offers a definitive account of this issue. See Andrews, *To Tell a Free Story*, 265–91. See also John Sekora, "Black Message/White Envelope: Genre, Authenticity, and Authority in the Antebellum Slave Narrative," *Callaloo: A Journal of African American and African Arts and Letters* 10, no. 3 (1987).

22. Douglass, *Frederick Douglass Papers*, II: 2, 52.

23. Ibid., 74.

24. Ibid., 32.

25. According to Andrews, "When we find a gap in a slave narrator's objective reportage of the facts of slavery, or a lapse in his prepossessing self-image, we must pay special attention. These deviations may indicate either a momentary loss of narrative control or a deliberate effort by the narrator to grapple with aspects of his or her personality that have been repressed out of deference to or fear of the dominant culture." Andrews, *To Tell a Free Story*, 8.

26. Ibid., 65.

27. The long international history of the politics of sentiment is usefully anatomized in Terry Eagleton, *Trouble with Strangers: A Study of Ethics* (Chichester, U.K.: Wiley-Blackwell, 2009). Sympathy in the United States has been subjected to exhaustive examination. A good starting point is Shirley C. Samuels, ed., *The Culture of Sentiment: Race, Gender, and Sentimentality in Nineteenth-Century America* (New York: Oxford University Press, 1992). For a useful discussion of empathy as it pertains to American abolitionism, see Stauffer, *The Black Hearts of Men*, 39.

28. Douglass, *Frederick Douglass Papers,* II: 2, 5.

29. Ibid., 311.

30. Warner, *Publics and Counterpublics,* 75–76.

31. Andrews, *To Tell a Free Story,* 56.

32. Douglass, *Frederick Douglass Papers,* II: 2, 206.

33. Caroline Levander, "Witness and Participant: Frederick Douglass's Child," *Studies in American Fiction* 33, no. 2 (Autumn 2005): 183.

34. Rooney, "A Semiprivate Room," 128.

35. For a full account of Smith on with-ness, see Baucom, *Specters of the Atlantic.*

36. Bentley, "The Fourth Dimension," 283.

37. Ibid., 282.

38. Douglass, *Frederick Douglass Papers,* II: 2, 206.

39. Ibid., 207.

40. Ibid.

41. Fanuzzi explains how the nostalgia that characterized the Garrisonians contributed to this problem. Fanuzzi, *Abolition's Public Sphere,* 16–23.

Chapter 3

1. Translated by Amandine Lepers-Thornton.

2. Fabre, "The New Orleans Press," 33.

3. Chris Michaelides, *Paroles D'honneur: Écrits de Créoles de couleur Néo-Orleanais, 1837–1872,* Les Cahiers du Tintamarre (Shreveport, La.: Les Éditions Tintamarre, 2004), 167. Translated by Amandine Lepers-Thornton.

4. See Thompson, *Exiles at Home;* Thomas F. Haddox, *Fears and Fascinations: Representing Catholicism in the American South* (New York: Fordham University Press, 2005); Bell, *Revolution, Romanticism, and the Afro-Creole Protest Tradition.* For a critical history of the framing of New Orleans as a historical exception, see Barbara J. Eckstein, *Sustaining New Orleans: Literature, Local Memory, and the Fate of a City* (New York: Routledge, 2006).

5. Floyd Cheung, "*Les Cenelles* and Quadroon Balls: 'Hidden Transcripts' of Resistance and Domination in New Orleans, 1803–1845," *Southern Literary Journal* 29 (Spring 1997); Thomas F. Haddox, "The 'Nous' of Southern Catholic Quadroons: Racial, Ethnic, and Religious Identity in *Les Cenelles," American Literature* 73 (December 2001).

6. Eliza Richards's work on "gender and the poetics of reception" significantly informs my thinking on this issue. See *Gender and the Poetics of Reception in Poe's Circle* (Cambridge: Cambridge University Press, 2004).

7. In his discussion of the dividuated personal pronoun, Marshall Sahlins writes: "The problem here is not just the category mistake of rendering the relationships of kinship as the attributes of singular persons. The problem is that kin persons are not the only kind who are multiple, divisible, and relationally constructed. In this connection, not enough attention has been paid to Alan Rumsey's demonstration—following Émile Benveniste and Greg Urban on the meaning and the use of personal pronouns—that the capacities of partibility and hierarchy (or the encompassment of others) are general

conditions of humans in language. 'Moments of both encompassment and partibility are inherent in language,' Rumsey writes, 'corresponding to two distinct dimensions in which the pronouns are meaningful (the "direct indexical" and "anaphoric").' Using Polynesian as well as Melanesian examples, Rumsey shows how in a single discourse the shifting frames of reference of the pronoun 'I' can refer alternately to the current (partible) speaker, the collective kin group to which he belongs, or the long-dead chief who heroically instantiates the group. Of course, this does not mean these capacities are necessarily enacted in social practice, as in the modes of 'dividual' persons and the 'kinship I.' Then again, as a general condition of possibility, partible and relational identities may characterize persons who are not 'dividual' kin persons—but perhaps even bourgeois individuals like us." Sahlins, *What Kinship Is—and Is Not* (Chicago: University of Chicago Press, 2013), 27.

8. Gates, "Tradition: From the Seen to the Told," 25.

9. Jerah Johnson, "*Les Cenelles*: What's in a Name?," *Louisiana History* 31, no. 4 (Winter 1990): 407–10.

10. Armand Lanusse, ed., *Les Cenelles: Choix de poésies indigènes* (Shreveport, La.: Tintamarre, 2003), 3. Translated by Amandine Lepers-Thornton.

11. Alex Preminger and T. V. F. Brogan, eds., *The New Princeton Encyclopedia of Poetry and Poetics* (Princeton, N.J.: Princeton University Press, 1993), 82. See also Virginia Jackson and Yopie Prins, eds., *The Lyric Theory Reader: A Critical Anthology* (Baltimore, Md.: Johns Hopkins University Press, 2014).

12. Jonathan D. Culler, *The Pursuit of Signs: Semiotics, Literature, Deconstruction* (Ithaca, N.Y.: Cornell University Press, 1981), 61.

13. Ibid., 157.

14. Norman R. Shapiro and M. Lynn Weiss, eds., *Creole Echoes: The Francophone Poetry of Nineteenth-Century Louisiana* (Urbana: University of Illinois Press, 2004), 216–17.

15. Virginia Walker Jackson, *Dickinson's Misery: A Theory of Lyric Reading* (Princeton, N.J.: Princeton University Press, 2005), 159.

16. J. Douglas Kneale, *Romantic Aversions: Aftermaths of Classicism in Wordsworth and Coleridge* (Montreal: McGill-Queen's University Press, 1999), 17.

17. Régine Latortue and Gleason Rex Adams, eds., *Les Cenelles: A Collection of Poems of Creole Writers of the Early Nineteenth Century* (Boston: G. K. Hall, 1979), 4–5. Unless otherwise noted, the original French transcriptions and English translations of materials from *Les Cenelles* are from this edition.

18. Ibid., 6–7.

19. Ibid., 16–17.

20. Ibid., 26–27.

21. See Erving Goffman, *Behavior in Public Places: Notes on the Social Organization of Gatherings* (New York: Free Press of Glencoe, 1963), 83–84: "When persons are mutually present and not involved together in conversation or other focused interaction, it is possible for one person to stare openly and fixedly at others, gleaning what he can about them

while frankly expressing on his face his response to what he sees—for example, the 'hate stare' that a Southern white sometimes gratuitously gives to Negroes walking past him. It is also possible for one person to treat others as if they were not there at all, as objects not worthy of a glance, let alone close scrutiny. Moreover, it is possible for the individual, by his staring or his 'not seeing,' to alter his own appearance hardly at all in consequence of the presence of the others. Here we have 'nonperson' treatment; it may be seen in our society in the way we sometimes treat children, servants, Negroes, and mental patients.

"Currently, in our society, this kind of treatment is to be contrasted with the kind generally felt to be more proper in most situations, which will here be called 'civil inattention.' What seems to be involved is that one gives to another enough visual notice to demonstrate that one appreciates that the other is present (and that one admits openly to having seen him), while at the next moment withdrawing one's attention from him so as to express that he does not constitute a target of special curiosity or design."

22. Latortue and Adams, *Les Cenelles*, 48–49.

23. Ibid., 50–51.

24. Ibid.

25. Robert Darnton, *Poetry and the Police: Communication Networks in Eighteenth-Century Paris* (Cambridge, Mass.: Harvard University Press, 2010), 4.

26. Latortue and Adams, *Les Cenelles*, xxxvi–xxxvii.

27. Ibid.

28. Ibid., 17.

29. Ibid., 28–35.

Chapter 4

1. Jacques Rancière, *Proletarian Nights: The Workers' Dream in Nineteenth-Century France*, trans. John Drury (New York: Verso, 2012), xii.

2. Ibid., xi.

3. Fraser and Honneth, *Redistribution or Recognition?*, 10.

4. Nancy Fraser, *Scales of Justice: Reimagining Political Space in a Globalizing World* (New York: Columbia University Press, 2008), 19.

5. Madhu Dubey, "Speculative Fictions of Slavery," *American Literature* 82, no. 4 (December 2010): 779.

6. Katherine Clay Bassard, "Imagining Other Worlds: Race, Gender, and the 'Power Line' in Edward P. Jones's *The Known World*," *African American Review* 42, nos. 3/4 (Fall–Winter 2008): 407–9.

7. Bassard argues that "Jones shifts the ground of literary representation from the question of historical 'accuracy' and 'authenticity' and onto the terrain of language. This re-mapping away from the sociohistorical and onto the linguistic through the mistrust of historical documents, data, and the like demonstrates the powerlessness of written texts to yield what it is we really want most to know about the past: the complexities of relationships, emotions and motivations that make up the human experience." Ibid., 408.

8. For one of the most compelling accounts of how to engage the archive's absences so as to tell black and modern world history, see Baucom, *Specters of the Atlantic*.

9. Harper revises standard accounts of postmodernity by suggesting that one of the key features associated with the experience of postmodernity—decentered subjectivity—defined life for minority subjects well before the technological advances often associated with the advent of the decentered subject. Harper proposes in essence that postmodernity represents the extension of minority experiences of modernity to a greater number of majority peoples. In this reading the experience of minoritized subjects constitutes the chronological precursor to the experience of postmodernity, and attending to the conditions of minority illuminates the condition of postmodernity. Phillip Brian Harper, *Framing the Margins: The Social Logic of Postmodern Culture* (New York: Oxford University Press, 1994).

10. Susan V. Donaldson, "Telling Forgotten Stories of Slavery in the Postmodern South," *The Southern Literary Journal* 40, no. 2 (Spring 2008): 273.

11. Ibid. Marnie Hughes-Warrington writes convincingly of the long-standing African American interest in universal history.

12. For a more detailed account of the sort of historical writing being done in the nineteenth century, see Stephen G. Hall, *A Faithful Account of the Race: African American Historical Writing in Nineteenth-Century America* (Chapel Hill: University of North Carolina Press, 2009), 5–6.

13. György Lukács, *History and Class Consciousness: Studies in Marxist Dialectics* (London: Merlin, 1971).

14. For a different account of thingness in *The Known World*, see Sarah Mahurin Mutter, "'Such a Poor Word for a Wondrous Thing': Thingness and the Recovery of the Human in *The Known World*," *The Southern Literary Journal* 43, no. 2 (Spring 2011).

15. John Ernest, *Liberation Historiography: African American Writers and the Challenge of History, 1794–1861* (Chapel Hill: University of North Carolina Press, 2004), 25.

16. Ibid., 5.

17. Ibid., 7. For a cogent summary of recent accounts of unrepresentability in the context of the Holocaust, see Karl Schoonover, *Brutal Vision: The Neorealist Body in Postwar Italian Cinema* (Minneapolis: University of Minnesota Press, 2012), 1–3.

18. Ernest, *Liberation Historiography*, 22.

19. Ibid., 2.

20. Ibid., 10. As Dubey points out, Ernest's and Hall's claims can be seen to rewrite for African American criticism much more familiar writings on history such as those of Hayden White. According to Dubey, "White contends that, for 'subordinant, emergent, or resisting social groups,' the realist imperative that has characterized history since its inception as a discipline can only appear as the crowning element of the very ideology they wish to oppose. Effective opposition must therefore be based on a refusal of realism, on 'a conception of the historical record as being not a window through which the past "as it really was" can be apprehended,' but rather as an

impediment to proper understanding of the past." Dubey, "Speculative Fictions of Slavery," 784.

21. Hall, *A Faithful Account of the Race*, 3. Hall convincingly argues that this emphasis on the nontextual has its limitations. As he shows, "Central to the articulation of a black historical voice was textual production, especially extended, book-length works, and its influence on and connection to the subsequent scholarly development of the field." Ibid., 4.

22. Dubey, "Speculative Fictions of Slavery," 784.

23. Ibid., 780.

24. Ibid., 785–86.

25. Ibid., 784.

26. Edward P. Jones, *The Known World* (New York: Amistad, 2003), 384.

27. Ibid., 386.

28. Paul Christian Jones, "Copying What the Master Had Written: Frederick Douglass's 'The Heroic Slave' and the Southern Historical Romance," *Southern Quarterly* 38, no. 4 (Summer 2000).

29. György Lukács, *The Historical Novel* (Boston: Beacon, 1963), 35.

30. Ibid., 36.

31. Noble, "Sympathetic Listening," 65.

32. Hall, *A Faithful Account of the Race*, 6–7.

33. Ibid., 11.

34. Ibid., 14.

Chapter 5

1. Minutes of the Nantucket Atheneum, Nantucket Atheneum, Nantucket, Mass.

2. Register for Free Colored Persons Entitled to Remain in the State, City Archives, New Orleans Public Library. For the translations cited below, see Judy Riffel, *New Orleans Register of Free People of Color, 1840–1864* (Baton Rouge: Le Comité des Archives, 2008).

3. Douglass, *Frederick Douglass Papers*, II: 2, 205.

4. The current Nantucket Atheneum was built in 1847, after Nantucket's Great Fire of 1846, in which much of the downtown area was destroyed. Accounts of the earlier building suggest the description provided here. For a more detailed account of the Atheneum buildings and their histories, see Betsy Tyler, *The Nantucket Atheneum: A History* (Nantucket, Mass.: Nantucket Preservation Trust, 2009).

5. Douglass, *Frederick Douglass Papers*, II: 2, 37.

6. Ibid., 38.

7. In this respect, America's atheneums blurred the already thin line between the lecture hall and the library. For a discussion of the American lyceum movement, see Carl Bode, *The American Lyceum: Town Meeting of the Mind* (New York: Oxford University Press, 1956). For a more general account of how libraries came to play a central role in the constitution of nineteenth-century American culture, see Thomas Augst and

Kenneth E. Carpenter, eds., *Institutions of Reading: The Social Life of Libraries in the United States* (Amherst: University of Massachusetts Press, 2007).

8. Douglass, *Frederick Douglass Papers*, II: 2, 214.

9. Tyler, *The Nantucket Atheneum*, 3.

10. Ibid., 13.

11. Ibid., 14.

12. *Catalogue of the Library of Nantucket Atheneum: With the Bylaws of the Institution* (Nantucket, Mass., 1841), v.

13. This resentment preceded Douglass's visit to the island, and it was exacerbated in the year that followed. See the debate over John A. Collins's lectures on the island that appears in *The Islander*. One of Collins's more notable roles was as the man who told Douglass to stick to the facts and leave the philosophy to his white sponsors. "For the Islander," *The Islander*, March 26, 1842.

14. The minutes of the society include a detailed account of its transformation. "Philosophical Institute of Nantucket Minutes" (Nantucket, Mass.: Nantucket Historical Association, 1826–32).

15. William S. McFeely, *Frederick Douglass* (New York: W. W. Norton, 1991), 89–90. Although McFeely also suggests that Douglass did not speak at the Atheneum that night, he would later recant that claim in a public lecture on Nantucket.

16. The Nantucket school desegregation controversy is treated in Barbara Linebaugh White, *The African School and the Integration of Nantucket Public Schools, 1825–1847* (Boston: Boston University, 1978).

17. Although there is still some debate over whether this closure happened or was merely discussed, records from the island suggest that it did. See Renée L. Bergland, *Maria Mitchell and the Sexing of Science: An Astronomer Among the American Romantics* (Boston: Beacon, 2008); White, *The African School*. See also Nathaniel Barney, "Letter Book of Nathaniel Barney," in *Nathaniel Barney (1792–1869)* (Nantucket, Mass.: Nantucket Historical Association, 1845).

18. Barbara Linebaugh White, "The Integration of Nantucket Public Schools," *Historic Nantucket* 40, no. 3 (Fall 1992).

19. Mary Beaudry and Ellen Berkland, "Archaeology of the African Meeting House on Nantucket," in *Archaeology of Atlantic Africa and the African Diaspora*, ed. Akinwumi Ogundiran and Toyin Falola (Bloomington: Indiana University Press, 2007), 405.

20. Ibid., 411.

21. Ibid., 408.

22. Ibid., 400.

23. Ibid., 406, 408.

Epilogue

1. Rufus W. Griswold, *The Prose Writers of America*, 3rd ed. (Philadelphia: Carey and Hart, 1849), 5.

2. Ibid., 6.

3. Rufus W. Griswold, *The Poets and Poetry of America* (Philadelphia: Carey and Hart, 1845), v.

4. Rufus W. Griswold, *The Female Poets of America* (Philadelphia: Carey and Hart, 1849), 9, 8.

5. Ibid., 8.

6. Griswold, *Prose Writers*, 5.

7. Griswold, *Poets and Poetry of America*, v.

8. Ibid., xiii.

9. Ibid.

10. Bentley, "The Fourth Dimension," 282.

11. Ellen Rooney, *Seductive Reasoning: Pluralism as the Problematic of Contemporary Literary Theory* (Ithaca, N.Y.: Cornell University Press, 1989).

BIBLIOGRAPHY

Agamben, Giorgio. *Homo Sacer: Sovereign Power and Bare Life*. Translated by Daniel Heller-Roazen. Stanford, Calif.: Stanford University Press, 1998.

Alexander, Jeffrey. "Rethinking Strangeness: From Structures in Space to Discourses in Civil Society." *Thesis Eleven* (November 2004): 87–104.

Ames, Julius Ruben. *"Liberty."* N.p., 1837.

Andrews, William L. *To Tell a Free Story: The First Century of Afro-American Autobiography, 1760–1865*. Urbana: University of Illinois Press, 1986.

Appiah, Kwame Anthony. *Cosmopolitanism: Ethics in a World of Strangers*. New York: W. W. Norton, 2006.

Arendt, Hannah. *The Human Condition*. 2nd ed. Chicago: University of Chicago Press, 1998.

Asad, Talal. *Formations of the Secular: Christianity, Islam, Modernity*. Stanford, Calif.: Stanford University Press, 2003.

Augst, Thomas, and Kenneth E. Carpenter, eds. *Institutions of Reading: The Social Life of Libraries in the United States*. Amherst: University of Massachusetts Press, 2007.

Baker, Houston A. *Blues, Ideology, and Afro-American Literature: A Vernacular Theory*. Chicago: University of Chicago Press, 1984.

Ball, Charles, and Thomas Fisher. *Fifty Years in Chains; or, the Life of an American Slave*. New York: H. Dayton, 1858.

Barney, Nathaniel. "Letter Book of Nathaniel Barney." Nathaniel Barney (1792–1869). Nantucket, Mass.: Nantucket Historical Association, 1845.

Bassard, Katherine Clay. "Imagining Other Worlds: Race, Gender, and the 'Power Line' in Edward P. Jones's *The Known World*." *African American Review* 42, nos. 3/4 (Fall–Winter 2008): 407–19.

———. *Transforming Scriptures: African American Women Writers and the Bible*. Athens: University of Georgia Press, 2010.

Baucom, Ian. *Specters of the Atlantic: Finance Capital, Slavery and the Philosophy of History*. Durham, N.C.: Duke University Press, 2005.

Beaudry, Mary, and Ellen Berkland. "Archaeology of the African Meeting House on Nantucket." In *Archaeology of Atlantic Africa and the African Diaspora*, edited by Akinwumi Ogundiran and Toyin Falola, 395–412. Bloomington: Indiana University Press, 2007.

Bell, Caryn Cossé. *Revolution, Romanticism, and the Afro-Creole Protest Tradition in Louisiana, 1718–1868*. Baton Rouge: Louisiana State University Press, 1997.

Bentley, Nancy. "The Fourth Dimension: Kinlessness and African American Narrative." *Critical Inquiry* 35 (Winter 2009): 270–92.

Bergland, Renée L. *Maria Mitchell and the Sexing of Science: An Astronomer Among the American Romantics*. Boston: Beacon, 2008.

Best, Stephen Michael. *The Fugitive's Properties: Law and the Poetics of Possession*. Chicago: University of Chicago Press, 2004.

Bode, Carl. *The American Lyceum: Town Meeting of the Mind*. New York: Oxford University Press, 1956.

Bogues, Anthony. "And What About the Human?: Freedom, Human Emancipation, and the Radical Imagination." *boundary 2* 39, no. 3 (2012): 29–46.

Bourne, George. *A Condensed Anti-Slavery Bible Argument*. Printed by S. W. Benedict, 1845.

Bromell, Nick. "A 'Voice from the Enslaved': The Origins of Frederick Douglass's Political Philosophy." *American Literary History* 23, no. 4 (2011): 687–723.

Brown, William Wells. *Clotel, or, the President's Daughter: A Narrative of Slave Life in the United States*. Boston: Bedford/St. Martin's, 2000.

Carby, Hazel. *Race Men*. Cambridge, Mass.: Harvard University Press, 2000.

———. *Reconstructing Womanhood: The Emergence of the Afro-American Woman Novelist*. New York: Oxford University Press, 1987.

Castiglia, Christopher. *Interior States: Institutional Consciousness and the Inner Life of Democracy in the Antebellum United States*. Durham, N.C.: Duke University Press, 2008.

Castronovo, Russ. *Necro Citizenship: Death, Eroticism, and the Public Sphere in the Nineteenth-Century United States*. Durham, N.C.: Duke University Press, 2001.

Catalogue of the Nantucket Atheneum: With the Bylaws of the Institution. Nantucket, Mass., 1841.

Cheung, Floyd. "*Les Cenelles* and Quadroon Balls: 'Hidden Transcripts' of Resistance and Domination in New Orleans, 1803–1845." *Southern Literary Journal* 29 (Spring 1997): 5–16.

Colbert, Soyica Diggs. "'When I Die, I Won't Stay Dead': The Future of the Human in Suzan-Lori Parks's *The Death of the Last Black Man in the Whole Entire World*." *boundary 2* 39, no. 3 (2012): 191–220.

Craft, William, and Ellen Craft. *Running a Thousand Miles for Freedom; or, the Escape of William and Ellen Craft from Slavery*. Miami: Mnemosyne, 1969.

Culler, Jonathan D. *The Pursuit of Signs: Semiotics, Literature, Deconstruction*. Ithaca, N.Y.: Cornell University Press, 1981.

Darnton, Robert. *Poetry and the Police: Communication Networks in Eighteenth-Century Paris*. Cambridge, Mass.: Harvard University Press, 2010.

Davis, David Brion. *Slavery and Human Progress*. New York: Oxford University Press, 1984.

DeLombard, Jeannine. *In the Shadow of the Gallows: Race, Crime, and American Civic Identity*. Philadelphia: University of Pennsylvania Press, 2012.

———. *Slavery on Trial: Law, Abolitionism, and Print Culture*. Chapel Hill: University of North Carolina Press, 2007.

Dillon, Elizabeth Maddock. *The Gender of Freedom: Fictions of Liberalism and the Literary Public Sphere*. Stanford, Calif.: Stanford University Press, 2004.

Dimock, Wai Chee. *Empire for Liberty: Melville and the Poetics of Individualism*. Princeton, N.J.: Princeton University Press, 1989.

Donaldson, Susan V. "Telling Forgotten Stories of Slavery in the Postmodern South." *The Southern Literary Journal* 40, no. 2 (Spring 2008): 267–83.

Douglass, Frederick. *The Frederick Douglass Papers*. Ed. John W. Blassingame et al. New Haven: Yale University Press, 1979–2009.

Douglass, Frederick, and Philip Sheldon Foner. *The Life and Writings of Frederick Douglass*. New York: International Publishers, 1950.

Douglass, Frederick, Philip Sheldon Foner, and Yuval Taylor. *Frederick Douglass: Selected Speeches and Writings*. Chicago: Lawrence Hill, 1999.

Drew, Benjamin. *A North-Side View of Slavery: The Refugee; or, the Narratives of Fugitive Slaves in Canada Related by Themselves; with an Account of the History and Condition of the Colored Population of Upper Canada*. Boston: John P. Jewett, 1856.

Dubey, Madhu. "Speculative Fictions of Slavery." *American Literature* 82, no. 4 (December 2010): 779–805.

Eagleton, Terry. *Trouble with Strangers: A Study of Ethics*. Chichester, U.K.: Wiley-Blackwell, 2009.

Eckstein, Barbara J. *Sustaining New Orleans: Literature, Local Memory, and the Fate of a City*. New York: Routledge, 2006.

Ernest, John. *Liberation Historiography: African American Writers and the Challenge of History, 1794–1861*. Chapel Hill: University of North Carolina Press, 2004.

Fabre, Michel. "The New Orleans Press and French-Language Literature by Creoles of Color." In *Multilingual America: Transnationalism, Ethnicity, and the Language of American Literature*, edited by Werner Sollors, 29–49. New York: New York University Press, 1998.

Fanuzzi, Robert. *Abolition's Public Sphere*. Minneapolis: University of Minnesota Press, 2003.

"For the Islander." *The Islander*, March 26, 1842.

Foster, Frances Smith. *Love and Marriage in Early African America*. Hanover, N.H.: University Press of New England, 2008.

Fraser, Nancy. *Scales of Justice: Reimagining Political Space in a Globalizing World*. New York: Columbia University Press, 2008.

Fraser, Nancy, and Axel Honneth. *Redistribution or Recognition? A Political-Philosophical Exchange*. Translated by Joel Golb, James Ingraham, and Christian Wilke. New York: Verso, 2003.

Garrison, William Lloyd. *Thoughts on African Colonization: Or an Impartial Exhibition of the Doctrines, Principles and Purposes of the American Colonization Society. Together with the Resolutions, Addresses, and Remonstrances of the Free People of Color.* Boston: Garrison and Knapp, 1832.

Gates, Henry Louis, Jr. "Tradition: From the Seen to the Told." In *Afro-American Literary Study in the 1990s*, edited by Houston A. Baker and Patricia Redmond, 14–38. Chicago: University of Chicago Press, 1989.

Gilroy, Paul. *Against Race: Imagining Political Culture Beyond the Color Line.* Cambridge, Mass.: Harvard University Press, 2000.

Glissant, Édouard. *Poetics of Relation.* Translated by Betsy Wing. Ann Arbor: University of Michigan Press, 1997.

Goffman, Erving. *Behavior in Public Places: Notes on the Social Organization of Gatherings.* New York: Free Press of Glencoe, 1963.

Griest, Ellwood. *John and Mary; or, the Fugitive Slaves, a Tale of South-Eastern Pennsylvania.* Lancaster, Pa.: Inquirer Printing and Publishing Company, 1873.

Griswold, Rufus W. *The Female Poets of America.* Philadelphia: Carey and Hart, 1849.

———. *The Poets and Poetry of America.* Philadelphia: Carey and Hart, 1845.

———. *The Prose Writers of America.* 3rd ed. Philadelphia: Carey and Hart, 1849.

Habermas, Jürgen. *The Structural Transformation of the Public Sphere: An Inquiry into a Category of Bourgeois Society.* Cambridge, Mass.: MIT Press, 1989.

Haddox, Thomas F. *Fears and Fascinations: Representing Catholicism in the American South.* 1st ed. New York: Fordham University Press, 2005.

———. "The 'Nous' of Southern Catholic Quadroons: Racial, Ethnic, and Religious Identity in *Les Cenelles.*" *American Literature* 73 (December 2001): 757–78.

Hall, Stephen G. *A Faithful Account of the Race: African American Historical Writing in Nineteenth-Century America.* Chapel Hill: University of North Carolina Press, 2009.

Halttunen, Karen. *Confidence Men and Painted Women: A Study of Middle-Class Culture in America, 1830–1870.* New Haven, Conn.: Yale University Press, 1982.

Hanger, Kimberly S. *Bounded Lives, Bounded Places: Free Black Society in Colonial New Orleans, 1769–1803.* Durham, N.C.: Duke University Press, 1997.

Harper, Phillip Brian. *Framing the Margins: The Social Logic of Postmodern Culture.* New York: Oxford University Press, 1994.

Hartman, Saidiya. *Lose Your Mother: A Journey Along the Atlantic Slave Route.* New York: Farrar, Straus and Giroux, 2007.

———. *Scenes of Subjection: Terror, Slavery, and Self-Making in Nineteenth-Century America.* New York: Oxford University Press, 1997.

Henson, Josiah, and Harriet Beecher Stowe. *Truth Stranger Than Fiction: Father Henson's Story of His Own Life.* Boston: John P. Jewett, 1858.

Jackson, Leon. "The Talking Book and the Talking Book Historian: African American Cultures of Print—the State of the Discipline." *Book History* 13 (2010): 251–308.

Jackson, Virginia Walker. *Dickinson's Misery: A Theory of Lyric Reading.* Princeton, N.J.: Princeton University Press, 2005.

Jackson, Virginia, and Yopie Prins, eds. *The Lyric Theory Reader: A Critical Anthology.* Baltimore, Md.: Johns Hopkins University Press, 2014.

Jacobs, Harriet A. *Incidents in the Life of a Slave Girl.* Boston: Pub. for the author, 1861.

Jauss, Hans Robert. *Toward an Aesthetic of Reception.* Minneapolis: University of Minnesota Press, 1982.

Johnson, Barbara. *Persons and Things.* Cambridge, Mass.: Harvard University Press, 2008.

Johnson, Jerah. "*Les Cenelles*: What's in a Name?" *Louisiana History* 31, no. 4 (Winter 1990): 401–10.

Johnson, Walter. *Soul by Soul: Life Inside the Antebellum Slave Market.* Cambridge, Mass.: Harvard University Press, 2001.

Jones, Edward P. *The Known World.* 1st ed. New York: Amistad, 2003.

Jones, Paul Christian. "Copying What the Master Had Written: Frederick Douglass's 'The Heroic Slave' and the Southern Historical Romance." *Southern Quarterly* 38, no. 4 (Summer 2000): 78–92.

Kaye, Anthony E. *Joining Places: Slave Neighborhoods in the Old South.* Chapel Hill: University of North Carolina Press, 2007.

Kneale, J. Douglas. *Romantic Aversions: Aftermaths of Classicism in Wordsworth and Coleridge.* Montreal: McGill-Queen's University Press, 1999.

Lanusse, Armand, ed. *Les Cenelles: Choix de poésies indigènes.* Shreveport, La.: Tintamarre, 2003.

Latortue, Régine, and Gleason Rex Adams, eds. *Les Cenelles: A Collection of Poems of Creole Writers of the Early Nineteenth Century.* Boston: G. K. Hall, 1979.

Levander, Caroline. "Witness and Participant: Frederick Douglass's Child." *Studies in American Fiction* 33, no. 2 (Autumn 2005): 183–93.

The Light and Truth of Slavery: Aaron's History. Worcester, Mass.: n.p., 1843.

Looby, Christopher. *Voicing America: Language, Literary Form, and the Origins of the United States.* Chicago: University of Chicago Press, 1996.

Lorde, Audre. "The Master's Tools Will Never Dismantle the Master's House." In *Sister Outsider: Essays and Speeches*, 110–14. Berkeley, Calif.: Crossing Press, 2007.

Lukács, György. *The Historical Novel.* Boston: Beacon, 1963.

———. *History and Class Consciousness: Studies in Marxist Dialectics.* London: Merlin, 1971.

McDowell, Deborah E. *"The Changing Same": Black Women's Literature, Criticism, and Theory.* Bloomington: Indiana University Press, 1995.

McFeely, William S. *Frederick Douglass.* New York: W. W. Norton, 1991.

McGill, Meredith L. *American Literature and the Culture of Reprinting, 1834–1853.* Philadelphia: University of Pennsylvania Press, 2003.

Michaelides, Chris. *Paroles D'honneur: Écrits de Créoles de couleur Néo-Orleanais, 1837–1872.* Les Cahiers du Tintamarre. Shreveport, La.: Les Éditions Tintamarre, 2004.

Moody, Joycelyn. *Sentimental Confessions: Spiritual Narratives of Nineteenth-Century African American Women.* Athens: University of Georgia Press, 2001.

Mutter, Sarah Mahurin. "'Such a Poor Word for Such a Wondrous Thing': Thingness and the Recovery of the Human in *The Known World*." *The Southern Literary Journal* 43, no. 2 (Spring 2011): 125–46.

Nantucket Atheneum Strangers Book. Papers. Nantucket Atheneum. Nantucket, Mass.

Nelson, Dana D. *National Manhood: Capitalist Citizenship and the Imagined Fraternity of White Men*. Durham, N.C.: Duke University Press, 1998.

Newfield, Christopher. *The Emerson Effect: Individualism and Submission in America*. Chicago: University of Chicago Press, 1996.

Noble, Marianne. "Sympathetic Listening in Frederick Douglass's 'The Heroic Slave' and *My Bondage and My Freedom*." *Studies in American Fiction* 34, no. 1 (Spring 2006): 53–68.

Noll, Mark A. *America's God: From Jonathan Edwards to Abraham Lincoln*. New York: Oxford University Press, 2002.

Nord, David Paul. *Communities of Journalism: A History of American Newspapers and Their Readers*. Urbana: University of Illinois Press, 2001.

The Papers of Andrew Jackson. Vol. III, 1814–15. Knoxville: University of Tennessee Press, 1991.

Penningroth, Dylan C. *The Claims of Kinfolk: African American Property and Community in the Nineteenth-Century South*. Chapel Hill: University of North Carolina Press, 2003.

Peterson, Daniel H. *The Looking-Glass: Being a True Report and Narrative of the Life, Travels and Labors of the Rev. Daniel H. Peterson, a Colored Clergyman; Embracing a Period of Time from the Year 1812 to 1854, and Including His Visit to Western Africa*. New York: Wright, 1854.

"Philosophical Institute of Nantucket Minutes." Nantucket, Mass.: Nantucket Historical Association, 1826–32.

Preminger, Alex, et al., eds. *The New Princeton Encyclopedia of Poetry and Poetics*. Princeton, N.J.: Princeton University Press, 1993.

Prentiss, Benjamin F., and Boyrereau Brinch. *The Blind African Slave, or, Memoirs of Boyrereau Brinch Nick-Named Jeffrey Brace*. St. Albans, Vt.: Harry Whitney, 1810.

Prince, Mary. *The History of Mary Prince, a West India Slave*. 3rd ed. N.p., 1831.

Questy, Joanni. "Monsieur Paul." In Michaelides, ed. 167–86.

Rancière, Jacques. *The Politics of Aesthetics: The Distribution of the Sensible*. Translated by Gabriel Rockhill. London: Continuum, 2006.

———. *Proletarian Nights: The Workers' Dream in Nineteenth-Century France*. Translated by John Drury. New York: Verso, 2012.

Randolph, Peter. *From Slave Cabin to the Pulpit*. Boston: J. H. Earle, 1893.

Register for Free Colored Persons Entitled to Remain in the State [of Louisiana]. City Archives. New Orleans Public Library.

Richards, Eliza. *Gender and the Poetics of Reception in Poe's Circle*. Cambridge: Cambridge University Press, 2004.

Rooney, Ellen. "A Semiprivate Room." *differences: A Journal of Feminist Cultural Studies* 13, no. 1 (Spring 2002): 128–56.

———. *Seductive Reasoning: Pluralism as the Problematic of Contemporary Literary Theory*. Ithaca, N.Y.: Cornell University Press, 1989.

Roper, Moses, and Thomas Price. *A Narrative of the Adventures and Escape of Moses Roper, from American Slavery*. 4th ed. London: Harvey and Darton, 1840.

Sahlins, Marshall David. *What Kinship Is—and Is Not*. Chicago: University of Chicago Press, 2013.

Samuels, Shirley C., ed. *The Culture of Sentiment: Race, Gender, and Sentimentality in Nineteenth-Century America*. New York: Oxford University Press, 1992.

Schoonover, Karl. *Brutal Vision: The Neorealist Body in Postwar Italian Cinema*. Minneapolis: University of Minnesota Press, 2012.

Sedgwick, Eve Kosofsky. *Epistemology of the Closet*. Berkeley: University of California Press, 1990.

———. *Tendencies*. Durham, N.C.: Duke University Press, 1993.

Sekora, John. "Black Message/White Envelope: Genre, Authenticity, and Authority in the Antebellum Slave Narrative." *Callaloo: A Journal of African American and African Arts and Letters* 10, no. 3 (1987): 482–515.

Shapiro, Norman R., and M. Lynn Weiss, eds. and trans. *Creole Echoes: The Francophone Poetry of Nineteenth-Century Louisiana*. Urbana: University of Illinois Press, 2004.

Simpson, David. *Romanticism and the Question of the Stranger*. Chicago: University of Chicago Press, 2013.

Smallwood, Thomas, and Richard Almonte. *A Narrative of Thomas Smallwood (Coloured Man)*. Toronto: Mercury, 2000.

Smith, Valerie. *Not Just Race, Not Just Gender: Black Feminist Readings*. New York: Routledge, 1998.

———. *Self-Discovery and Authority in Afro-American Narrative*. Cambridge, Mass.: Harvard University Press, 1987.

Spillers, Hortense J. *Black, White, and in Color: Essays on American Literature and Culture*. Chicago: University of Chicago Press, 2003.

———. *Comparative American Identities: Race, Sex, and Nationality in the Modern Text*. New York: Routledge, 1991.

St. Céran, M. Tullius. *Les Louisianaises*. New Orleans: J. L. Sollée, 1840.

Stauffer, John. *The Black Hearts of Men: Radical Abolitionists and the Transformation of Race*. Cambridge, Mass.: Harvard University Press, 2001.

Stepto, Robert B. *From Behind the Veil: A Study of Afro-American Narrative*. Urbana: University of Illinois Press, 1979.

Stringfellow, Thornton. *A Brief Examination of Scripture Testimony on the Institution of Slavery, in an Essay*. Richmond, Va.: Religious Herald, 1841.

Sunderland, La Roy. *The Testimony of God Against Slavery, or a Collection of Passages from the Bible, Which Show the Sin of Holding Property in Man*. Boston: Webster and Southard, 1835.

Thompson, Shirley Elizabeth. *Exiles at Home: The Struggle to Become American in Creole New Orleans*. Cambridge, Mass.: Harvard University Press, 2009.

Tyler, Betsy. *The Nantucket Atheneum: A History*. Nantucket, Mass.: Nantucket Preservation Trust, 2009.

Veney, Bethany. *The Narrative of Bethany Veney, a Slave Woman*. Worcester, Mass.: n.p., 1889.

Wagner, Bryan. *Disturbing the Peace: Black Culture and the Police Power After Slavery*. Cambridge, Mass.: Harvard University Press, 2009.

Waligora-Davis, Nicole. *Sanctuary: African Americans and Empire*. New York: Oxford University Press, 2011.

Warner, Michael. *Publics and Counterpublics*. New York: Zone, 2002.

Warren, Kenneth W. *What Was African American Literature?* Cambridge, Mass.: Harvard University Press, 2011.

Weheliye, Alexander G. "After Man." *American Literary History* 20, nos. 1–2 (Spring–Summer 2008): 321–36.

White, Barbara Linebaugh. *The African School and the Integration of Nantucket Public Schools, 1825–1847*. Boston: Boston University, 1978.

———. "The Integration of Nantucket Public Schools." *Historic Nantucket* 40, no. 3 (Fall 1992): 59–62.

Wiegman, Robyn. "Feminism, Institutionalism, and the Idiom of Failure." *differences: A Journal of Feminist Cultural Studies* 11, no. 3 (Fall 1999/2000): 107–36.

Wynter, Sylvia. "Unsettling the Coloniality of Being/Power/Truth/Freedom: Towards the Human, After Man, Its Overrepresentation—an Argument." *CR: The New Centennial Review* 3, no. 3 (2003): 257–337.

Yates, William. *Rights of Colored Men to Suffrage, Citizenship and Trial by Jury: Being a Book of Facts, Arguments and Authorities, Historical Notices and Sketches of Debates—with Notes*. Philadelphia: Merrihew and Gunn, 1838.

Zafar, Rafia. *We Wear the Mask: African Americans Write American Literature, 1760–1870*. New York: Columbia University Press, 1997.

ACKNOWLEDGMENTS

─────────

This book would not have happened without the American Antiquarian Society. As anyone who has done research there knows, the only thing that matches the quality of its archives is its staff. In addition to the staff at the AAS, I am grateful to those at the Amistad Research Center at Tulane University, the Boston Athenaeum, the Historic New Orleans Collection, the Library Company of Philadelphia, the Nantucket Atheneum, the Nantucket Historical Association, the New Orleans Public Library's City Archives, the Providence Athenaeum, the Vere Harmsworth Library at the University of Oxford, and Xavier University of Louisiana's Archives and Special Collections. Across these institutions, I am especially grateful for the generous and intelligent guidance of Paul Erickson, Vincent Golden, Jim Green, John Hench, Elizabeth Oldham, Elizabeth Watts Pope, Jane Rawson, Caroline Sloat, and Betsy Tyler. At a late stage of the process, Judy Riffel provided timely research assistance in the Louisiana State Archives. Amandine Lepers-Thornton provided expert translations where noted. A Mellon Fellowship at the Library Company of Philadelphia, National Endowment for the Humanities and Northeast Modern Language Association fellowships at the AAS, a Massachusetts Foundation for the Humanities/Bay State Historical League Scholar-in-Residence Grant at the Nantucket Atheneum, and a Verney Fellowship at the Nantucket Historical Association supported my research at these institutions. I also received leave time and research support from Yale University, Michigan State University, and the University of Oxford.

The fellows at the AAS during my time in Worcester made for brilliant company. Among them I learned a great deal from Ezra Greenspan, April Haynes, Jessica Lepler, Adam Nelson, David Paul Nord, Emily Pawley, and Beth Barton Schweiger. I also benefited from the energetic intelligence of the members of the AAS's Summer Seminar in the History of the Book in America on the Global American South and Early American Print Culture, which I was lucky enough to codirect with Jeannine DeLombard.

Audiences for talks at the following venues helped me to clarify my thinking on the topics covered here: the American Antiquarian Society, Columbia

University, the Dartmouth Institute in American Studies, Indiana University, Michigan State University, the Nantucket Historical Association, Northwestern University, Syracuse University, the University of Cambridge, the University of Leeds, the University of Manchester, the University of Nottingham, the University of Oxford, the University of Sussex, Vanderbilt University, and Yale University. Audiences at meetings of the following scholarly societies who entertained my thoughts on these materials were equally helpful: the American Comparative Literature Association; the American Literature Association; the American Studies Association; C19: The Society of Nineteenth-Century Americanists; the Modern Language Association; the Society for the History of Authorship, Reading and Publishing; and the Society for the Study of the Novel.

I have drawn on previous publications at various points throughout the book. The writing included here has been significantly revised, reorganized, and collated with mainly unpublished material. I am grateful to the following presses and journals for their permission to draw on the previously published materials. I am also thankful to the reviewers for and editors of those volumes and journals for their comments and suggestions: "'I Am a Stranger with Thee': Frederick Douglass and Recognition After 1845," *American Literature* 85, no. 2 (2013); "The Lyric Public of *Les Cenelles*," in *Early African American Print Culture*, ed. Lara Langer Cohen and Jordan Alexander Stein (Philadelphia: University of Pennsylvania Press, 2012); "Historical Totality and the African American Archive," in *Unsettled States: Nineteenth-Century American Literary Studies*, ed. Dana Luciano and Ivy Wilson (New York: New York University Press, 2014); "Stranger History," *J19: The Journal of Nineteenth-Century Americanists* 1, no. 1 (2013); and "Early American Literature and Its Exclusions," *PMLA* 128, no. 4 (2013).

My thinking on this topic first took shape at Yale University, and it evolved in significant ways at Michigan State University. I am grateful to my Yale and MSU colleagues for their kind attention to my work. At Oxford, the Faculty of English, Linacre College, and the Rothermere American Institute have offered stimulating environments in which to complete the book. A number of people at the aforementioned institutions deserve special notice for their many personal and professional kindnesses: Tanya Agathacleous, Stephen Arch, Zarena Aslami, Rebecca Beasley, Elleke Boehmer, Nigel Bowles, David Bradshaw, Ron Bush, Jill Campbell, Elizabeth Maddock Dillon, Wai Chee Dimock, Jennifer Fay, Laura Frost, Ken Harrow, Patrick Hayes, Scott Juengel, Rhodri Lewis, Eng-Beng Lim, Sanda Lwin, Lynn Makau, Laura Marcus, Ellen McCallum, Patrick McConeghy, Michèle Mendelssohn, Ankhi Mukherjee, Justus Nieland,

Patrick O'Donnell, Heather O'Donoghue, Seamus Perry, Ellen Pollack, Peter Riley, Joseph Roach, Tessa Roynon, Nicole Sierra, Helen Small, Geneva Smitherman, Edward Sugden, Courtney Traub, Ned Watts, Jennifer Williams, Jeff Wray, and Karin Wurst. I have also benefited from conversations with many people in the wider scholarly community. All lists of this kind are necessarily truncated, but even so, here are just a few of the people to whom I am gratefully in debt: Nancy Armstrong, Jennifer Baker, Hester Blum, Chris Castiglia, Denise Davis, Jeannine DeLombard, Jonathan Elmer, Paul Erickson, Jennifer Fleissner, Philip Gould, Gordon Hutner, Jeffrey Insko, Barbara Ladd, Christopher Looby, Dana Luciano, Heather McCoy, Meredith McGill, Dana Nelson, Donald Pease, Eliza Richards, Sarah Rivett, Ellen Rooney, Stephanie Smith, Jordan Stein, Elisa Tamarkin, Leonard Tennenhouse, Kyla Wazana Tompkins, Priscilla Wald, Ivy Wilson, and Michael Winship.

I could not have asked for better readers for the manuscript than Branka Arsić and Nancy Bentley. As readers they combined intellectual rigor, clarity of thought, and insightfulness in equal measures, just as they do in their own work. Jerry Singerman was once again responsible for choosing such ideal readers. Jerry is a prince among editors (and among men). I have been grateful for his counsel many times. This is the second time through production at the University of Pennsylvania Press with Erica Ginsburg, and I am grateful for her tremendous care with the process. The same is true for Holly Knowles.

A few people need to be acknowledged for specific considerations that lay outside the actual writing of the book but that were pivotal to its completion. Gail Bragg, Nancy Browner, Ruth Fisk, Kathy Ornish, and Molly Poorman eased the way with their special talents. My parents, Joe and Sue Pratt, moved to New Orleans when I was four years old. If for no other reason than that move, I am forever in their debt. But of course there are many other reasons besides just that one. Ada Pratt Boutchard, Barry Boutchard, Avery Boutchard, and Quinn Boutchard make visits home to New Orleans an exciting adventure. Charlotte Kastner and Tom Kastner have offered an unending chorus of support. Charlotte has also done more than her fair share in terms of the content of this book. She pointed me to the Strangers Book at the Nantucket Atheneum, where she was director during the ten years that saw the institution rebuilt and revitalized. My first visit to the African Meeting House on Nantucket was for Tom and Charlotte's wedding, and so I owe them that too. Eric Schoonover and Susan Pollack have kept me company over many years, and I am grateful to them for their intelligence and their depth of knowledge about things historical, literary, musical, and culinary. Lara Langer Cohen and John Pat Leary became fast friends in Michigan and remain so today. Wally Pansing and Jeffery Conway are models for how to be good people. They calm my soul and raise my spirits whenever I see them. Tango's not so bad, either. Patricia Villalobos Echeverría and Nayda Collazo-Llorens made the final year in Michigan a special one. It is technically true to say that my friendship with Patricia has most often been a long-distance one, but it has always felt exactly the opposite. Rosalind Galt and Adrian Goycoolea have made life in the United Kingdom possible. To my mind the only high-speed rail that Britain needs at present is one that would go from Oxford to Brighton. I discussed many of these ideas with Aimé Ellis during my first three years at MSU. He was not there for the last two of those five years in East Lansing, but he made all of them better. Mike Wade is a treasure.

I met Charles Tolle when I was an undergraduate at Louisiana State University. He was then and remains now one of my most valued teachers. Charles's house in those days combined the best qualities of a *rive gauche* literary salon, a gallery, the British Library, a frontier saloon, and Sir John Soane's Museum. His reading and archival suggestions for this particular book project are at its core. Charles's knowledge of Louisiana history and culture, and of world literature, is outstanding. He also makes a mean Pimm's Cup. After Hurricane Katrina, Charles and another great Baton Rouge icon, Annette Wilson, gave my sister a place to stay and a warm meal on a difficult Sunday night when she arrived back in Louisiana after one of the many exoduses that followed the storm. This was after Charles and Annette had already spent weeks trying to assist in whatever ways they could the many others taking shelter in Baton Rouge. For all of these reasons, and for many more, Charles incarnates the humanist ideal as much as anyone I know.

It is difficult to know how to put into words my gratitude to and for Karl Schoonover. All of my best ideas are really Karl's ideas. If the publication schedule holds, this book will go to press in our twentieth year together. My only hope is for at least two hundred more such anniversaries.